BARBECUE

ROBERT F. MOSS

BAR
★ BE ★
CUE

THE
HISTORY
OF AN
AMERICAN
INSTITUTION

The University of Alabama Press ★ Tuscaloosa

The recipes in this book are intended to be followed
as written by the author. Results will vary.

Manufactured in the United States of America

Typeface: Adobe Caslon Pro
Designer: Michele Myatt Quinn

∞

The paper on which this book is printed meets the minimum
requirements of American National Standard for Information
Sciences—Permanence of Paper for Printed Library Materials,
ANSI Z39.48-1984.

Library of Congress Cataloging-in-Publication Data

Moss, Robert F.
    Barbecue : the history of an American institution / Robert F. Moss.
      p.   cm.
    Includes bibliographical references and index.
    ISBN 978-0-8173-1718-8 (cloth : alk. paper) 1. Barbecue
cooking—United States. 2. Barbecue cooking—History—United
States. I. Title.
    TX840.B3M687 2010
    641.7′6—dc22
                                                            2010005683

For my father

CONTENTS

Acknowledgments

This project began almost ten years ago when I went to the University of South Carolina library to read about the history of barbecue. I discovered, to my surprise, that not only had no one written a full book on the subject but there really wasn't much historical research published on barbecue at all. For several years I haphazardly collected old newspaper stories and diary entries about barbecue and slowly began piecing together the story. This research eventually evolved into a book. During that time, I had two children, changed jobs three times, and moved cities and houses three times, too.

As with any project with this long a gestation, there are dozens of people who helped along the way, and I am sure I will forget more than a few of those who deserve thanks. John Shelton Reed shared valuable research, encouragement, and much-needed advice as I was finishing this book and trying to figure out how to get it published. I owe him and Dale Vosberg Reed a big blowout at Hominy Grill. Jeff Allen and John T. Edge read chapters from the manuscript, and their comments helped make it better.

By the time I'd gotten seriously underway on this project, Robert W. Trogdon had already been exiled to the barbecueless backwoods of Ohio, but he and I ate a lot of mustard-sauced pork together in Columbia, South Carolina, and he helped fuel my early passion for the subject.

The Interlibrary Loan Staff at the Charleston County Public Library were invaluable in helping me complete my work far from the walls of a research library, and Ray Quiel of San Bernardino, California, was very generous in providing material on the early McDonald's restaurants back before they gave up barbecue in favor of hamburgers.

The whole team at The University of Alabama Press has done a remarkable job of taking an unwieldy manuscript and turning it into a finished book, and I thank them all for their efforts.

And, lastly, I owe a tremendous debt to my wife, Jennifer, who has always been my strongest supporter and has patiently endured countless side trips down country roads seeking out obscure barbecue joints in the days before GPS. I'm not contesting her claim that this whole project was just a big ruse to allow me to eat barbecue every weekend in the name of "research," but at least I have a book to show for it.

Mount Pleasant, South Carolina
December 2009

Introduction

Americans love barbecue. They love to eat it, argue about it, and even read about it. Dozens of titles on the subject are published each year, covering every imaginable aspect of the topic: recipes, grilling tips, restaurant guides, instructions for constructing barbecue pits, and exotic variants such as Mongolian barbecue and Indian tandoor cooking. But, for a dish on which so much ink has been spilled, remarkably little has been written about the history of barbecue in the United States.

Most barbecue books focus on recipes or contemporary restaurants and show little more than a passing interest in the origins of their subject. Very little has been written about barbecue before 1900, and the small amount of information presented has typically been vague and speculative. One of the best cultural histories of southern cookery, John Egerton's *Southern Food: At Home, On the Road, In History* (1987), has an entire chapter about barbecue, but this chapter treats the history of southern barbecue before 1900 in only two paragraphs, one of which summarizes the etymology of the word. Bob Garner's *North Carolina Barbecue: Flavored by Time* (1996) offers an excellent account of the origins of North Carolina barbecue restaurants in the early twentieth century, but it provides just two pages of material on barbecue before 1900, and most of that discussion is largely conjecture. John Shelton Reed and Dale Vosberg Reed's recent *Holy Smoke: The Big Book of North Carolina Barbecue* (2008) offers by far the most detailed and reliable history of barbecue published thus far, though their account is limited to the context of a single state and is part of a larger work on all aspects of barbecue in North Carolina.

These are the best books; most ignore the history of barbecue altogether and focus only on the dish as it is known today. One reason why the full story has not been told is that the details are not easily found. Barbecue men have not left their personal papers to archives. The first recipes for pit-cooked barbecue did not appear in print until after the Civil War; the first books devoted to the subject were not published until the 1940s. The history of barbecue before 1900 can be found only as fragments scattered lightly through newspapers, letters, private journals, and travel narratives. Reconstructing this history requires sifting through reams of material to find the few disparate scraps and arranging them into a coherent story.

The results are well worth the effort, for the story of barbecue is far more than just the way people came to roast whole pigs or beef briskets over open pits. It is the story of a vital institution in American life. While roasting meat over a fire is universal, the specific term "barbecue" originated among the various Native American tribes in the Caribbean and along the eastern coast of North America, and it was adopted from them by English colonists in the seventeenth century. The word was used through-out the American colonies to refer to both the cooking technique and the social event, but the institution took root most firmly in Virginia and became an essential part of Tidewater plantation culture. From there it spread southward through the Carolinas and into Georgia and across the Appalachians into Tennessee and Kentucky, following the main pattern of southern settlement. In the early nineteenth century, the barbecue tradition moved westward with American settlers across the Gulf states and into Texas, and later through the Southwest all the way to the Pacific Coast.

Barbecue has always been more than just something to eat. For three centuries it has been a vital part of American social and political life, particularly in the South and the West. Entire communities would come together at barbecues for celebration, recrea-tion, and the expression of common values. In the early years of the Republic, Fourth of July barbecues were not just a time to celebrate the nation's independence but also a means of reinforcing the democratic values of the community. The tradition has evolved over time, following the larger evolution of American society. In colonial days, barbe-cues were rough, rowdy festivals accompanied—like much of frontier life—by drunk-enness and fistfights. In the early nineteenth century, the reform movements that trans-formed American society—most notably the temperance movement—also changed the character of barbecues. The events became more staid and ritualized, evolving into respectable affairs that bound communities together. They also became an essential part of the political life of the nation, as events staged by politicians to woo potential voters and as expressions of community support for leaders and causes. For decades, barbecues were the traditional way to honor local politicians for their service, and they played a prominent role in the sectionalist controversies that led to the Civil War. Such events rallied support for secession, honored troops as they were sent off to battle, and survived the war as the standard form of large-scale civic celebration in the South and West.

Before the Civil War and after, barbecue was a tradition shared by white and black Americans alike, and the issues of race are intertwined with the food's history. African American slaves were usually the pitmasters and cooks for the large barbecues hosted and attended by whites, and thus played a formative role in developing the techniques and recipes of southern barbecue. Barbecues were a common form of recreation for slaves, too, as events they staged and created for themselves and as a form of paternalistic entertainment granted by slave owners as a means of reward and control. After Emancipation, barbecue continued to play a key role in the lives of African Americans, serving as the center of a wide range of community celebrations and becoming a core part of African American foodways.

One of the most significant changes in barbecue culture occurred around the turn of the twentieth century, when it became a product of commerce. Before the 1890s, barbecue was almost never sold but instead given away at public festivals, which generally were hosted by organizations or prominent citizens and open to all members of the community. This began to change when itinerant barbecue men started selling their services for events such as school commencements and other celebrations. These cooks would set up tents on special occasions such as the Fourth of July, Labor Day, and court days in county seats and on street corners in cities. The tents evolved into more permanent structures, and the modern barbecue restaurant was born.

The restaurant trade helped create today's distinctive regional variations of barbecue. Cooks settled on a few types of meat based on local tastes and availability. In the Southeast, pork was the standard, but goat and mutton were common in Kentucky, and in Texas and the West beef reigned supreme. Regional variations became more pronounced over the decades, with cooking styles, sauces, and side dishes becoming distinctive to each region. Business was boosted by the rise of the automobile, and barbecue stands became an iconic feature of the roadside not just in the South but across the country. Some—but not many—of these establishments survive today as legendary barbecue restaurants, such as Sprayberry's in Newnan, Georgia, and McClard's in Hot Springs, Arkansas. Most did not last, their slow-cooking methods and diverse regional variations ill suited to the standardized demands of the fast-food industry.

But, the very qualities that prevented barbecue from becoming a fast-food staple are what make it a classic American dish today. No one travels from town to town sampling cheeseburgers, and no one has heated debates over which state serves the best chicken fingers. A newspaper article on tomatoes or fried chicken is unlikely to generate much controversy, but one on barbecue is almost guaranteed to provoke dozens of angry letters to the editor. Something about barbecue brings out the passion in both cooks and eaters. Few American dishes can boast of the sheer variety of barbecue, whose ingredients and cooking styles can differ completely in restaurants separated by only a few hundred miles and therefore create strong geographic preferences and loyalties. Barbecue as an event remains an important form of celebration and gathering, be it for reunions, campaign fundraisers, or outdoor festivals, and barbecue as a dish is enjoying a remarkable resurgence in popularity throughout the country.

Most of all, barbecue has shown an enduring power to bring people together. From the very beginning, barbecues were powerful social magnets, drawing people from a wide range of classes and geographic backgrounds. Because of this, it has played an important role in three centuries of American history, reflecting and influencing the direction of an evolving society. As Americans founded their nation, defined their civic values, expanded democracy, built canals and railroads, and threw themselves westward, barbecue was there. It helped cast the country apart during the Civil War, then bring it back together again in the years of reconciliation that followed. The same forces that shaped the larger contours of American life influenced barbecue, too, and over time the institution evolved to reflect the country's progression from a rural, agricultural society to an industrialized, commercial world power. To trace the story of barbecue is to trace the very thread of American history.

This is that story.

Barbecue in Colonial America

Sometime around 1706, a group of English colonists in Peckham, Jamaica, gathered for a most un-British feast. Drunk on rum, they built a rack of sticks and started a fire beneath it. Once the fire had burned down to coals, they laid long wooden spits across the range then hoisted three whole pigs on top. As the pigs roasted, the cook basted them with a combination of green Virginia pepper and Madeira wine, using a fox's tail tied to a long stick. After many hours of cooking, the pigs were removed from the fire, laid on a log, and divided into quarters with an ax. They were then distributed to the gathered revelers, who delighted in the "Incomparable Food, fit for the Table of a *Sagamoor.*"

The details of this feast were captured by Edward Ward in his pamphlet *The Barbacue Feast: or, the three pigs of Peckham, broiled under an apple-tree,* which was published in London in 1707. Roasting meat over flames was nothing new to Englishmen, but the event Ward witnessed was something different—and something definitely *not* British. The feast, he explains, was staged because the colonists had "their English appetites so deprav'd and vitiated" by rum that they craved "a Litter of Pigs nicely cook'd after the West Indian manner." The hogs were cooked whole "with their Heads, Tails, Pettitoes, and Hoofs on . . . according to the *Indian* Fashion."[1]

This Caribbean feast was quite similar to today's community barbecues in Georgia or North Carolina: whole hogs cooked slowly over a pit of coals and basted with a spicy sauce. From its earliest days barbecue was not just a type of food or a cooking technique but also a social event. The colonists' feast was a community affair that included "the best Part of the town of Peckham." It began long before the food was served, for the cooking itself was part of the experience. The citizens watched with great interest as the range was constructed and the fire stoked, and once the pigs were laid upon the spits, the crowd gathered around, "expressing as much Joy in the Looks and Actions, as a Gang of wild *Canibals* who, when they have taken a Stranger, first dance round him, and afterwards devour him." Like many of the barbecue writers who would follow him, Ward liked to exaggerate, but his descriptions capture the ritualistic nature of barbecue, rituals that were fast becoming ingrained in the culture of the British colonies and, later, would play a defining role in the social life of the United States.

In the broadest sense, *barbecue* simply means the act of cooking anything over a fire, be it hamburgers, shrimp kebabs, or corn on the cob. For most Americans, though, the word has a more precise definition. It is, for starters, a particular type of food, and one that varies greatly from one part of the country to another. When an eastern North Carolinian says, "Let's go get some barbecue," he is referring to finely chopped bits of smoked pork mixed with a spicy, vinegar-based sauce. A Texan saying the same thing usually means sliced beef brisket, while someone from Memphis may be talking about a basket of pork ribs. Varied as these definitions are, there are a few common qualities to what Americans call barbecue: meat cooked slowly over wood coals and (usually) served with a sweet or spicy sauce.

But, barbecue is more than just something to eat. It is also a social event—the occasion when barbecue is cooked and served. This may be something small and informal— a handful of friends grilling out in the backyard for a Saturday-night barbecue. Or, it might be a major production. When a southern church holds a barbecue, it sets up rows of folding tables on the grounds and lets people park their cars on the grass once they overflow the parking lot. In many parts of the country, it is a standard way to celebrate a wedding, kick off a political campaign, or pass the hat for a charitable cause. If you want to get a lot of people together, a barbecue is the way to do it. And it has been this way for a long time.

The Derivation of the Word

THE WORD *BARBECUE* COMES from the Taino Indians in the Caribbean, where it was the name for a frame of green sticks that was used both as a sleeping platform and for smoking or drying meat. Initially, the word had the dual meaning of a physical piece of equipment and a method of cooking. The English version first appeared in print in Edmund Hickeringill's travel narrative *Jamaica Viewed* (1661), which described the hunting of animals as, "Some are slain, And their flesh forthwith Barbacu'd and eat." Though initially encountered on Caribbean islands such as Jamaica, Western explorers recorded the word (often spelled "borbecue" or "barbecu") and the technique being used by Indians ranging from New England to Guiana in South America.

By the end of the seventeenth century the word *barbecue* was no longer limited to travel narratives but had moved into the common usage as a synonym for roasting or grilling, even outside the context of food. In Aphra Behn's play *The Widow Ranter* (1690) a riotous crowd seizes a rebel and demands, "Let's barbicu this fat Rogue." Cotton Mather used the term to describe the burning deaths of Native Americans in Massachusetts: "When they came to see the bodies of so many of their countrymen terribly barbikew'd." Although *barbecue* would continue to be used in Europe in the general sense of *roast*, it was in the American colonies that it truly took hold and acquired a range of specific meanings.

Though *barbecue*'s origins are well established by lexicographers, there have been many more fanciful derivations proposed. The most common of these is that the word comes from the French *barbe-a-queue*, or beard-to-tail, referring to the cooking of whole hogs over the pit. This explanation has been around almost two centuries, appearing in print as early as 1829, and it is frequently listed in general reference works as a legitimate alternative derivation to the Indian origins. (The editors of the *Oxford English Dictionary* dismiss *barbe-a-queue* as "an absurd conjecture suggested merely by the sound of the word.") Other often-repeated stories are that the word originated from a restaurant offering whiskey, beer, and pool along with its roasted pork (*bar-beer-cue*) and from a rancher with the initials B.Q. who branded his cattle with the two letters topped by a bar, or Bar-B-Q Ranch. But, the word *barbecue* is clearly much older than such explanations would allow.

Source: *The Oxford English Dictionary*. 2nd ed. 1989. *OED Online*. Oxford University Press. http://dictionary.oed.com/cgi/entry/00181778.

Einhöltzern Roost/daraufffie die XIIII.
Fische besengen.

So Ann sie eine grosse menge Fische haben gefangen/begeben sie sich auff einen därzu vers ordneten Platz/welcher die Speiß zu bereiten bequeme ist/ daselbst stecken sie vier Ga. beln auff einem vierecketen Platz in die Erden hinein/ auff diese legen sie vier Hölzer/ vnd auff dieselbigen andere zwerchoweise/ also/ daß es einem Roost/ der da hoch gnug sam sey/ gleichförmig werde. Wann sie die Fische auff den Roost gelegt/machen sie ein Fewer darunter/doch nicht nach der weise der Völcker von Florida/welche die Fisch al. lein besengen/vnnd im Rauch außtrücknen/die sie den ganzen Winter vber behalten. Diese Völcker aber braten alles/verzehrens/vñ behalten nichts in vorrath/ darnach/ wann sie dessen dörff. tig sind/braten oder sieden sie frische/ wie wir hernach sehen werden. Wann aber der Roost so groß nicht ist/daß die Fisch alle möchten darauff gelegt werden/stecken sie kleine steckkein am Fewer in die Erden/ vnnd hencken die vbrigen Fische durch die Ohren auff/vnd braten sie vollendt so lang es gnug sey. Sie sehen aber mit fleiß zu/ daß sie nicht verbrannt werden. Wann die ersten gebraten sind/ legen sie andere/ so sie frisch herzu gebracht/auff den Roost. Vnd also widerholen sie diß braten so lange/ biß sie der Speise gnugsam zu haben vermeynen.

Native Americans barbecuing fish in North Carolina, from a 1590 engraving by Theodor de Bry. The image is from the German edition of Thomas Harriot's *Brief and True Report of the New Found Land of Virginia.* De Bry's engraving was based on a watercolor of the scene by English artist John White, who sailed with Richard Grenville in 1588 to explore the coast of present-day North Carolina. (Courtesy Library of Congress, Prints & Photographs Division.)

Barbecue in the American Colonies

The word *barbecue* originated in the Caribbean, but the cooking technique itself was widespread along the eastern coast of North America. In *The History of Virginia* (1705), Robert Beverley notes about the local tribes, "They have two ways of broiling, vis. one by laying the Meat itself upon the coals, the other by laying it upon sticks raised upon forks at some distance above the live coals, which heats more gently, and dries up the gravy; this they, and we also from them, call barbecuing."[2] The same technique was used in the Carolinas. John Brickell's *Natural History of North Carolina* (1737) indicates that the Native Americans in this area, like those in the Caribbean, used barbecue racks for dual purposes. The first was to dry meat for preservation: "They commonly barbecu or

Early Florida Barbecue. Engraving by Theodor de Bry after a painting by Jacques le Moyne de Morgues, a French artist who traveled through North Florida in 1564 and documented the Timucua culture.

dry their *Venison* on Mats or Hurdles in the Sun, first salting it with their Salt, which is made of the Ashes of the Hickory Wood." The second, more common usage was for cooking meat, particularly wild turkeys, which "they Barbecue and eat with *Bears-grease,* this is accounted amongst them a good Dish." The technique was also used for fish and shellfish, which they would "open and dry upon Hurdles, keeping a constant Fire under them; these Hurdles are made of *Reeds* or *Hollow Canes,* in shape of a Gridiron." Barbecuing several bushels at a time, the Native Americans would preserve skate, oysters, and cockles for times of scarcity.[3]

Neither Beverley nor Brickell were fans of Native American cooking. Beverley claimed that it had "nothing commendable in it, but that it is performed with little trouble."[4] Their fellow colonists must have disagreed, for barbecuing was soon adopted by British settlers in an area spanning from the Carolinas all the way to New England.

It may seem surprising, considering how difficult it is to find barbecue in New England today, but during the eighteenth century barbecues were quite common in the region. In 1733, Benjamin Lynde Jr. of Salem, Massachusetts, wrote a cryptic entry in his diary for August 31: "Fair and hot; Browne, Barbacue; hack overset."[5] Lexicographers have interpreted this to mean that Lynde went to a barbecue with Mr. Browne, making it the first written usage of *barbecue* in the sense of a gathering or an event in addition to a method of cooking. Other Massachusetts diaries from the period show a similar usage. The Reverend Ebenezer Bridge of Chelmsford recorded "A Barbacue in Dracut" on October 20, 1752, while the diary of Mary Holyoke of Salem references three "barbeques" between May 1761 and June 1762.[6] Barbecues were held as far north as Falmouth, Maine, where in 1759, following the fall of Quebec City during the French and Indian War, the citizens of Falmouth celebrated with a "festal barbecue" on an island in the harbor. This island would later become known as "Hog Island" because of the event.[7]

By the end of the 1760s, barbecues were regular occurrences in Massachusetts. In 1767, seventy gentlemen were invited to a barbecue to celebrate the launching of the brigantine *Barnard* at Braintree.[8] Two years later, Thomas Carnes announced in a newspaper advertisement that he was opening a tea and coffeehouse about four miles outside of Boston where, he promised, "If any select Company at any Time should incline to have a Barbecue, either Turtle or Pigg, they may depend having it done in the best Manner."[9] This flourishing of barbecue in New England proved short-lived. The events faded from the region following the American Revolution and were rarely seen thereafter.

Barbecue Takes Root in Virginia

It was farther south, in Virginia, that the institution of barbecue first took strong root in America. Both as a food and as a social event, barbecue was more consistent with the tastes of Virginians than with those of New Englanders, for reasons deeply rooted in the cultural backgrounds of the colonists. The English people who colonized America are often portrayed as if they all came from a single, homogenous British culture, but there were strong differences in the customs and tastes of the various American colonies. Their residents came from different parts of Britain and, therefore, had different regional habits and preferences, including how they cooked and entertained and what they liked to eat. In New England, baking was the favored method, while boiling predominated in the Delaware Valley and Southern Highlands. Tidewater Virginians inherited a culture of roasting and broiling from their forebears, who came mostly from southern and western England, so the wood fires of the barbecue pit were a natural fit. Feasting was also a more vital part of the culture of Virginia than of Massachusetts. New Englanders might eat and drink heavily every now and then (such as at annual Thanksgiving celebrations or to commemorate the death of a neighbor), but almost any event was occasion for feasting in Virginia: a marriage, a christening, Christmas, Easter, and visits from family members—or from anyone else, for that matter.[10]

Another factor in the popularity of barbecue in Virginia was the preponderance of pigs in the colony. Pigs first arrived in the New World in 1493 on the second voyage of Christopher Columbus, who brought eight hogs to the island of Hispaniola. Descendants of these pigs were brought to the North American continent by Hernando de Soto in 1539, and many escaped and turned feral. These Spanish pigs are believed by some scholars to be the ancestors of the Arkansas razorback and other wild southern pigs.[11] The pigs cooked at Virginia barbecues, however, had British roots. Many were brought to Jamestown on the first three ships of the Virginia Company in 1607. Just two years later, the colonists possessed only seven horses and a few goats and sheep, but they had between 500 and 600 swine.[12]

Pigs were the ideal livestock for the Virginia colonists. They are prolific animals, with a four-month gestation time and an average litter size of ten or more. Being omnivores, they are easy to feed and, left to their own devices, are adept at rooting out food. Of all the domesticated animals they are the most efficient in terms of translating energy intake into pounds of meat. Virginians were notoriously lax at animal husbandry and tended to let their livestock roam free in the woods rather than erecting fences or sties. Their pigs flourished in the forests, with their plentiful acorns and chestnuts, and Virginian planters hunted them like wild game at slaughter time, earning a good return of meat with minimal care and feeding.[13]

Grazing pigs in the woods required a lot of land, and Virginia had plenty of it. After the colonists settled upon tobacco as their primary cash crop, the colony grew rapidly. By the 1670s settlements stretched out from Jamestown along the shores of the Chesapeake Bay and pushed their way up the banks of the James, Rappahannock, and Potomac Rivers. A Virginia planter needed lots of land with nearby water for transport and plenty of forest in which his livestock could roam, and the number of pigs owned by these planters grew by leaps and bound. At the time of his death in 1651, Ralph Wormeley of the "Rosegill" plantation on the Rappahannock had 439 heads of cattle, 86 sheep, and "too many pigs to count." Inventories of estates regularly excluded swine because no one knew where to find the pigs to count them.[14]

When you combine Virginians' inherent love of feasting with the easy availability of pork, the colony was perfectly positioned to become the birthplace of American barbecue. A final factor was the value that the emerging plantation society placed on home and hospitality.[15] Once the agricultural economy had developed sufficiently to support large plantations and the building of "great houses," the dinner table became the central focus of elite Virginia society, and it was common for planters to throw open their homes to dozens of guests for dinners and dancing. As these entertainments grew, they moved outdoors, allowing a planter to extend his hospitality widely without encroaching on the formalities of the household.

By the 1750s, outdoor barbecues were one of the chief forms of entertainment in the Tidewater colony. On July 21, 1758, John Kirkpatrick wrote to George Washington and complained about life in Alexandria during the French and Indian War: "To tell you our Domestick occurrences would look silly—& ill sute your time to peruse—We have dull Barbecues—and yet Duller Dances—An Election causes a Hubub for a Week or so—& then we are dead a While."[16] Washington himself was a frequent barbecue guest. In his diary he recorded attending six such events between 1769 and 1774—including, on September 18, 1773, "a Barbicue of my own giving at Accotinck."[17]

Barbecues had evolved from casual gatherings of families and friends into a formal social institution. A "barbecue day" was spent feasting and celebrating from morning until late into the evening and drew attendees from all levels of society. Most accounts of barbecues from this period can be found in brief journal entries or newspaper items,

Three Views of Virginia Barbecues

ONE OF THE MORE detailed early descriptions of Virginia barbecue appears in the journals of Nicholas Cresswell, a young Englishman who came to the colony in 1774 to tour the Tidewater region and the frontier lands to its west. In July 1774, as Cresswell was taking passage on a boat down the Potomac River, he attended a barbecue, which he described as follows: "About noon a Pilot Boat came along side to invite the Captn. to a Barbecue. I went with him and have been highly diverted. These Barbecues are Hogs, roasted whole. This was under a large Tree. A great number of young people met together with a Fiddler and Banjo played by two Negroes, with Plenty of Toddy, which both Men and Women seem to be fond of. I believe they have danced and drunk till there are few sober people amongst them." Philip Vickers Fithian, another visitor to Virginia, recorded a similar account in a September 1774 journal entry: "I was invited this morning by Captain *Fibbs* [Gibbs] to a *Barbecue:* this differs but little from the Fish Feasts, instead of Fish the Dinner is roasted *Pig,* with the proper appendages, but the Diversion & exercise are the very same at both—I declined going and pleaded in ex[c]use unusual & unexpected Business for the School." Fithian was a Princeton seminarian from New Jersey who spent a year tutoring the children at Nomini Hall, the Northern Neck plantation seat of Robert Carter III. Though Fithian recorded no judgment on the dish itself, his journals make clear that the "Diversion & exercise" of the barbecues offended his Presbyterian sensibilities.

Assembling the necessary food and drink for barbecues required money and planning, and that meant either sponsorship by a wealthy individual or a coordinated subscription effort to finance the entertainment. Colonel Landon Carter, the uncle of Robert Carter III, discussed the evolving tradition in his diaries on September 5, 1772:

> It is our third Barbacue day [this year]. I think it an expensive thing; but submit to the opinions of others.
>
> I went to the barbacue and cou[ld not help] observing that [torn] many on the credit of their Su[bsc]ription brought eaters enough there, some 5 and 6 for one Subscription. So that they all eat at about the price of 15d a head, when others paid at least 7/ for themselves alone which I think is a very unequal disposal of money. But as others submit to it I will not be the first to alter it: I confess I like to meet my friends now and then; but certainly the old method of every family carrying its own dish was both cheaper and better because then nobody intruded, but now everyone comes in and raises the club; and really many do so only for the sake of getting a good dinner and a belly full of drink.

Carter was wary of the drinking and dancing that went on at these events, fearing that "barbecues and what not deprived some of their senses" and were a form of "treachery to decoy young people off from Duty."

Sources: Nicholas Cresswell, *The Journal of Nicholas Cresswell, 1774–1777* (London: Dial, 1924), 16. Philip Vickers Fithian, *Journals and Letters of Philip Vickers Fithian 1773–1774: A Plantation Tutor of the Old Dominion,* ed. Hunter Dickinson Farish (Williamsburg, VA: Colonial Williamsburg, 1957), 183. Landon Carter, *The Diary of Colonel Landon Carter of Sabine Hall, 1752–1778,* ed. Jack P. Greene (Charlottesville: University Press of Virginia, 1965), 2:722, 900.

and they spend little time describing the type of meat that was served, how it was prepared, or how it was served to guests. From the brief descriptions that exist, however, we can surmise that pork was generally the meat of choice, that it was roasted whole over a pit of coals, and that the dinners were accompanied by dancing and heavy drinking. By the eve of the Revolution, the events were firmly entrenched as one of the most popular forms of entertainment in Virginia society.

Over time, the barbecue grew beyond the social sphere and became part of the political world as well, and it was in Virginia that the first political barbecues were held. Election days in Colonial Virginia were infrequent, occurring whenever the governor dissolved the Assembly or a member quit or died. Each county was allotted two seats in the House of Burgesses, the only real elected body in the colony. To choose their representatives, eligible voters would gather at the county courthouse, coming into town in wagons and on horseback from miles around. Elections were usually held on court days, when many men would already be traveling to the county seat to conduct business such as buying and selling land, slaves, and supplies. These gatherings were rowdy events, with lots of liquor and fistfights. The casting of ballots occurred publicly in the courthouse in front of the sheriff and competing candidates and only added to the excitement.[18]

According to the unwritten code of conduct, candidates in Virginia were obliged to compete upon their natural virtues, abilities, and honor, staying aloof from voters and not stooping to active campaigning. In practice, though, office seekers knew they had to go out among the voters and drum up support. The practice of "treating"—plying voters with liquor and food—was widespread and, though practiced discreetly, became an indispensable component of an election campaign.[19] These election treats always included large quantities of rum punch and other liquors, and often sweets such as cookies and ginger cakes. Some candidates took the practice a step further, hosting outdoor picnics for the public and providing barbecued bullocks and pigs—the first instances of American campaign barbecues.

Treating was expensive, but because Virginian officeholders were drawn almost exclusively from the upper classes, the candidates generally paid for the gifts out of their own pockets. In the 1758 election for the House of Burgesses, for example, George

Washington spent £39.6s to purchase "28 gallons of rum, 50 gallons and one hogshead of rum punch, 34 gallons of wine, 46 gallons of 'strong beer,' and 2 gallons of cider royal," a generous ration for a district that contained only 391 voters.[20] The rationale for these expenditures was more complicated than simply trying to buy voters' loyalty, for any suggestion that the treats were being explicitly traded for votes was considered dishonorable and could result in a candidate's being denied office. In 1758, Matthew Marrable of Lunenburg County made just such a misstep in his campaign for a burgess seat. He treated too extravagantly, providing seven barbecued lambs and thirty gallons of rum to a militia company on election day. He was also found to have written a letter to an influential citizen promising support for specific pieces of legislation in exchange for his backing in the upcoming election. Such explicit promises were a violation of campaign ethics, and the Burgesses' Committee on Privileges and Elections declared Marrable's actions to be improper and voided his election.[21]

Properly done, treating was supposed to be not an exchange of favors for votes but rather a demonstration of the candidate's generosity and hospitality, virtues that were considered the defining traits of a gentleman. George Washington recognized this distinction, explaining to one of his allies, "I hope no exception were taken to any that voted against me but that all were alike treated and all had enough; it is what I much desir'd—my only fear is that you spent with too sparing a hand."[22] It was a curious mix of aristocracy and democracy. Because they presented themselves for approval before the common citizenry, the gentry could claim the consent of those they governed and argue that their natural fitness to rule had been recognized by the people. At the same time, each Virginian had to cast his vote aloud before a table in the courthouse at which the candidates were seated, and the chosen candidate generally thanked each person as his vote was cast—a clear reminder that it was being noted who had given support and who had not.[23]

Barbecue in the Carolinas

Though it was firmly entrenched in the daily life of Virginia planters, barbecue does not seem to have played a significant part in the lowcountry plantation culture of Charleston, South Carolina. Early diaries and other accounts of Charleston life make no reference to barbecue, and even descriptions of the city's horse races—occasions that were almost always accompanied by barbecues in Virginia—do not mention the dish. Charleston society in the eighteenth century was dominated by rice planters, and it tended toward more formal entertainment such as banquets and balls. Its cookery was characterized by shrimp, wild game, rice dishes, and rich desserts such as syllabubs, not roasted meats such as pork and mutton.

Fifty miles down the coast in Beaufort, however, a barbecue tradition did flourish around the time of the Revolutionary War, though it differed from the Virginia style in that it was not an institution for the entire community—male and female, upper and lower classes—but rather was a form of entertainment for an exclusively male and mostly well-to-do group. In his autobiography, William J. Grayson, a prominent lawyer and man of letters born in Beaufort in 1788, recalled growing up among older men who had participated in the Revolution. He remembers them as "a jovial and somewhat rough race, liberal, social, warm-hearted, hospitable, addicted to deep drinking, hard-swearing, and practical-joking and not a little given to loose language and indelicate allusions.... They were fond of dinner, barbacues, and hunting clubs."[24] These barbecues were hard-drinking, all-male events. Each guest had to match his fellow drink for drink; refusing to continue was a breach of what Grayson termed "barbacue-law" and would result in ostracism for the violator—or, at least, some form of mockery as punishment.[25] These barbecue and hunt clubs were gentlemen's organizations that consisted of the leading citizens of the community.

The Beaufort hunting club had a barbecue house located about a mile outside of town. It is unclear when the structure was built, but it was destroyed by a hurricane in 1804. The event was recorded by a man named Findlay, a schoolteacher recently arrived from the North, whose mock-heroic poem "On the Fall of the Barbacue-House At Beaufort, S.C. During the Late Tremendous Storm" was published in the *Charleston Courier* on November 1, 1804. It describes the "sacred temple—where, in mirthful glee, the jovial sons of Pleasure oft convene." As expected, there was plenty of drinking and practical joking:

Grog's mellow radiance set their souls on fire,

Till kindling into generous rage, the group

Caught inspiration from each other's eye;

Then, bright witticisms flash—the merry tale—

Satirical description—*jeu de wel*—

Song—and conundrum—in their turn succeed.[26]

This poem sheds some light on the ingredients of early barbecue. In his introduction to *The Confederate Housewife,* John Hammond Moore speculates that early South Carolina barbecues were likely "little more than alfresco animal roasts, without the tomato, ketchup, mustard, and pepper-vinegar concoctions now associated with a good plate of barbecue" and that it wasn't until the Mexican-American War (1846–1848), when South Carolinians discovered new, hotter varieties of peppers, that barbecue became heavily seasoned.[27] Findlay's poem, however, makes clear that the South Carolina version of the dish was highly spiced long before the influence of Mexican peppers, and the meat wasn't limited to pork. The poet describes the "famed SIRLOIN" and "Turkey-cock" that were regularly consumed at the barbecue house and notes,

These roasted—bak'd—grill'd—devil'd—barbacu'd—

Like Heretic or Jew beneath the claws

Of Spain's dread Inquisition, feel the pangs

Of pungent Cayenne, Mustard's biting power,

And many a stimulant to me unknown,

Judiciously applied, exhale their sweets,

Grateful to hungry Poet and his Muse.[28]

The remainder of the poem describes the hurricane and the destruction of the barbecue house where, in the words of William J. Grayson, "generations had feasted and made merry." The structure was apparently never rebuilt.[29]

The barbecue house in Beaufort seems an anomaly for lowcountry South Carolina. The strong Carolina barbecue tradition that developed in the nineteenth century did not move from the coast inland; instead, it spread into the Carolinas from Virginia, following the main migration patterns of backwoods settlers. In the 1740s, frontier families began moving south from Virginia and Pennsylvania, following the eastern edge of the Appalachian Mountains, seeking new lands to farm. Through the 1750s the backcountry was unstable and unorganized, and the outbreak of the Cherokee War in 1760 and the lawlessness that followed created further chaos. It was not until the 1770s that the backcountry was stable and safe enough for a reliable agricultural economy to develop. Barbecue as an institution—that is, large social gatherings where whole hogs and sheep were cooked and eaten—was not feasible on the frontier, for it required not only large amounts of food but also a concentrated enough population to gather for a feast. Once farms and plantations began to prosper in the Carolina backcountry, the residents resumed many of the social traditions they had enjoyed in Virginia. In many cases, these settlers had moved southward with ambitions of founding their own plantations and becoming landed gentry themselves. Their adoption of barbecue was not just a continuation of the food preferences they had learned in their native Virginia but also an attempt to recreate Tidewater society in the newly settled backcountry.

One common occasion for a backcountry barbecue was a militia muster, which brought together the white men from all over a county for a day of drilling and socializing. A barbecue feast was usually prepared to follow the drills. One such muster in 1766 in New Hanover, North Carolina, occurred at a time of high tensions over the recently passed Stamp Act, and angry colonists turned the occasion into a political protest. The tyrannical Governor William Tryon had prepared a feast for the mustering troops, including a whole barbecued ox and several barrels of beer. When Tryon called the citizens to the feast, they spurned his hospitality, pouring the beer into the ground and throwing the ox untasted into the river.[30]

Barbecues were fairly common throughout upstate South Carolina. Charles Woodmason, an itinerant Anglican minister assigned to the western parishes of South Carolina, described in his journals in the late 1760s, "I had last Week Experience of the Velocity and force of the Air—By smelling a Barbicu dressing in the Woods upwards of six Miles."[31] In 1775, William Henry Drayton was sent to South Carolina's Upper District (near present-day Spartanburg) to enlist the support of backcountry residents for independence. That August he held a meeting at Wofford's Iron Works and barbecued a beef for the event.[32]

By most accounts, these backwoods events were pretty crude affairs. They took place in clearings in the woods or in dusty open fields, with improvised tables and furnishings and whatever dishes and utensils the settlers had on hand. The meat might be pork, beef, or mutton, depending on what was available, and accounts of stifling heat, undercooked meat, and other unappetizing conditions are common. Carolina barbecues still had a way to go before they would match the elegance of their Virginia predecessors. The institution had been established, however, and was beginning to spread southward and westward through the frontier states.

An Early South Carolina Barbecue

ONE OF THE MOST detailed accounts of a colonial South Carolina barbecue can be found in the letters of William Richardson, a Charleston
merchant who left the city in the early 1770s to become a planter in
South Carolina's Camden District. Richardson attended a local horse
race in March 1773 and described it in a letter to his wife, who was still
living in Charleston:

> First then suppose us in the midst of a new ploughed field, the Wind
> blowing excessively hard, clouds of dust arising every [torn] & [a]
> Quarter of Beef Barbacuing in this dust and nicely browned indeed,
> but not with the fire, Three planks laid a Cross some sticks for a
> Table, this elegant table covered, not with damask or diaper, I would
> not have you think, [illegible] to your self two superb Oznabrigs
> sheets (not white) no! they scornd to have any thing so formal as
> to be clean) that had perhaps been laid in a month at least & the
> couler of a dishclout that had served the uses of the kitchen, for a
> month at least without washing . . . well then this Table coverd, the
> pewter arranged, a knife to some plates & half a one to others, Enter
> two Hogs & a Quarter of Beef of the couler of a piece of Beef Tied
> to a string & dragged thro' Chs Town streets on a very dry dusty
> day & then smoke dried, a Dish of Bacon & Turnip Tops & a Dish of
> Beef, plenty of Brown loaves their looks not inviting & in taste re-
> sembling Saw dust.

Richardson found the meal appalling, but his companions disagreed:

> I absolutely saw one lady devour a whole Hog head except the

bones, don't tell this to any of your squeemish C Town ladies for they will not believe you, had some of them been near our feast & their appetites Gorged with what you in town call delicases (but what we Crackers dispise) they perhaps might think us cannibals & with some propiety they might think, if they could suppose a half rosted hog, with the blood running out at every cut of the Knife, any thing like human flesh but ye squeemish C Town ladies I would not have ye think our buxom Cracker wenches so degenerate! no they can eat when hungry a piece of the devil roasted, in the shape of a Hog & to wash down this [superb e]legant repast, we did not gulp down necter, no, that would [torn] liquor of life mingled with the dust of the field whole pails we Quaf'd, not quite so transparent indeed as the Kennell water that runs thro' your streets after a shower of rain.

Source: Emma B. Richardson, ed., "Letters of William Richardson, 1765–1784," *South Carolina Historical and Genealogical Magazine* 47 (January 1946): 6–7.

Barbecue and the Early Republic

In the first decades of the nineteenth century, barbecue continued to move across the South. As settlers made their way through the Cumberland Gap into Tennessee and Kentucky, they carried the barbecue tradition with them, as did the planters who pushed southwestward through Georgia and into Alabama, seeking new land for cotton farming. Both on the frontier and in the older communities of Virginia and the Carolinas, the events took on increased social importance. Barbecues became the quintessential form of democratic public celebration, bringing together citizens from all stations to express and reaffirm their shared civic values.

One of the most common expressions of these values occurred on the Fourth of July, and the barbecue became the traditional way to celebrate the country's independence and its egalitarian principles. As election campaigns became more open and democratic, the barbecue was adopted by political candidates and used to reach larger and larger groups of voters. These events used food and drink to appeal to voters' baser appetites and were frequently criticized as a form of corruption and demagoguery. At the same time, they provided a new forum for political debate and helped increase the number of white southern men involved in the political life of their communities. By the 1840s, the barbecue—once a form of genteel recreation limited largely to Tidewater Virginia—had become firmly entrenched in the culture of an area stretching from the

Chesapeake Bay all the way to the highlands of Kentucky and the newly cleared farm-lands of Mississippi.

"Republican Plenty": Fourth of July Barbecues

Barbecue restaurants today do a brisk business on the Fourth of July, advertising for customers to place their orders in advance to ensure there will be enough pulled pork or ribs for family celebrations. The meat and the accompanying sides—coleslaw, baked beans, rolls, banana pudding—are taken home in big aluminum foil–covered pans and served on paper plates on front porches and in backyards at gatherings of families and friends. These gatherings have a long history in the South, a history stretching back to the very first Independence Day celebrations. The surprising thing about early Fourth of July celebrations is how formal and standardized they became. Town after town cele-brated the Fourth with an almost identical set of ceremonies that featured a barbecue at their center. As settlers moved west into the frontier territories, they took these holiday customs with them, making July Fourth barbecues not just a southern tradition but an American one.

From the very beginning, public dinners were a common feature of July Fourth cele-brations, and these dinners quickly grew from small affairs hosted by prominent citi-zens to large outdoor barbecues attended by entire communities. On July 9, 1808, *Mill-er's Weekly Messenger* of Pendleton, South Carolina, reported the July Fourth celebration at Occoney Station in the mountainous western part of the state. Following a parade by the local militia, "a short address suited to the occasion was delivered by the Rev. Mr. ANDREW BROWN; after which they marched to an agreeable and natural arbor, where, in the company with a number of others, they partook of an elegant barbecue." Occoney (now spelled Oconee) was a newly settled frontier district, and the *Miller's Weekly Messenger* correspondent wrote, "It was a sight highly pleasing, to see such re-spectable members meet for the first time in this remote place, to celebrate the anni-versary of our national existence."[1]

The naturalist John James Audubon, traveling in Kentucky in the early part of the

Audobon's "Kentucky Barbecue on the Fourth of July"

JOHN JAMES AUDUBON, THE great American naturalist and painter, recorded the following account of a Fourth of July barbecue in Kentucky during the early part of the nineteenth century as part of a sketch in *Delineations of American Scenery and Character*.

The free, single-hearted Kentuckian, bold, erect, and proud of his Virginia descent, had, as usual, made arrangements for celebrating the day of his country's Independence. The whole neighborhood joined with one consent. No personal invitation was required where everyone was welcomed by his neighbor, and from the governor to the guider of the plough all met with light hearts and merry faces.

It was indeed a beautiful day; the bright sun rode in the clear blue heavens; the gentle breezes wafted around the odours of the gorgeous flowers; the little birds sang their sweetest songs in the woods, and the fluttering insects danced in the sunbeams. Columbia's sons and daughters seemed to have grown younger that morning. For a whole week or more, many servants and some masters had been busily engaged in clearing an area. The undergrowth had been carefully cut down, the low boughs lopped off, and the grass alone, verdant and gay, remained to carpet the sylvan pavilion. Now the waggons were seen slowly moving along under their load of provisions, which had been prepared for the common benefit. Each denizen had freely given his ox, his ham, his venison, his turkeys, and other fowls. Here were to be seen flagons of every beverage used in the country; "La belle Riviere" had opened her finny stores;

the melons of all sorts, peaches, plums and pears, would have been sufficient to stock a market. In a word, Kentucky, the land of abundance, had supplied a feast for her children.

A purling stream gave its water freely, while the grateful breezes cooled the air. Columns of smoke from the newly kindled fires rose above the trees; fifty cooks or more moved to and fro as they plied their trade; waiters of all qualities were disposing the dishes, the glasses, and the punch-bowls, amid vases filled with rich wines. "Old Monongahela" filled many a barrel for the crowd. And now, the roasted viands perfume the air, and all appearances conspire to predict the speedy commencement of a banquet such as may suit the vigorous appetite of American woodsmen. Every steward is at his post, ready to receive the joyous groups that at this moment begin to emerge from the dark recesses of the woods.

Each comely fair one, clad in pure white, is seen advancing under the protection of her sturdy lover, the neighing of their prancing steeds proclaiming how proud they are of their burdens. The youthful riders leap from their seats, and the horses are speedily secured by twisting their bridles round a branch. As the youth of Kentucky lightly and gaily advanced towards the Barbecue, they resembled a procession of nymphs and disguised divinities. Fathers and mothers smiled upon them, as they followed the brilliant cortége. In a short time the ground was alive with merriment. A great wooden cannon, bound with iron hoops, was now crammed with home-made powder; fire was conveyed to it by means of a train, and as the explosion burst forth, thousands of hearty huzzas mingled with its echoes.

From the most learned a good oration fell in proud and gladdening words on every ear, and although it probably did not equal the eloquence of a Clay, an Everett, a Webster, or a Preston, it served to remind every Kentuckian present of the glorious name, the patriotism, the courage, and the virtue, of our immortal Washington. Fifes and drums sounded the march which had ever led him to glory; and as they changed to our celebrated "Yankee Doodle," the air again rang with acclamations.

Now the stewards invited the assembled throng to the feast. The fair led the van, and were first placed around the tables, which groaned under the profusion of the best productions of the country that had been heaped upon them. On each lovely nymph attended her gay beau, who in her chance or sidelong glances ever watched an opportunity of reading his happiness. How the viands diminished under the action of so many agents of destruction I need not say, nor is it necessary that you should listen to the long recital. Many a national toast was offered and accepted, many speeches were delivered, and many essayed in amicable reply. The ladies then retired to booths that had been erected at a little distance, to which they were conducted by their partners, who returned to the table, and having thus cleared for action, recommenced a series of hearty rounds. How-ever, as Kentuckians are neither slow nor long at their meals, all were in a few minutes replenished, and after a few more draughts from the bowl, they rejoined the ladies, and prepared for the dance.

Source: John James Audubon, *Delineations of American Scenery and Character* (New York: G. A. Baker, 1926), 241–43

century, was a guest at a similar event, which he described at length in *Delineations of American Scenery and Character* (see page 26). Audubon's account links the barbecue tradition to its Virginia roots, noting, "The free, single-hearted Kentuckian, bold, erect, and proud of his Virginia descent, had, as usual, made arrangements for celebrating the day of his country's Independence." Unlike the tradition in colonial Virginia, where society's elite hosted barbecues as part of their duties of hospitality, the frontier celebration Audubon attended was organized and prepared by the entire community. Area residents donated the provisions "for the common benefit"—including ox, ham, venison, turkeys, and other fowls—and helped to clear a large area in the woods for the barbecue grounds. The day began with a cannon salute and a patriotic oration delivered by "the most learned" of the community. The company then proceeded to the tables for the feast, which was followed by a series of toasts and dancing that continued until sundown.[2]

Most frontier barbecues were free to all comers, with the provisions donated by various members of the community. A few, however, were for-profit events held by entrepreneurs who charged for admittance. The following advertisement, for example, appeared in a Lexington, Kentucky, newspaper in June 1815:

BARBACUE

The subscribed respectfully informs the citizens of Fayette and the adjoining counties, that he will prepare an elegant *Barbacue Dinner, on the Fourth of July, at his own house, on the Limestone road, nine miles from Lexington. . . . The subscriber furnishes foreign liquors of the best quality for the LADIES—the gentlemen will have* free access *to the use of domestic liquors. Tickets of admittance, two dollars—there will be no expense nor personal trouble omitted to render his entertainment* brilliant *and interesting.*[3]

Commercial events such as this one seem to have been the exception, not the rule. It was almost the end of the century before barbecue became a regular commercial enterprise.

The elements seen in these early descriptions—communal barbecues, drinking, orations, toasts, and dancing—were typical of early frontier celebrations, and they soon became part of the ritual in settled towns, too. By the 1820s Independence Day celebrations had become standardized throughout the Carolinas, Kentucky, and Tennessee. Newspaper accounts of these events read almost like boilerplate. The day began with the citizens of the surrounding region gathering to form a procession. Led by local militia units in uniform, the community would march to a central location—usually the courthouse or a church—for the day's ceremonies. These opened with a prayer, then the Declaration of Independence would be read aloud. In many communities, local musicians would play and sing patriotic songs. The ceremonies always concluded with an oration delivered by a prominent citizen on a topic such as the principles of the Revolution or the importance of the Constitution to civic life. After the proceedings, the citizens would retire to a shady grove for a large dinner, which usually featured barbecued pigs, sheep, and goats.

After the dinner, toasts would be made in celebration of Independence Day, the United States, and its leaders. These began with a series of "regular" toasts, usually thirteen in number, which were prepared in advance and given by prominent persons chosen for the honor. The list of subjects for the toasts varied from celebration to celebration, but they usually included the U.S. Constitution, prominent political leaders, and abstract patriotic principles such as "Political Liberty" and "The Right to Fight" (see page 31). The thirteenth toast was almost always devoted to honoring American women (or, "The American Fair," as it was usually phrased). As each toast was made, the crowd would respond, in the words of the *Camden, South Carolina, Journal* in 1831, with "loud huzzas and the firing of guns."[4]

Once the prepared set of regular toasts was completed, "volunteer toasts" followed—often as many as thirty or forty. In addition to celebrating war heroes and democratic ideals, these toasts often addressed contemporary political issues. At the 1824 celebration in Jackson, Tennessee, for example, the volunteer toasts included support for the country of Greece ("May it be sustained by the Eagle of America"), a plea for the people of the Western District to choose their candidates wisely at the next general election, and a call for the navigation of the Mississippi to remain free to the citizens of the United States and not entangled in any foreign partnerships.[5] In 1834, in the wake of the Nullification Crisis, there were thirty-six volunteer toasts made at the Sherman's Store celebration in the Greenville District of South Carolina. Almost all were strongly pro-Union, pro-Jackson, and anti-Calhoun—reflecting the sentiments of Greenville,

Fourth of July Toasts

THE FOLLOWING REGULAR TOASTS were delivered at the 1824 Fourth of July barbecue in Madison County, Tennessee.

1. "The Day we celebrate"—The birthday of American Independence; duly appreciated, and held sacred by its votaries.

2. "The memory of George Washington"—Encomium would be fulsome: Let expressive silence muse his praise.

3. "Thomas Jefferson and James Madison"—Ex-Presidents of the United States.

4. "James Monroe, President of the U. S."—The voice of an independent people will award him an escutcheon worthy of his services.

5. "The American Revolution"—Founded upon principle; its origin the source of lasting happiness of millions yet unborn.

6. "The memory of our fellow-citizens who fell in the late war"—Their services are still fresh in our recollections.

7. "General Andrew Jackson"—Our Chief in War; our Ruler in Peace.

8. "The 8th of January, 1815"—A day on which Britain's Invincibles crouched to American valor.

9. "Grecian Emancipation?"—In a cause so glorious, she has our best wishes.

10. "The Western District of Tennessee"—The most desirable part of our state.

11. "Internal Improvements"—The surest basis of National Wealth.

12. "Our Country"—Breathes there a man with soul so dead, Who never to himself hath said, "This is my own, my native land."

13. "Woman"—Her smiles our richest reward, her protection our [solemn duty].

Source: *Jackson (TN) Gazette*, July 10, 1824.

the hotbed of Unionist sentiment in South Carolina.[6] Such toasts were of considerable interest to the community, and most newspaper accounts of July Fourth celebrations from the period published transcriptions of the regular toasts and, in many cases, the volunteer ones as well.

The sheer number of toasts at the typical Fourth of July barbecues suggests that there was a lot of drinking going on, and the events were indeed notorious for drunkenness and the violence that naturally came with it. Recalling the Fourth of July barbecues of his childhood in antebellum South Carolina, Dr. Samuel B. Latham noted that the various local militia companies would attend the celebration at Caldwell Cross

Roads and, after the drills, oration, and dinner, "hard liquor would flow; and each section would present its 'bully of the woods' in a contest for champion in a fist and skull fight. Butting, biting, eye gouging, kicking and blows below the belt were barred. It was primitive prize fighting."[7] Booze and July Fourth accidents go hand in hand, and there was no shortage of such incidents at early barbecues. In 1834 at the celebration in South Carolina's Union District, Washington Sample had his right hand blown off and his left arm broken when an old cannon, taken from the British during the Revolution, discharged while he was reloading it. He had "neglected in his hurry to swab out the gun, and a burning cinder still inside came into contact with the new gunpowder being loaded," and there were only "some faint hopes of his life."[8]

Rough as they were, Fourth of July barbecues had an important civic function beyond simple merrymaking. The entire community would come together at these events and—through the reading of the Declaration and the patriotic orations—would reaffirm the guiding principles of the early republic. The toasts were both a celebration of the new country's history and, in their commentary on current events, a form of political discourse. Barbecues were also important reflections of American democratic values. In colonial Virginia, barbecues had been part of an aristocratic social structure, with wealthy planters showing their hospitality and hosting barbecues for those on the lower rungs of the hierarchy. After the Revolution, the gatherings became increasingly egalitarian. This change can be seen in the following newspaper account of an armistice celebration in New Bern, North Carolina, in June 1778:

> By way of celebration for this event, starting at one o'clock there was a barbecue (a roast pig) and a barrel of rum, from which the leading officials and citizens of the region promiscuously ate and drank with the meanest and lowest kind of people, holding hands and drinking from the same cup. It is impossible to imagine, without seeing it, a more purely democratic gathering, and it confirms what the Greek poets and historians tell us of similar concourses among those free peoples of Greece. There were some drunks, some friendly fisticuffs, and one man was injured. With that and the burning of some empty barrels as a feu de joie at nightfall, the party ended and everyone retired to sleep.[9]

Such portrayals of barbecues as fundamentally democratic gatherings can be found again and again in newspaper reports from the early nineteenth century.[10]

In keeping with this republican spirit, most Fourth of July celebrations were not hosted by a single individual but rather were organized by a "Committee of Arrangements." This committee generally consisted of three to five men who were elected at a public gathering. In 1824, the citizens of Jackson, Tennessee, met on Saturday, June 12, "to make arrangements preparatory to a celebration of the approaching anniversary of American Independence."[11] In other communities the committee was chosen as much as a year in advance, sometimes on the morning of July 4. An advertisement in the July 2, 1831, *Camden Journal,* for example, announced, "The citizens of Camden and its vicinity are requested to meet at the Court House on *Monday the fourth day of July* next; at 9 o'clock AM . . . to elect an orator and appoint a Committee of Arrangements for the succeeding Anniversary."[12] As was typical for elected offices in the early nineteenth century, the members of the committee were usually prominent local citizens such as planters, lawyers, and doctors.

The Origins of Political Barbecues

The citizens who organized the Fourth of July barbecues and delivered the orations at them did so in part out of dedication to their community. At the same time, they were ambitious men with an eye on social, business, and political advancement. In his memoirs, Robert B. McAfee of Mercer County, Kentucky, recalled that during his early days as a young lawyer, he drummed up business by making orations at any and all occasions, speaking on political issues and other topics of public interest. His first public speech was made at a July Fourth barbecue at William Adams Spring in 1801, and as a result he "soon obtained more business than I expected, which convinced me that if I had gone to Harrodsburgh at once I would have acquired Distinction and practice much sooner than I did, as I was ardently ambitious and determined to rise before the public as soon as I could."[13] McAfee at this time was only seventeen years old. His speeches at Fourth of July barbecues and other events not only increased business for his law practice but also advanced him politically, and he went on to become a state senator and lieutenant governor of Kentucky.

Many other ambitious men found that barbecues offered a promising platform for political advancement. In addition to delivering orations and mingling with voters at public gatherings, politicians in the early nineteenth century began hosting their own barbecues for the sole purpose of attracting voters. In part they were just being practical: in an era with limited forms of mass communication, such gatherings were one of the few ways to reach large numbers of voters. But the popularity of the campaign barbecue also reflected a fundamental shift in the American political scene, as the rise of populist politics led to a reshaping of electoral standards and the establishment of a permanent party system.

American politics was evolving from the aristocratic model of colonial days to a more inclusive, rough-and-tumble democracy. The ruling gentry in colonial Virginia had professed the classical Republican ideal of a disinterested elite governing with the deferential consent of the common citizens, though barbecues and other forms of treating were early signs that voters actually exerted a certain amount of power. If this trend was noticeable in Tidewater Virginia, where the social structure was relatively stable and defined, it was even more evident on the frontier, where the social order was less certain and ordinary citizens were more likely to demand that their representatives cater to their personal interests. In these environments, public gatherings such as barbecues took on increased importance as venues where ambitious men could establish themselves politically.

On the frontier, the qualifications for political leadership were still being sorted out, and education, good breeding, and family connections were not nearly as important as they had been in old Virginia. Military service was one route to distinction, as was success in farming and business. In his autobiography, David Crockett recalled that a candidate for colonel in the Tennessee militia, whose officers were chosen by popular election among the regiment, was considered qualified for the post because, "He was an early settler in that country, and made rather more corn than the rest of us."[14] Equally important were virtues such as hunting skill, joviality, and the ability to make good stump speeches, which would be demonstrated in the weeks before an election at public barbecues. In his first campaign for the Tennessee legislature in 1821, Crockett made up for his lack of political experience by making a series of folksy speeches at events such as a squirrel hunt barbecue (see page 37), and he won his first seat in public office.

David Crockett. (Courtesy
Tennessee State Library and
Archives.)

By the 1820s, barbecue stump speeches were common throughout the settled portions of the South, which at that time included Virginia, the Carolinas, Tennessee, Kentucky, Georgia, and northern Alabama. Some local newspapers advertised three or four
barbecues a week during the election season.[15] Many of these, like the squirrel hunt attended by David Crockett, were held primarily for amusement and were used oppor-
tunistically by politicians as a chance to reach assembled voters. Others were organized
specifically for electioneering. A newspaper advertisement for a barbecue at Byrd's Big
Spring in northern Alabama, for example, announced, that "voters and candidates 'two
by two in couples one after another' are respectfully invited to attend . . . and partake
of whatever may be found to regale the soul and the senses."[16] An 1825 notice in the
Hunstville Democrat promised "a greater collection of people than has ever been seen

Davy Crockett's First Barbecue Stump Speech

THE FOLLOWING PASSAGE IS taken from Davy Crockett's *A Narrative of the Life of David Crockett of the State of Tennessee* (1834):

> *About this time there was a great squirrel hunt on Duck river, which was among my people. They were to hunt two days: then to meet and count the scalps, and have a big barbecue, and what might be called a tip-top country frolic. The dinner, and a general treat, was all to be paid for by the party having taken the fewest scalps. I joined one side, taking the place of one of the hunters, and got a gun ready for the hunt. I killed a great many squirrels, and when we counted scalps, my party was victorious.*
>
> *The company had every thing to eat and drink that could be furnished in so new a country, and much fun and good humor prevailed. But before the regular frolic commenced, I mean the dancing, I was called on to make a speech as a candidate; which was a business I was as ignorant of as an outlandish negro.*
>
> *A public document I had never seen, nor did I know there were such things; and how to begin I couldn't tell. I made many apologies, and tried to get off, for I know'd I had a man to run against who could speak prim, and I know'd, too, that I wa'n'y able to shuffle and cut with him. He was there, and knowing my ignorance as well as I did myself, he also urged me to make a speech. The truth is, he thought my being a candidate was a mere matter of sport; and didn't think, for a moment, that he was in any danger from an ignorant back-woods bear hunter. But I found I couldn't gert off, and so I determined just to go ahead, and leave it to chance what I should*

say. I got up and told the people, I reckoned they know'd what I come for, but if not, I could tell them. I had come for their votes, and if they didn't watch mighty close, I'd get them, too. But the worst of all was, that I couldn't tell them any thing about government. I tried to speak about something, and I cared very little what, until I choaked up as bad as if my mouth had been jam'd and cram'd chock full of dry mush. There the people stood, listening all the while, with their eyes, mouths and ears all open, to catch every word I would speak.

At last I told them I was like a fellow I had heard of not long before. He was beating on the head of an empty barrel near the road-side, when a traveler, who was passing along, asked him what he was doing that for? The fellow replied, that there was some cider in that barrel a few days before, and he was trying to see if there was any then, but if there was he couldn't get at it. I told them that there had been a little bit of a speech in me a while ago, but I believed I couldn't get it out. They all roared out in a mighty laugh, and I told some other anecdotes, equally amusing to them, and believing I had them in a first-rate way, I quit and got down, thanking the people for their attention. But I took care to remark that I was as dry as a powder horn, and that I thought it was time for us all to wet our whistles a little; and so I put off to the liquor stand, and I was followed by the greater part of the crowd.

Crockett's maneuver left few people to hear his opponent's speech. He won the election with twice the votes of his competitor.

Source: David Crockett, *A Narrative of the Life of David Crockett of the State of Tennessee* (Philadelphia: Carey and Hart, 1834), 138–42

at a barbecue in any of the southern states," with no less than "ONE THOUSAND weight of meat put upon the pitt, besides other necessaries to give zest to the entertainment. All this will be like God's blessing, 'without money and without price.'"[17] As campaign barbecues grew larger and became more frequent, they were increasingly hosted not by the candidates but by groups of supporters, who arranged the entertainment, purchased the food and drink, and placed advertisements in local newspapers. Such actions were some of the early roots of political party organization in southern states.

The Anti-Barbecue Backlash

By this point, stump speaking had become a requirement for attaining public office. A broadside entitled, "To the Voters of Frederick county" composed by "AN INDEPENDENT VOTER" on October 3, 1818, reveals how much the relationship between office seekers and voters had shifted. Candidates at one time had hosted "treats" to show their generosity and hospitality to voters; now, candidates were guests at the voters' barbecues. In assessing the qualifications of two candidates for the Maryland House of Delegates, "An Independent Voter" commented, "They are both amiable men, and the modest *unassuming* manner in which Mr. Worthington has gone through the drudgery of public speaker at your barbecues, sets him, in my estimation, above the common democratic seekers for fame or office."[18]

"An Independent Voter" did not look favorably upon the new political ritual, and he was not alone. The changes taking place on the frontier were making their way back east to the older states. In 1825, the editor of the *Norwich Courier* bemoaned that New Yorkers were starting to adopt "the modest custom of their Southern neighbors" and were starting not only to announce publicly that they were candidates for elections but also to run notices in newspapers to proclaim their qualifications for office. "We shall doubtless next hear," the editor harrumphed, "of stump orations, barbecues, and prime bang up knock me down whiskee frolicks."[19]

In the late 1820s, a remarkable backlash against campaign barbecues and other electioneering practices occurred in Madison County, Alabama. This anti-barbecue movement began in July 1827 when the *Southern Advocate* published the first of a series of letters from a correspondent calling himself "Barbecuensis." The letter, which attacked election barbecues as licentious and corrupt, opened with a poem that condemned the rowdiness of the gatherings:

> Did you ever see a Barbecue? For fear
> You should not, I'll describe it you exactly:—
> A gander-pulling mob that's common here,
> of candidates and sovereigns stowed compactly,—
> Of harlequins and clowns, with feats gymnastical
> In hunting-shirts and shirt-sleeves—things fantastical;—
> with fiddling, feasting, dancing, drinking, masquing
> And other things which may be had for asking.[20]

One of Barbecuensis's complaints against barbecues was that at them "sobriety is exchanged for intemperance . . . and liberty chastened to licentiousness." But his more serious charge was that they debased the electoral process, creating a new, lower standard for selecting a leader. "The question now," he wrote, "is not, what is his mental capacity? But, what are the dimensions of his stomach? Not, does he read and think? But, does he eat and digest? Not, if he will enact wholesome laws and promote and preserve the peace, happiness, and prosperity of the State, but if he will drink raw whiskey, eat rawer shote, dance bare foot on a puncheon floor . . . and pull at a gander's neck?"[21] In frontier barbecues, opportunism was on display for all to see, and it appalled many traditionalists.

The protests of Barbecuensis were echoed by the editors of the two local newspapers, and within a few months a full-fledged anti-barbecue movement was underway in Madison County. The *Southern Advocate* condemned the effects of campaign barbecues on the health and morals of the community, conjuring up specters of poor victims "shattered and shipwrecked, driven helpless and nerveless before the slightest blast . . . and which encountered their first and fatal gales on the stormy seas of barbacue politics." Undercooked pork and bad whiskey must have been common at these events, for

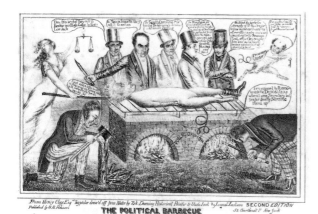

An 1834 political cartoon show-ing President Andrew Jackson being barbecued over the fires of public opinion after his removal of the deposits from the Bank of the United States. (Courtesy Library of Congress, Prints & Photographs Division.)

the editor echoed Barbecuensis in condemning the "gorging upon raw shote, and of a swilling of a species of liquor little less pernicious than liquid fire is worse than actual and immediate death."[22] The *Huntsville Democrat* struck a similar chord, arguing that due to electioneering, "many a man who would otherwise remain employed on his farm is induced to forsake his business and his family by the temptation" until "the sober in-dustrious citizen becomes a sot."[23]

Ultimately, these critics feared that barbecues and similar campaign tactics would lead to disorder and mob rule—a common anxiety during the age of Jackson.[24] Madison County's anti-barbecue movement culminated in a petition drive in July 1829 that gathered more than a thousand signatures from citizens opposed to the campaign prac-tice. Two years later, some candidates for the state legislature pledged not to attend bar-becues or other public gatherings organized for electioneering purposes.[25] These efforts had little effect. Democratic politics required campaigning, and barbecues were one of the most effective ways of doing so. Those candidates who tried to place themselves above such populist events usually paid the price on election day. As a matter of prin-ciple, for example, Josef Leftwich publicly announced his refusal to attend barbecues while running for the office of tax collector for Madison County. He finished seventh out of nine candidates.[26] Campaign barbecues remained controversial over the succeeding decades, but they had become permanent features of the southern political scene and would only grow in size and popularity.

Campaign Barbecues in the 1830s

The evolution of the political barbecue in the 1830s paralleled the rise of the organized political party system in the United States. In the early days of the Republic there had been two competing factions, the Federalists and the Democratic Republicans, which were more loose coalitions of politicians and voters sharing similar interests than actual political organizations. By 1816 the Federalists were effectively extinct, and the 1820s were a time of virtual one-party rule, a period known as the "Era of Good Feelings" that would be brief. By the end of the decade, the Democrats had become divided by ideological differences and personal rivalries, culminating in the contentious 1828 presidential race between Andrew Jackson and John Quincy Adams, which Jackson won by a 178 to 83 margin in the electoral college. A new political party began to coalesce in the mid-1830s, united primarily by opposition to Jackson's policies, particularly his attack on the Bank of the United States and his forceful response to the Nullification movement. Calling themselves the Whigs, a reference to the English political party that tried to limit the power of the king, the members of the new party considered it their first duty to rein in the excesses of "King Andrew."

The founding of the Whigs coincided with a dramatic expansion in the American electorate. In the early decades of the Republic, most states had property ownership or taxpaying requirements that limited the vote to only a minority of white men. These requirements began to be loosened or dropped altogether in the 1820s, first in the West and then in the older states on the East Coast, which had to follow suit to slow the out-migration of their residents to the frontier. In 1800, only four out of the then sixteen states chose their presidential electors by popular vote rather than legislative appointment; by 1824, eighteen out of twenty-four states had instituted the popular vote. Between 1824 and 1828 alone, the number of voters casting ballots in the presidential election increased from 400,000 to 1.1 million.[27] By the time of the Jackson presidency, almost all white male Americans were eligible to vote. To appeal to this newly expanded electorate, candidates had to adopt more broad-reaching electioneering tactics, such as barbecues, and these tactics required more formal organizations for planning and paying for campaigns. The Founding Fathers had considered political parties to be dangerous because they placed partisanship ahead of principle, but they gradually gained acceptance in the United States, being established first at the state level and then developing into national organizations.

It would be a mistake to assume that because new campaign practices appealed to a broader audience they necessarily required politicians to stoop to mindless demagoguery. Campaign barbecues involved much more than swapping food and drink for votes. As they became more formalized, barbecues began to contribute to, not diminish, the process of informed democracy. To be sure, politicians engaged in plenty of back-slapping and joviality at these gatherings, but at the same time they were going out into their communities, meeting voters in person, and getting to understand their wants and opinions. Some stump speeches were little more than florid oratory, but many turned into sophisticated debates on vital issues. Newspapers began printing the full text of speeches delivered at barbecues, sometimes taken directly from the orator's prepared text but more often transcribed word-for-word by a correspondent on the scene.

The conventions for holding barbecues, such as published invitations, also became more formal. Compare, for example, the earlier-cited advertisements from the 1820s that touted the amount of meat and quantity of liquor to be had with the following notice that appeared in the *Pendleton Messenger* in 1838: "As a Committee of Invitation on behalf of the citizens of Pickens district, we do most respectfully invite to attend a Barbecue to be given to the Hon. John C. Calhoun at this place, on Wednesday the 12th inst. all the revolutionary soldiers of Pickens, Anderson, and the adjoining districts, the Candidates for both branches of the State Legislature, and the citizens generally."[28] The barbecue was now a serious part of the public discourse over ideas and issues.

Political barbecues also became larger. In September 1836, the Whigs in Kentucky staged a massive barbecue on Lafayette Green on the outskirts of Versailles to welcome their leader Henry Clay home after the adjournment of the United States Senate. Clay brought with him several other national Whig leaders, including Daniel Webster and John J. Crittenden. In their addresses before an "immense throng of people," these noted statesmen railed against the excesses of the Jackson administration. The following spring, Daniel Webster embarked on a tour of the western states, making his way down the Ohio River by steamboat. The Whig diarist Philip Hone recorded that Webster was greeted with great enthusiasm at one town after another, and "Public dinners and barbecues have been tendered to him in great profusion."[29] In St. Louis on June 13, over five thousand people turned out to welcome Webster at a barbecue at a grove owned by Judge J.B.C. Lucas, and Webster delivered a two-hour speech for the occasion.[30]

A year later, another prominent southern statesman, John C. Calhoun, enlisted barbecues as a means of public political debate. Though his own seat in the U.S. Senate was not up for reelection, he took to the stump to campaign in favor of Martin Van Buren's plan for a subtreasury system and against the reelection of several officeholders who did not share his position.[31] Taking to the stump meant making the rounds at political barbecues. The first one Calhoun attended was on August 28, 1838, at Sandy Spring Church in South Carolina's Greenville District. The event was organized by a committee of seven prominent citizens who presumably paid for the provisions and invited the speakers. A blanket invitation was issued to the citizens of the district, and some fifteen hundred people showed up. In his address, Calhoun defended his support for the subtreasury system, attacking the relationship between the federal government and private banks as "unequal, unjust, corrupting in its consequences, anti-republican, hostile to States rights, and subversive of our liberties." Representative Waddy Thompson Jr., one of the rival politicians Calhoun was trying to unseat, had also been invited to the barbecue, and after Calhoun finished his oration, Thompson arose in response, pointing to Calhoun's previous support for the Bank of the United States and accusing him of inconsistency on the issue.[32]

As Thompson's presence shows, campaign barbecues were not necessarily one-sided partisan rallies. In many cases, they were forums for public political debate, allowing the assembled citizens to hear voices on competing sides of an issue. Two days after the

Sandy Spring Church barbecue, Calhoun accepted an invitation "in the name of many of the citizens of Anderson District, who approve of my course on the great and agitating question of the day[,] to partake of a barbecue dinner to be given at Anderson on the 21st of September."[33] Though initially planned as a partisan affair, the barbecue was merged with a similar gathering organized by another group of citizens for Waddy Thompson Jr. Moved to September 27, the combined event allowed the two men to again debate the subtreasury issue head-to-head.

Even when Calhoun was not able to attend barbecues in person, he used them to advance his arguments in the debate over the Bank. In late August 1838, he received an invitation from "the Republican and States Rights citizens of Richland district" on September 8. In a long letter to the Committee of Arrangements, Calhoun declined the invitation, citing "the season of the year, the great distance, and other causes not necessary to state" then began a two-thousand-word discourse attacking the philosophy behind a National Bank and defending states' rights.[34] The letter was intended as a public statement, and it was presumably read to the crowd at the barbecue. It was also printed in at least eleven newspapers, including local organs such as the *Columbia Telescope* and the *Charleston Courier* as well as out-of-state newspapers such as the Richmond, Virginia, *Enquirer* and the Washington, D.C., *Daily National Intelligencer.* Calhoun wrote similar letters declining barbecues in Columbia, South Carolina, in July 1838 and Yanceyville, North Carolina, in September, on both occasions writing long public statements on the subtreasury and states' rights issues. In this way, he was able to make his arguments reach far beyond the attendees of the barbecues to newspaper readers throughout the country.

"Tippecanoe and Tyler, Too": The Political Barbecue Comes of Age

The presidential election of 1840 marked the full flowering of the political barbecue in antebellum America. It was the second national contest between the newly formed Democratic and Whig Parties. Four years previously, Democrat Martin Van Buren, Andrew Jackson's vice president and handpicked successor, had defeated the Whigs

Questioning the Campaign Barbecues

WHILE ELECTION BARBECUES UNDENIABLY drew huge crowds during the 1830s and 1840s, not everyone was convinced that they were effective means of winning votes—especially if they were being held by a rival party. In November 1842, Henry Clay addressed a crowd of three thousand people at a Whig barbecue in Frankfort, Kentucky. The solidly Democratic *Brooklyn Eagle* delightedly reported an incident that allegedly brought the event to a rapid close: "In the midst of [Clay's] speech, Nichol's circus company entered the town; whereupon nine-tenths of his auditory scampered off to look at the circus cavalcade and monkeys that accompanied it. We are informed that `that same old coon' was exceedingly enraged at the ill-manners of the flint pickers, and broke off in the midst of his harangue, and started off in double-quick time for the 'peaceful shades of Ashland.'"

Source: *Brooklyn (NY) Eagle,* November 18, 1842, 2.

Whig Election Chant

Democrats—
They eat rats!
But Whigs
Eat pigs!

Source: Election day chant recalled by Marion Harland in her autobiography. Marion Harland, *Marion Harland's Autobiography: The Story of a Long Life* (New York: Harper & Brothers, 1910), 122.

Woodcut emblem from William Henry Harrison's 1840 "Log Cabin" presidential campaign, showing the candidate sharing hard cider with soldiers in front of his log cabin. (Courtesy Library of Congress, Prints & Photographs Division.)

in a landslide. Still stinging from this loss, the Whigs in 1840 united behind William Henry Harrison for president and John Tyler for vice president, and they decided to adopt a new message and strategy.

Harrison had little political philosophy and campaigned primarily on his military career, most notably his victory over the Shawnee leader Tecumseh at the Battle of Tippecanoe in 1811. The result, as Samuel Eliot Morison phrased it, was "the jolliest and most idiotic presidential contest in our history . . . the Whigs beat the Democrats by their own methods. They adopted no platform, nominated a military hero, ignored real issues, and appealed to the emotions rather than the brains of voters."[35] Determined to "agitate the people," the Whigs assembled strong local organizations and insisted on using "every lawful means" to bring voters to the polls.[36] These means included extensive treating, picnics, processions, and, of course, barbecues, all accompanied by popular campaign songs and catchy slogans such as "Tippecanoe and Tyler, Too."[37]

In Barren County, Kentucky, James Murrell constructed an eight-foot by twelve-foot log cabin for the Harrison barbecue at Bowling Green on the Fourth of July. The cabin was drawn to the barbecue grounds on a wagon by six white horses decorated with flags and banners, and some four thousand attendees listened while speeches were made from the front door of the cabin.[38] In Henderson County, Kentucky, the local Harrison barbecue was heavily attended by the ladies, who wore white aprons with log cabins painted on them and dined at long tables decorated with log cabins built out of stick candy.[39] Similar events were held across the upper South and the Midwest, ranging from the mountains of Virginia as far west as Mendon, Illinois, where hundreds of Whigs came from miles around to "consume the roasted carcasses of oxen, sheep, and hogs."[40]

Though the popular vote was close, Harrison beat Van Buren by a handy electoral college margin (234 to 60). The Whigs' successful tactics would be repeated by both parties in the presidential elections of 1844 and 1848 as well as the congressional elections in intervening years, establishing the barbecue as the premier form of political campaigning in the mid-nineteenth century.

A Typical Antebellum Barbecue

By the 1840s sufficient descriptions of barbecues had been published for us to piece together a composite picture of a typical event. The setting was almost always outdoors, usually in a wooded grove near a running spring. The shade was essential during the heat of summer and early fall, and the spring was not only cooling but also provided drinking water for the dinner (for those who were interested in water, that is).

The preparations typically began several days before the actual event, as animals had to be procured, brought to the site, and slaughtered and dressed. Barbecue fans today debate whether pork or beef or even mutton is the proper meat for genuine barbecue, but in the early days there were few regional preferences. Members of the community donated whatever livestock they had on hand, and it is quite common in descriptions of early barbecue to see a long list of animals including beef cattle, oxen, hogs, sheep, goats, and chickens. In frontier areas, game such as deer, wild turkeys, and squirrels were often donated for the cause, too.

For the pit, a long, shallow trench was dug in the earth, four to six feet wide and anywhere from six to several hundred feet long, depending upon the size of the gathering and the amount of meat to be cooked. Piles of hardwood such as oak or hickory

Tending the pits at a Georgia barbecue, late nineteenth century.

were set ablaze in the pits and allowed to burn until reduced to coals, which were then spread throughout the trenches to prepare for the cooking. Once the pits were ready, the animal carcasses, which generally were kept whole or split lengthwise, were run through with either green sticks or iron bars and laid across the pit.

Tending the pit was a difficult job. In the South, the actual work was usually performed by slaves. In some cases white men supervised the pits, but just as frequently an older slave would be recognized as the area's barbecue master, and he would oversee the entire cooking operation. Pots of basting liquid—usually melted butter, vinegar, and/or water along with salt and pepper—were kept along the trench, and the cooks would move up and down either side, basting the meat with long-handled brushes. The whole carcasses had to be lifted periodically and turned over, and a small pit of hardwood was kept burning off to the side to supply fresh coals, which were shoveled into the trenches to ensure a constant source of slow, steady heat. This procedure lasted many hours—frequently beginning early in the morning or even the night before—so that the meat would be finished and ready for the crowds by early afternoon.

A typical barbecue grove would be transformed from an ordinary stand of woods into an outdoor auditorium and banquet hall. Stakes were driven into the ground, crosspieces attached, and boards laid along the top to form long, temporary tables. Puncheons—large logs hewn in half—were used for benches, and they were sometimes buried into the dirt, too, flat sides up, to form a floor for dancing. A platform was generally erected at one end of the grove, from which the politicians would make their speeches, which typically began before noon and lasted well into the afternoon before the crowds were released to go to the tables and begin feasting.

By most accounts, the gatherings were boisterous and—through the early decades of the Republic, at least—whiskey flowed freely alongside the barbecued pork and beef. After the meal was over, toasts were frequently drunk, and the gatherings generally lasted through the afternoon and sometimes into the early evening. The combination of alcohol with political passions was sometimes a dangerous one and, like Fourth of July barbecues, political gatherings were occasionally marred by violence. At a barbecue at Bynum's Spring in Alabama, for example, an altercation erupted between "Squire" Maury, a Whig partisan, and a Jacksonian Democrat silversmith named Murdock. Maury drew a spear hidden within his walking cane and ran Murdock through three times in his abdomen. Fortunately for Murdock, the spear was not particularly sharp, and he survived and "in a short time he was out again hurrahing for Jackson."[41]

Whiskey and violence were still present, but by the 1840s, the campaign barbecue had evolved from a rustic celebration into an important form of political discourse in the United States both in the older eastern states and the new western frontier. Its significance to American public life would only continue to grow during the succeeding decades.

A Democratic Barbecue, 1844

As a young woman in 1844, Marion Harland of Powhatan, Virginia, attended a Democratic campaign barbecue, and she recorded a detailed description of the event in her autobiography. The barbecue was held in a field on the outskirts of the village just beyond Jordan's Creek, and though Harland's family were the staunchest of Whigs, they, along with most of the other area residents, showed up for the festivities. Her account is also perhaps the first recorded appearance of Brunswick stew at a barbecue. A dish that generally includes chicken or squirrel meat, corn, lima beans, and tomatoes, Brunswick stew is a traditional accompaniment to barbecue in Virginia and eastern North Carolina—one of the many variations that distinguish that region's barbecue tradition from the rest.

We crossed the stream upon a shaking plank laid from bank to bank, and strolled down the slope to the scene of operations. An immense kettle was swung over a fire of logs that were so many living coals. The smell of Brunswick stew had been wafted to us while we leaned on the fence. A young man, who had the reputation of being an epicure, to the best of his knowledge and ability, superintended the manufacture of the famous delicacy.

"Two dozen chickens went into it!" he assured us. "They wanted to make me think it couldn't be made without green corn and fresh tomatoes. I knew a trick worth two of that. I have worked it before with dried tomatoes and dried sweet corn soaked overnight."

He smacked his lips and winked fatuously.

"I've great confidence in your culinary skill," was the good-natured rejoinder.

I recollected that I had heard my father say of this very youth:

"I am never hard upon a fellow who is a fool because he can't help it!" But I wondered at his gentleness when the epicure prattled on:

"Yes, sir! a stew like this is fit for Democrats to eat. I wouldn't give a Whig so much as a smell of the pot!"

"You ought to have a tighter lid, then," with the same good-humored intonation, and we passed on to see the roasts. Shallow pits, six or seven feet long and four feet wide, were half filled with clear coals of hard hickory billets. Iron bars were laid across these, gridiron-like, and half-bullocks and whole sheep were cooking over the scarlet embers. There were six pits, each with its roast. The spot for the speakers' rostrum and the seats of the audience was well selected. A deep spring welled up in a grove of maples. The fallen red blossoms carpeted the ground, and the young leaves supplied grateful shade. The meadows sloped gradually toward the spring; rude benches of what we called "puncheon dogs"—that is, the trunks of trees hewed in half, and the flat sides laid uppermost—were ranged in the form of an amphitheatre.

"You have a fine day for the meeting," observed my father to the master of ceremonies, a planter from the Genito neighborhood, who greeted the visitors cordially.

"Yes, sir! The Lord is on our side, and no mistake!" returned the other, emphatically. "Don't you see that yourself, Mr. Hawes!"

"I should not venture to base my faith upon the weather," his

eyes twinkling while he affected gravity, "for we read that He sends
His rain and sunshine upon the evil and the good. Good-morning! I
hope the affair will be as pleasant as the day."

Source: Marion Harland, *Marion Harland's Autobiography: The Story of a Long Life*
(New York: Harper & Brothers, 1910), 24–26.

The Barbecue Comes of Age

The presidential elections of the 1840s cemented the status of the barbecue as a political institution not only in the American South but in the Midwest, too. Over the next two decades, the barbecue continued to mature and became the preeminent form of public celebration in America. Propelled by the expansionist aims of Manifest Destiny—and instrumental in helping promote such ideas—the barbecue moved west, becoming a part of frontier life from Texas all the way to the Pacific Coast. Along the way, it became more civilized, too.

This change was a natural part of the transition from frontier to settled society. Barbecues played an increasingly important role in the social life of communities, but they still had many of the rough trappings of their early days, including hard drinking and fighting, which made them still unacceptable for many citizens.

The growing presence of women at barbecues—particularly at political barbecues—was one factor in making the events more sedate. The Whigs made a special effort to include women in their campaign events, with the hope that even though they were not able to vote, they would be able to exert their influence and persuasion over male voters. On August 5, 1844, Missouri Riddick of Suffolk, Virginia, wrote to her husband and described the preparations for a Democratic gathering at Cowling's Landings, to be held on August 10. Mrs. Riddick predicted that it would be "a poor affair" because "the ladies are not invited. I believe all of the ladies will attend the Whig Barbecue, as they are particularly invited, and tables and seats are to be provided for them."[1] With women in attendance, the men had to tone down the drinking and fighting, and barbecues became more respectable.

Despite the gradual loosening of gender restrictions, barbecues were still predominantly male affairs. Women were typically greatly outnumbered by the men and were treated as special guests. At an October 1856 barbecue in Ninety Six, South Carolina, to welcome home Senator Preston Brooks from Washington (more about that event in a moment), some ten thousand persons were estimated to have attended, one thousand of them women, for whom special temporary seating was constructed on either side of the speakers' platform.[2]

The presence of women alone, however, was not the only force of change. The maturation of the barbecue occurred amid the welter of reform movements launched in the wake of the Second Great Awakening of the 1830s, including prison reform, mental illness reform, and—most significantly—the temperance movement.

The Fourth of July barbecue came under particular attack from both religious and civic reformers. The Old Salt River Primitive Baptist Church was one of the oldest organized churches in Anderson County, Kentucky, and it kept a tight reign on its members' moral conduct. In August 1815, several members were chastised for attending a July Fourth barbecue, and the following question was put before the congregation: "Is it right or wrong to attend a barbecue?" The church's answer was succinct: "It is wrong."[3] In July 1837, the editor of the *Cheraw Gazette* argued against the town's having a public feast for Independence Day: "A people whose patriotism needs to be forced into activity and life by the stimulants of alcoholic liquors and rich dinners may make good *subjects*, but not good *citizens*."[4]

Other reformers attacked barbecues for their deleterious effect on political and religious life. Dr. Frederic Lees, in arguing for the outright prohibition of liquor, complained that "Drunkenness is so invariably a concomitant of great political excitement, that a vast concourse of men at a Presidential barbecue, without a single case of intoxication in it, is not merely a striking curiosity, but a subject worthy of profound study for the statesman."[5] In 1833, the Tennessee legislature passed an act dictating that any person preparing a barbecue within one mile of a worshipping church assembly "shall be dealt with as rioters at common law, and shall be fined in a sum not less than five dollars."[6]

The American temperance movement, which culminated in the nationwide prohibition of alcohol in 1919, had its roots in the early nineteenth century, and when early reformers turned their sights on alcohol at public celebrations they naturally focused on the barbecue. Most early temperance advocates were drawn largely from the ranks of the well-to-do and the clergy, and most were lifelong abstainers from alcohol. Such reformers were easily cast as opponents of fun and sociability, and some received rough treatment at the hands of pro-drinking crowds. One unfortunate Methodist minister in Key West fell victim to "washing" by a crowd of sailors and local tavern-goers, who tied a rope around his waist and shoulders, cast him from a wharf into the water, then reeled him in and cast him back again. Josiah Flourney, a Methodist planter from Georgia, attempted a statewide campaign in 1839 to elect pro-temperance candidates to the legislature. As he traveled the state, his meetings were broken up by angry crowds, who threatened Flourney, destroyed his buggy, and shaved and painted his mule.[7]

Some temperance crusaders could give as good as they got. Prohibition advocates from the late nineteenth century loved to tell the tale of Paul Denton, an itinerant Methodist preacher who held a camp meeting in 1836 in one of the roughest, most disreputable districts in Texas. Denton issued handbills promoting a grand barbecue to take place in a shady grove, promising that "to all who attend, the best drink in the world will be furnished, free." A huge crowd turned out for the feast. When the rougher element demanded to know where the liquor was, Denton gestured to a spring near the grove and said, "There is the drink I promised! Not in simmering stills, over smoky fires, choked with poisonous gasses, and surrounded with the stench of sickening odors and rank corruptions, doth your Father in heaven prepare the precious essence of life, the pure cold water, but in the green glade and grassy dell, where the red deer wanders and the child loves to play, there God brews it."[8] The crowd's reaction to Denton's trick is not recorded.

Around 1840, a new approach to temperance emerged. Reformers began to realize that their efforts would remain ineffective if, in their zeal to stamp out drunkenness, they also attacked the forms of amusement and social interaction that naturally came along with drinking. It wasn't the barbecue itself that the temperance advocates found objectionable; it was the excessive boozing that took place at the typical gathering.

So, reformers began to enlist barbecues in their cause, often staging competing events to draw crowds away from the whiskey-soaked affairs. In 1846, the Salubrity Temperance Society staged a July Fourth Temperance barbecue near Liberty, South Carolina. Allen Fuller, the secretary of the society, contrasted his organization's event with a competing Fourth of July barbecue at nearby Wolf Creek, "at which the lovers of strong drink assembled in multitudes. The candidates for office were there, and dealt out the liquor in profusion, and profanity, drunkenness and quarrelling were the order of the day. One of its advocates admitted that it was the most disorderly company he had ever seen." The Salubrity Temperance Society's competing event not only provided an alternate way to celebrate Independence Day but also was "the means of advancing the temperance cause in this vicinity."[9]

The Washingtonian Temperance Society, founded in Baltimore in 1840, was an organization of "dry drunks" who sought to convert other drinkers to the life of temperance. Rather than advocating legislation and sweeping social changes, the Washingtonians focused on the individual drinker, with the goal of getting converts to sign the "teetotal" pledge of total abstinence. To do so, they embraced public meetings, parades, and—particularly in the southern states—barbecues. A Washingtonian "cold water barbecue" held in July 1842 in Quincy, Florida, illustrates the evangelical and ritual aspects of the temperance gatherings that made the Washingtonian events such a draw. Dressed in their finest clothes, the participants created a grand procession, with the women in carriages flanked by the men on horseback, "with badges on their left breast and the banner of Temperance unfurled to the breeze." They paraded to the Methodist Church, where a series of speeches encouraged attendees to come forward and sign the pledge. Lee Willis, who studied the temperance and prohibition movement in Florida for his doctoral dissertation, concluded that these events helped Washingtonian revivals flourish because "they substituted for masculine drinking rituals and provided an alternative form of intoxication."[10]

Temperance barbecues were not limited to the South. On July 4, 1843, attendees from local churches and Sunday Schools assembled in Norwich Township near Columbus, Ohio, for an event that paralleled the traditional Independence Day barbecue format. "Temperance melodies" were substituted for some of the patriotic songs on the procession to the barbecue grove. The speaker was one Mr. Moseley, "the distinguished Washingtonian and efficient temperance advocate," whose oration addressed "the history of our institutions, their nature, and the tendency of the mighty temperance reformation to the perpetuity."[11]

Before long the effect of the temperance movement could be seen at ordinary public barbecues, too. In 1837, Mary Morangé, the daughter of a planter in the Abbeville district of South Carolina, attended the local Fourth of July barbecue and noted that after the barbecue was served, "some cold water toasts were drunk which nearly froze on the lips."[12] In 1843, the *Greenville Mountaineer* noted that at the Pickens, South Carolina, event barbecue had been served "with nothing to wash it down but cold water."[13] By this point, hard-liquor toasts were frequently replaced with the cold water variety. While newspapers still published the text of the toasts made at the events, it became quite common to see, as the *Greenville Mountaineer* noted in 1844, "the drink part, as is usual, being dispensed with."[14]

Even without the draw of liquor, the popularity of barbecues continued to grow, and they were no longer looked upon with suspicion and distrust. By the 1840s newspaper stories and advertisements often referred to "old-fashioned" barbecues, for the rituals and characteristics of the events had long become part of society's traditions. The largest gatherings grew from a few thousand to over ten thousand guests. When a barbecue was held, virtually everyone in the surrounding county would turn out, if not to eat roasted pork or listen to campaign speeches then to meet their friends and see what everyone else was doing. Barbecue had become a social institution.

Brunswick Stew

As barbecue evolved, new elements became part of the tradition, including the side dishes that accompanied the roasted meat. One of the earliest barbecue sides was Brunswick stew. The origins of this dish have been hotly debated, with two different Brunswick counties—one in Georgia and the other in Virginia—claiming credit as the rightful

"Nat Joined the Temperance Society"

NAT MONTEITH WAS A good-natured free and easy individual from boyhood up. He was a great lover of "pot-liquor," and whenever cabbage would be prepared for dinner, the cook would invariably call to him, when she'd hear his well known footsteps, to come and get some of the homely beverage. There had been quite a revival among the advocates of temperance, and a "Cold Water Army," for the benefit of the boys, had been organized—backed by a barbecue in the Court House grounds, northeast corner Main and Washington streets. Next day the cook called to him that she had his "pot-liquor" ready. "No, Aunt Jane, can't take it: joined the temperance society."

Julian A. Selby, *Memorabilia and Anecdotal Reminiscences of Columbia, S.C. And Incidents Connected Therewith* (Columbia, SC: R. L. Bryan Company, 1905), 34

home. At the Highway 17 Welcome Center in Brunswick, Georgia, a twenty-five-gallon iron pot is affixed to a stone base with an inscription that reads, "In this pot the first Brunswick Stew was made on St. Simon Isle July 2 1898." A mess sergeant, the story goes, for a company of soldiers stationed at Gascoigne Bluff on the island created the stew with no particular recipe, using whatever meats and vegetables he had handy. It turned out so tasty that local residents started copying his formula.

It is a specific claim with a very tangible piece of evidence, but, unfortunately for Georgia, by 1898 Brunswick stew had been around for over a half-century in Virginia. While the Virginia claim is easily established, the actual origins of the recipe are more difficult to pin down. The most widely repeated story traces the stew not only to a particular person but to a particular event. The general narrative is usually presented with some very specific details: the first Brunswick stew was created in 1828 by James "Uncle Jimmy" Matthews for Dr. Creed Haskins of Mount Donum during a squirrel hunt. Matthews is generally identified as a black man and is described as a "family cook," "retainer," or "manservant" for Dr. Haskins, and sometimes more prosaically as a slave owned by Haskins. The stew is often presented as an improvisation, with Matthews concocting the stew from squirrels, butter, onions, and bread after the venison or other meat the hunting party planned to eat spoiled.[15]

This version has some basis in the historical record, but like many food origin stories, it contains a number of elaborations and false assumptions that were added over the years. The hunting expedition and the last-minute improvisation are latter-day embellishments, but it appears that James Matthews was indeed the originator of the stew. In 1886 the *Petersburg Index-Appeal* published a letter from "Tar Heel" that sketches the basic outline of the story. Two decades later, I. E. Spatig, the commissioner of Brunswick County, Virginia, in preparing a pamphlet that provided a capsule history of the county, solicited letters from residents of the Red Oak District to trace the history of the famous stew, and the responses confirm the story from the *Petersburg Index-Appeal.* This pamphlet seems to be the source for most of today's explanations of the dish's origins.

M. E. Brodnax, one of the correspondents published by Spatig, wrote that James Matthews was "a retainer of Dr. Creed Haskins, who lived at Mount Donum, on the banks of the Nottoway River."[16] The term "retainer" seems to have caused later commentators to conclude that Matthews was a black man, most likely a slave. "Tar Heel," however, makes clear that Matthews was a white "man of refinement" from the Red Oak neighborhood in Brunswick County, Virginia. A soldier who fought in the War of 1812, Matthews had "a roving disposition" and was a popular household guest who would perform odd jobs for his hosts. He was also a great squirrel hunter and, as "Tar

Brunswick stew pots at a Georgia barbecue. (*Strand Magazine,* 1898.)

Heel" phrases it, "it was his way of cooking the squirrels which gained him such popularity and eclat with the ladies."[17]

Matthews started making his stew sometime around 1820, and his recipe was quite simple.[18] He cooked the squirrels in water along with bacon and onions, stewing them until the flesh separated from the bones, which were skimmed out. He finished the pot with butter and breadcrumbs and seasoned it with salt and pepper. Matthews earned a reputation for his stew, which he delighted to make at picnics and public gatherings.

After his death, Matthews was succeeded by Dr. Aaron B. Haskins as the local stew master, who was in turn succeeded by Jack Stith and then Colonel W. T. Mason. Each man brought his own innovation to the recipe. Haskins was said to have added a touch of brandy or Madeira wine for flavor. Stith introduced vegetables sometime during the 1830s, adding tomato, onion, corn, and potatoes.

By the 1840s, Brunswick stew had spread beyond the borders of its namesake county and had become a staple of barbecues across the state of Virginia. Marion Harland of Powhatan—about fifty miles north of the Nottoway River—recalled attending a Democratic barbecue outside of Richmond in 1844 where a Brunswick stew made

The Original Brunswick Stew Recipe

PARBOIL SQUIRRELS UNTIL THEY are stiff (half done), cut small slices of bacon (middling), one for each squirrel; one small onion to each squirrel (if large one to two squirrels), chop up. Put in bacon and onions first to boil, while the squirrels are being cut up for the pot. Boil the above till half done, then put in butter to taste; then stale loaf bread, crumbled up. Cook then till it bubbles, then add pepper and salt to taste. Cook this until it bubbles and bubbles burst off. Time for stew to cook is four hours with steady heat.

Source: "Original Squirrel Stew, by Dr. A. B. Haskins, of Brunswick County, Va." quoted in *Brunswick County, Virginia: Information for the Homeseeker and Investor* (Richmond, VA: Williams Printing Company, 1907), 22.

from two dozen chickens was cooked in an immense kettle over a log fire.[19] The 1879 cookbook *Housekeeping in Old Virginia,* a compilation of recipes from two hundred and fifty Virginia housewives, contains four different recipes for Brunswick stew. Three of them call for either squirrel or chicken, while one calls for a shank of beef. All four include corn and tomatoes. Brunswick stew spread beyond the borders of Virginia sometime in the late nineteenth century, but in the years prior to the Civil War it remained a local delicacy.

Barbecues in the Life of American Slaves

As with most aspects of American history, barbecue is thoroughly intertwined with the issues of race and slavery—often in contradictory ways. On the one hand, slave owners used barbecues as a means of control, giving Fourth of July and Christmas barbecues to their slaves as a supposed reward for their labor. This occasional display of generosity helped reinforce the image of benevolent masters that was crucial to the South's conception of its peculiar institution. On the other hand, barbecues were opportunities for slaves to subvert the system. In antebellum Virginia, masters often allowed slaves to hold their own barbecues for recreation, but the practice was curtailed after several incidents—most notably Gabriel's Rebellion in Henrico County—where these gatherings were used as cover to plan uprisings. Illicit barbecues with stolen livestock remained a common way for slaves to have entertainment at their masters' expense. And, African American slaves were usually the pitmasters and cooks for the large barbecues hosted and attended by whites, and thus played a formative role in developing the techniques and recipes of southern barbecue.

In the colonial era and for the first few decades of the new republic, slaves in Virginia and the Carolinas were given a relative amount of license to travel and assemble outside appointed work hours. Many slaves—particularly skilled artisans—enjoyed considerable freedom of mobility, including the ability to travel between plantations and cities as well as to attend church meetings, funerals, and barbecues. Barbecues were common forms of recreation for slaves, particularly on Sundays, when they were typically released from labor. Few descriptions of these informal events survive, but it is reasonable to assume that the cooking techniques and styles were similar to those used when the slaves cooked for larger gatherings where whites were in attendance.

Because they allowed an inconspicuous means for slaves to gather and interact, barbecues played key roles in several of the most notable slave revolts during the antebellum years. In 1800, an enslaved blacksmith named Gabriel formulated a plan for a massive revolt in the Richmond, Virginia, area that would involve thousands of slaves. His plan was to kill two local slaveholders—Mr. Johnson and Mr. Prosser, Gabriel's owner—seize their arms, then kill all the neighboring whites, then proceed to Richmond to seize the arms and ammunition from the magazine. To enlist supporters, Gabriel and his co-conspirator Solomon invited slaves to attend several barbecues, using the occasions as cover to plan the uprising.[20] The plot unraveled before it could get underway when slave informants notified authorities in Richmond of the plan, and Gabriel and twenty other conspirators were arrested and executed.

Thirty-one years later, on a Sunday afternoon in August, six slaves met at noon in the woods on the plantation of Joseph Travis in the Cross Keys neighborhood in Southampton County, Virginia, bringing with them some brandy and a pig for a barbecue. At three o'clock they were joined by a seventh slave named Nat Turner, a charismatic carpenter and preacher, and—putting in place a plan that had been in the works for six months—they left the barbecue, gathered fifty more slaves, and proceeded on a two-day assault against the white families in Virginia. In the end, fifty-five white men, women, and children were killed before the local militia violently suppressed the revolt, and more than one hundred slaves were killed in retaliation.[21]

The Nat Turner rebellion was the bloodiest slave revolt in American history, and it marked a turning point in the institution of slavery. News of the revolt caused panic throughout the South, and whites formed vigilance committees and severely curtailed the remaining freedoms of both slaves and free blacks. State legislatures enacted laws prohibiting slaves, free blacks, and mulattoes from being taught to read, preaching without a white minister present, and practicing medicine. Many whites blamed abolitionists and the ongoing Missouri Compromise debates for causing slave unrest, and the Nat Turner rebellion helped heighten the tensions that eventually led to the Civil War. It also brought to a halt the freedom of movement that had allowed slaves to organize their own barbecues and gather with fellow slaves from other farms and plantations.

But, the barbecue still played an important role in the social life of American slaves. In the cotton states of the Deep South—especially Georgia, Alabama, and Mississippi— barbecues were common on plantations straight up until the Civil War. At a typical plantation, barbecues were the centerpiece of two holidays: Christmas and either the Fourth of July or a more general late-summer holiday held once the crops were "laid by," meaning cultivation was complete and the hardest labor was over until the autumn harvest. The plantation owner usually supplied the meat for the occasion, which might be a pig, sheep, or even beef, and the slaves often supplemented this with produce from their own garden patches. In most places slaves were given the entire day off to do as they pleased, and frequently they were allowed to invite friends from other plantations to join in the festivities. The meat was prepared using the standard method, with a long trench dug in the ground and the carcasses placed on long spits or poles over the glowing coals. The smoked meat was the centerpiece of the feast, but there was a range of side items as well. Some of the more common foods appearing in contemporary accounts include chicken pies, sweet potato pies, "light" bread, and corn bread along with desserts like ginger cake, molasses cake, peach cobbler, and apple dumplings.

In some cases, drinking was not a part of the festivities, for owners were wary of alcohol use among their slaves. Louis Hughes recalled that at the Fourth of July barbecues on the plantation where he was enslaved near Pontotoc, Mississippi, "the drinks were temperance drinks—buttermilk and water."[22] This was not true across the board. Lina Hunter from Oglethorpe County, Georgia, remembered that at the barbecues that followed the cotton harvest there was "lots of drinkin' and dancin'." When a WPA interviewer questioned Mose Davis's memory of whiskey being available on his master's plantation, he replied, "The Colonel was one of the biggest devils you ever seen—he's the one that started my daddy to drinking. Sometimes he used to come to our house to git a drink hisself."[23]

With or without whiskey, dancing was almost always an important part of plantation barbecues. One or more fiddlers would play the tunes, and the revelers would "pat Juba" or launch into breakdown dancing. Virginia Tunstall Clay-Clopton recalled visiting "Redcliffe," the South Carolina plantation home of James Henry Hammond, and witnessing the dancing at the Fourth of July and Christmas barbecues: "There is a tall black man, called Robin, on this plantation, who has originated a dance he calls the turkey-buzzard dance. He hold his hands under his coat-tails, which he flirts out as he jumps, first to one side, and then to the other, and looks exactly like the ugly bird he imitates."[24]

Barbecues were used for more than relaxation and celebration. In some cases they were an incentive for collaborative work. Corn shuckings were the most common of such events. After the corn was harvested, it needed to be shucked, dried, and stored or

A cornshucking on Mr. Fred Wilkins's farm near Stem, North Carolina, 1940. This common form of collaborative farmwork had its roots in antebellum plantation life and lasted well into the twentieth century. (Courtesy Library of Congress, Prints & Photographs Division.)

ground into meal. All the hands on a plantation, whether they worked in the fields or in the house, would be enlisted, and the owner would send invitations to neighboring planters to have their slaves attend, too. Hundreds of bushels of corn would be placed in a giant mound fifty or more feet high or in a long row that stretched hundreds of feet. Mahala Jewel, who lived on a plantation in Oglethorpe County, Georgia, recalled, "De fust thing dey done at cornshuckin's was to 'lect a gen'ral. All he done was to lead de singin' and try to git evvybody to jine in his song 'bout de corn, and as dey sung faster de shucks de flew faster too."[25] Often the shucking was made into a competitive event, with two teams racing to see who could finish their mound of corn first. After the work was over, all the hands would be treated to a barbecue feast, and music and dancing would continue long into the night. Hog killing and cotton pickings were similar collaborative occasions where barbecue was traditionally served.

Barbecue days were some of the best times in slaves' difficult lives. Louis Hughes, who was raised in slavery on a cotton plantation near Pontotoc, Mississippi, recalled that the annual Fourth of July barbecue "acted as a stimulant through the entire year. . . . It mattered not what trouble or hardship the year had brought, this feast and its attendant pleasure would dissipate all gloom."[26] Plantation barbecues also served an important role in the rhetoric of slavery, both during the sectionalist debate leading up to the

"Come to Shuck that Corn Tonight"

A CORN-SHUCKING SONG, GENERALLY sung on the way to the farm where
the shucking would be held:

>All dem puty gals will be dar,
>
>>Shuck dat corn before you eat.
>
>Dey will fix it fer us rare,
>
>>Shuck dat corn before you eat.
>
>I know dat supper will be big,
>
>>Shuck dat corn before you eat.
>
>I think I smell a fine roast pig,
>
>>Shuck dat corn before you eat.
>
>A supper is provided, so dey said,
>
>>Shuck dat corn before you eat.
>
>I hope dey'll have some nice wheat bread,
>
>>Shuck dat corn before you eat.
>
>I hope dey'll have some coffee dar,
>
>>Shuck dat corn before you eat.
>
>I hope dey'll have some whisky dar,
>
>>Shuck dat corn before you eat.
>
>I think I'll fill my pockets full,
>
>>Shuck dat corn before you eat.

William Wells Brown, *My Southern Home: or, The South and Its People* (Boston: A. G.
Brown, 1880), 92–93.

Civil War and in the postwar moonlight-and-magnolia brand of historiography, which portrayed slavery as a benevolent institution. The Fourth of July and Christmas celebrations were held up as examples of the generosity of slaveholders, and nostalgic accounts of life on the plantations routinely described barbecues as proof that African Americans were content in their lives of servitude. Walter L. Fleming, for example, a professor of history at West Virginia University, described plantation barbecues in his 1905 history *Civil War and Reconstruction in Alabama,* emphasizing the singing and merrymaking and concluding, "The slaves were, on the whole, happy and content."[27]

Frederick Douglass, a former slave and author of the *Narrative of the Life of Frederick Douglass* (1845), had a different view. He judged the holidays granted to slaves to be not a custom of benevolence but rather "the most effective means in the hands of the slaveholder in keeping down the spirit of insurrection" and "part and parcel of the gross fraud, wrong, and inhumanity of slavery." Such events were "safety valves" that allowed the pent-up spirit of rebelliousness to be released. Douglass noted that many masters not only allowed slaves to get drunk during holidays but actively encouraged it through drinking contests and other means. In Douglass's view, this was not a form of entertainment but a means of enforcing control. The supposed holiday times of freedom became periods of dissipation ending with illness and hangover, so that "we staggered up from the filth of our wallowing, took a long breath, and marched to the field,—feeling, upon the whole, rather glad to go, from what our master had deceived us into a belief was freedom, back to the arms of slavery."[28]

Despite the stricter controls on movements and gatherings put in place following Nat Turner's rebellion, not all barbecues were sanctioned by plantation owners. Estrella Jones recalled that when she was growing up on a Georgia plantation called Powers Pond Place the men would occasionally steal hogs, barbecue them, and serve them with hash and rice. "The overseer knowed all 'bout it," she remembered, "but he et as much as anybody else and kept his mouth shut."[29] Whether explicitly at white-approved events or illicitly as subversive forms of entertainment, the tradition of barbecue ran deep in the life of African Americans before the Civil War, and it would only deepen and expand after the end of slavery.

A Plantation Barbecue

LOUIS HUGHES WAS BORN into slavery in Virginia in 1832 and was sold at age twelve to a cotton planter from Pontotoc, Mississippi. He worked as an errand boy and house servant and learned enough medicine to be able to treat fellow slaves. He was sent to Memphis in 1850 to work at the planter's new house in the city, and there he married. Hughes twice attempted to escape and was captured before he finally succeeded during the closing days of the Civil War. Hughes and his wife settled in Milwaukee, where he worked as a professional nurse. In 1897 he published *Thirty Years a Slave: From Bondage to Freedom,* his memoirs of life on a cotton plantation. In the autobiography, Hughes captured the following description of a plantation barbecue:

> Barbecue originally meant to dress and roast a hog whole, but has come to mean the cooking of a food animal in this manner for the feeding of a great company. A feast of this kind was always given to us, by Boss, on the 4th of July. The anticipation of it acted as a stimulant through the entire year. Each one looked forward to this great day of recreation with pleasure. Even the older slaves would join in the discussion of the coming event. It mattered not what trouble or hardship the year had brought, this feast and its attendant pleasure would dissipate all gloom. Some, probably, would be punished on the morning of the 4th, but this did not matter; the men thought of the good things in store for them, and that made them forget that they had been punished. All the week previous to the great day, the slaves were in high spirits, the young girls and boys, each evening,

congregating, in front of the cabins, to talk of the feast, while others would sing and dance. The older slaves were not less happy, but would only say; "Ah! God has blessed us in permitting us to see another feast day." The day before the 4th was a busy one. The slaves worked with all their might. The children who were large enough were engaged in bringing wood and bark to the spot where the barbecue was to take place. They worked eagerly, all day long; and, by the time the sun was setting, a huge pile of fuel was beside the trench, ready for use in the morning. At an early hour of the great day, the servants were up, and the men whom Boss had appointed to look after the killing of the hogs and sheep were quickly at their work, and, by the time they had the meat dressed and ready, most of the slaves had arrived at the center of attraction. They gathered in groups, talking, laughing, telling tales that they had from their grandfather, or relating practical jokes that they had played or seen played by others. These tales were received with peals of laughter. But however much they seemed to enjoy these stories and social interchanges, they never lost sight of the trench or the spot where the sweetmeats were to be cooked.

The method of cooking the meat was to dig a trench in the ground about six feet long and eighteen inches deep. This trench was filled with wood and bark which was set on fire, and, when it was burned to a great bed of coals, the hog was split through the back bone, and laid on poles which had been placed across the trench. The sheep were treated in the same way, and both were turned from side to side as they cooked. During the process of roasting the cooks basted the carcasses with a preparation furnished from the great house, consisting of butter, pepper, salt and vinegar, and this was continued until the meat was ready to serve. Not far from this trench were the iron ovens, where the sweetmeats were cooked. Three or four women were assigned to this work. Peach cobbler and apple dumpling were the two dishes that made old slaves smile for joy and the young fairly dance. The crust or pastry of the cobbler was prepared in large earthen bowls, then rolled out like any pie crust, only it was almost twice as thick. A layer of this crust was laid in the oven, then a half peck of peaches poured in, followed by a layer of sugar; then a covering of pastry was laid over all and smoothed around with a knife. The oven was then put over a bed of coals, the cover put on and coals thrown on it, and the process of baking began. Four of these ovens were usually in use at these feasts, so that enough of the pastry might be baked to supply all. The ovens were filled and refilled until there was no doubt about the quantity. The apple dumplings were made in the usual way, only larger, and served with sauce made from brown sugar. It lacked flavoring, such as cinnamon or lemon, yet it was a dish highly relished by all the slaves. I know that these feasts made me so excited, I could scarcely do my house duties, and I would never fail to stop and look out of the window from the dining room down into the quarters. I was eager to get through with my work and be with the feasters. About noon everything was ready to serve. The table was set in a grove near the quarters, a place set aside for these occasions. The tableware was not fine, being of tin, but it served the

purpose, and did not detract from the slaves' relish for the feast.
The drinks were strictly temperance drinks—buttermilk and wa-
ter. Some of the nicest portions of the meat were sliced off and put
on a platter to send to the great house for Boss and his family. It
was a pleasure for the slaves to do this, for Boss always enjoyed it. It
was said that the slaves could barbecue meats best, and when the
whites had barbecues slaves always did the cooking. When dinner
was all on the table, the invitation was given for all to come; and
when all were in a good way eating, Boss and the madam would
go out to witness the progress of the feast, and seemed pleased
to see the servants so happy. Everything was in abundance, so all
could have plenty—Boss always insisted on this. The slaves had the
whole day off, and could do as they liked. After dinner some of the
women would wash, sew or iron. It was a day of harmless riot for all
the slaves, and I can not express the happiness it brought them. Old
and young, for months, would rejoice in the memory of the day and
its festivities, and "bless" Boss for this ray of sunlight in their dark-
ened lives.

Source: Louis Hughes, *Thirty Years a Slave: From Bondage to Freedom* (Milwaukee: South Side Printing Co., 1897), 46–51.

Railroad and Boostering Barbecues

Barbecue played an important role in one of the most important transformations of American life: the building of the railroads. Though tinctured by the legends of great individualists, railroad building was a community affair, and barbecue was involved on both the front end and the back. Railroad promoters used barbecues to attract citizens to giant rallies to support the building of railroads and, more important, to encourage them to buy "subscriptions," or shares, in the railroad companies. These shares provided the financial capital needed to build the expensive lines. On the back end, towns held barbecues to celebrate the completion of railroad lines to their communities, which could be pivotal events that would make or break the town's fortunes.

Building a railroad was an expensive proposition. A mile of track could cost anywhere from $20,000 to $50,000 to build, depending upon the difficulty of the terrain. Before the Civil War the federal government did little to fund railroads, and the large Eastern and European banks showed scant interest, too. Some state governments provided loans to railroad corporations, but most early funding came from individual investors. Most railroads were organized as corporations with state charters, and they raised the money to build their lines by selling capital stock or issuing bonds. The state charters gave railroads broad powers, including monopoly rights on rail service to defined areas, partial or total exemptions from state taxes, and the right to create banks and sponsor lotteries. In cases where state legislatures did provide loans or other funding to railroads, the money was often tied to the company's success in raising capital, with the state providing matching funds when the company had raised a specified amount in private money.[30]

Railroad promoters sought a large audience when raising funds. Many "subscribers" for early railroad companies were farmers and tradesmen living along the proposed routes or merchants and professional men in the lines' terminal cities. They were motivated not only by the income returned by the investment itself but also by the hope that the railroad would improve land values, open new markets, and lead to a general increase in trade for their city or region. The first generation of railroads were driven by investors in eastern port cities, who saw the lines as a way to gain a greater share of the

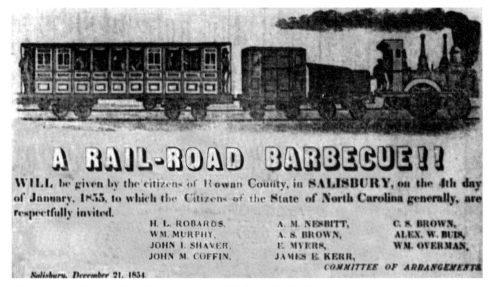

A RAIL-ROAD BARBECUE!!

WILL be given by the citizens of Rowan County, in SALISBURY, on the 4th day of January, 1855, to which the Citizens of the State of North Carolina generally, are respectfully invited.

H. L. ROBARDS,	A. M. NESBITT,	C. S. BROWN,
WM. MURPHY,	A. S. BROWN,	ALEX. W. BUIS,
JOHN I. SHAVER,	E. MYERS,	WM. OVERMAN,
JOHN M. COFFIN,	JAMES E. KERR,	
		COMMITTEE OF ARRANGEMENTS

Salisbury, December 21, 1854.

Advertisement for an 1854 railroad barbecue in Salisbury, North Carolina.

commerce from western markets. They were also supported by farmers along the routes, who sought a cheaper way to get their crops to market than by river or wagon.

To raise capital from these small investors, entrepreneurs needed to gather large crowds and create enthusiasm for their ventures. In midcentury America there was no surer way of gathering a crowd than holding a barbecue. The "railroad barbecue" became a staple of civic life in the South and Midwest during the 1840s and 1850s, joining Fourth of July celebrations and election stump speeches as prime occasions for sharing pit-roasted meat. In 1847, the citizens of Chester, South Carolina, combined their traditional Independence Day celebration with an event meant to raise money to complete the railroad from Columbia to Charlotte, which would pass through Chester. Following the standard speeches, the assembled citizens "partook of an excellent Barbacue, and again returned to the [speakers'] stand, where the Toasts were read, and the books opened for subscription to the Rail Road." Helped on perhaps by bellies full of barbecue and liquor, the townsmen poured forth their pledges, and the amount subscribed was $150,000—three-quarters of the $200,000 needed to secure the matching pledge from the state delegation.[31] The railroad line was eventually funded in full and reached Charlotte.

By 1850, some $300 million had been invested in building railroads, about half of that in stock and most of the rest in bonds. By 1860 that number exceeded $1.1 billion. Some thirty thousand miles of track had been laid, and railroads served all states east of the Mississippi.[32] Despite these successes, though, barbecues were a relatively inefficient way to recruit subscribers. The lure of free barbecue and whiskey would draw guests from miles around and fill them with "Railroad Enthusiasm," but that enthusiasm often waned when the sponsors opened their subscription books. Robert Hubard of Buckingham County, Virginia, who was helping raise funds for a "Straight Shoot" railroad, summed it up nicely in a letter to his brother: "4th of July barbecues afford good opportunities for the sovereigns to eat and drink to excess, but those who drink most liquor are not always most able to pay for the stock which their *whiskey generosity* and public spirit may tempt them to subscribe for."[33]

After the Civil War, Eastern financiers and European banks began to get in on the action, and railroads were increasingly built by corporations dominated by a few wealthy individuals. The federal government also became actively involved and provided grants of government land to the railroad companies for each mile of track constructed, and the companies could mortgage or sell this land to provide the capital for building the rails. Public gatherings and subscriptions ceased to be an important means of financing the rails. But, for the first thirty years of railroading—from 1830 until the start of the Civil War—it is not too much of an exaggeration to say that barbecue helped build America's railroads and, in the process, brought about a key transformation of American life.

Barbecues may have been an unreliable way to fund railroads, but they were a great way to celebrate their completion. Newspapers from the 1840s and 1850s are filled with accounts of massive gatherings to celebrate the arrival of the first train to a particular city. It was not only a recognition of the labor and effort involved in building the rails but also a celebration of the town and its future prosperity, which the arrival of the railroad helped secure. In June 1842, for example, the city of Columbia, South Carolina, staged a massive assembly to welcome the arrival of the first passenger train from

Charleston. The day chosen for this first run, June 29, was also the anniversary of the battle of Fort Moultrie during the Revolution, which at the time was a day of statewide celebration. At 6 A.M., two trains left the Line Street depot in Charleston and started for Columbia, its passengers including prominent Charleston citizens, members of the Artilleurs Francais militia company, and two pieces of ordnance. The train arrived in Columbia around 4:00 P.M. and was met by the Washington Light Infantry and some five thousand Midlands residents. Following welcome speeches from local dignitaries, the crowd "adjourned to the adjacent grove" for what was advertised as "a regular old fashioned BARBACUE." The meats for the barbecue were given particular attention, as the prized stock of Congaree planters were contributed for all to enjoy, including Bakewell sheep, Berkshire pigs, and Durham calves, all of which were new breeds recently imported from England.[34]

Barbecue Heads West

Barbecue had long been an important part of the American frontier and its expansion westward, so it is only natural that it had a significant role in the first major conflict that resulted from American expansionism: the Mexican-American War. The war had its roots a decade before, when in 1836 the largely American population of the province of Texas declared independence from Mexico and established themselves as an independent republic. Tensions simmered between the United States and Mexico over the next few years, coming to a head in 1845 when the United States admitted Texas to the Union as the twenty-eighth state. After several failed negotiations and a border skirmish that killed eleven Americans, the United States declared war in May 1846.

The standing American army was in no shape for the conflict. The so-called regular army—officers commissioned by Congress and soldiers who had joined for a five-year enlistment—numbered fewer than six thousand troops, and many senior officers were too old for active duty. In May, President Polk signed a war act authorizing fifty thousand volunteers to be recruited. Volunteers were raised according to the militia laws of each state and enlisted for twelve months of service, providing their own uniforms and, if cavalry, horses, too.[35] In most cases the state governor ordered that local militia units be assembled and a call made for volunteers. These volunteers were sent to a central rendezvous point for the state, where they were organized into regiments, elected their officers, and were accepted into service by the federal mustering officer.

The states in the Deep South and the Midwest contributed the most soldiers to the war, and barbecues were routinely used both for recruiting volunteers and for sending them off to battle. Attala County, Mississippi, for example, raised close to one hundred volunteers in the fall of 1846. Because the county had no railroads, the departing soldiers marched on foot to Canton, where they joined detachments from nearby Madison and Holmes. The people of Madison provided a huge barbecue for the soldiers, after which they organized a convoy of wagons to haul the troops to Jackson, where they could board the only railroad in the state and make their way to New Orleans to board ships to Mexico.[36]

One of the curiosities of the volunteer system was the twelve-month term of service. It was short enough to encourage a lot of volunteers, but, with training and transport time taken into account, it meant a high turnover of troops after only a few months of active combat duty. It also meant that state volunteer units were frequently welcomed home during the middle of the war, and these festivities generally involved the community staging a grand barbecue in the troops' honor.

In their details, these war barbecues were quite similar to the standard Fourth of July and political barbecues. What's most interesting about the celebrations is their geographical reach, which shows that by the 1840s the institution of barbecue had spread well beyond the American South. In the volume *Indiana in the Mexican War*, Oran Perry, the adjutant-general of Indiana, compiled more than a dozen instances of barbecues held to welcome home volunteers returning from the war. These celebrations occurred in the counties bordering the Ohio River near Louisville, Kentucky, and stretching westward across southern Indiana all the way to Sullivan County on the Illinois border.[37] These southern parts of Indiana were largely settled by emigrants from southern states—especially Kentucky, Tennessee, and North Carolina—who brought with them their traditions of public celebration by way of the barbecue.

Barbecue was present in Texas even before the outbreak of the Mexican-American War. In 1840, the citizens of Austin invited Colonel John H. Moore to a public barbecue to honor him for commanding companies of volunteers in raids against the Comanches.[38] Early Texas settlers hailed from American states with long barbecue traditions—particularly Tennessee and Kentucky—and they brought these traditions with them as they moved into formerly Spanish-held territory. The honoree of the 1840 barbecue, John H. Moore, was born in Rome, Tennessee, and came to Texas as part of the original "Old Three Hundred" group of settlers led by Stephen F. Austin. The lead member of the barbecue committee, Richard Fox Brenham, was born in Woodford County, Kentucky. Following Texas's admission to the Union in 1845, barbecue's role in the state's civic life would continue to grow, guided by old-timers from the Appalachian states. At Honey Grove in Fannin County, for example, the barbecue pits at the Fourth of July celebrations in the 1850s were overseen by "a Mr. Tate, a Kentuckian, who lived a few miles from town, was an expert in barbecuing meat, and could be had on most occasions."[39]

Texas today has a very distinctive regional barbecue style, but in the early days of statehood its barbecues were almost indistinguishable from the events held in the states back east. Beef barbecue dominates modern Texas barbecue but at mid-nineteenth century (as in other states) the meats used were whatever members of the local community donated to the cause. Early newspaper accounts of Texas barbecues mention beef, sheep, pigs, chicken, goats, and the occasional deer. The same reform movements that were transforming the barbecue tradition in the old South and Midwest influenced early Texas barbecue as well. In 1848, the first year that Texans could vote in an American presidential election, the Democratic Party held a free barbecue and mass meeting at Paris in Lamar County to promote support for the Democratic ticket of Lewis Cass and William O. Butler. An advertisement for the event noted, "The Ladies are particularly invited to attend, and cheer and animate with their smiles."[40] In 1850, citizens of Victoria and surrounding counties were invited to an "an old fashioned Free Barbacue" on the Fourth of July at which the ladies presented a Bible and banner to the Sons of Temperance.[41]

As Americans pushed the frontier beyond Texas into the territories gained during the Mexican-American War, they took barbecue along with them. In previous eras, it had taken several decades for barbecue and the social traditions it represented to catch

Kansas City's First Barbecue

KANSAS CITY, MISSOURI, TODAY is one of America's great barbecue cities, with its own distinctive cooking style and dozens of legendary barbecue joints. In the early days, though, its residents were still shaking out a few kinks. The city was chartered in 1853, and five years later had its first Fourtth of July barbecue: "Colonel McGee offered the grove in McGee's addition. 3,000 people attended, 500 of whom . . . were wives and daughters. Banta's Band furnished the music. The celebration commenced at 10 o'clock in the morning, and ended with a ball that night at the Metropolitan hotel. Colonel McGee bought a buffalo for the barbecue, which got away a few days before. Excited neighbors gave chase and captured the buffalo after a chase of a mile or more."

Source: Carrie Westlake Whitney, *Kansas City, Missouri: Its History and Its People* (Chicago: S. J. Clarke, 1908), 657.

up with the frontiersmen. By the 1850s, settlers were better equipped, and the rituals of barbecue were more ingrained into the national culture. Barbecues could be found on the western frontier from the very beginning, showing up, in fact, even before settlers arrived at their final destinations.

On July 3, 1849, a party of immigrants heading westward to the California gold fields arrived at Fort Bridger, Wyoming, a way station on the Oregon Trail. "Being

Americans in heart and feeling," the *North American and United States Gazette* reported, "they determined upon the celebration of the Fourth in proper style." A little improvisation was required—the menu for the feast included pork and beans—but they dug a pit in the classic fashion and barbecued plenty of beef for all. As at any July Fourth barbecue, the Declaration of Independence was read, toasts were drunk, and "some fine songs sung." The next day the party departed for the 114-mile trek to the Great Salt Lake and from there on to Sacramento, which they expected to reach in twenty-five days.[42]

Once in California, prospectors and other adventurers continued the traditions they brought with them from more settled places. In 1850, the Fourth of July was celebrated in Sacramento with an "old-fashioned" barbecue, though there were a few frontier twists. Following a grand procession to a shady grove, a traditional Independence Day address was delivered by J. M. Jones—in Spanish. After the assembly retired to the barbecue tables, a Major Dickey received four challenges to duels while he was eating his dinner.[43]

Things settled down within a few years. In 1853, the Fourth of July barbecue in Suisun Valley (midway between Sacramento and San Francisco) attracted eight hundred participants, one hundred fifty of them women. The address was delivered by the governor of California, and the barbecue was served on long tables under shade trees on the bank of a creek. For many, the mere fact that such events could be held—and held without drunken disturbances—was a testament to the region's becoming civilized. The reporter for the *Placer Times and Transcript* concluded of the Suisun Valley barbecue, "Nothing can more forcefully demonstrate the rapid advancement of California in those essential elements of natural prosperity and glory than occasions like this in the midst of the country."[44]

As in the East, California barbecues were quickly seized upon by political parties. Five thousand people gathered outside San Jose in 1856 to hear stump speeches by candidates from the Democratic, Republican, and American Parties. Four oxen, ten sheep, and twenty-four hogs were barbecued for the occasion. When the local marshal caught two men carrying away a roasted pig, they tried to argue that "they were Democrats and were bound to go the whole hog," but the marshal made them return it to the tables. The frontier population was a diverse one, made up of immigrants not only from all of the United States but from Mexico and Europe as well, and political barbecues helped introduce new generations to the traditions of barbecue. The roasted meat at the San Jose event, one commentator noted, was "so sweet and tender that many who had never eaten such meat before, eat as though they never would have a chance to eat any more."[45] A month later, at a Republican barbecue in Oakland, the speeches were delivered not just in English but in French, German, and Spanish, too.[46]

Barbecues weren't limited to the Golden State. The first recorded barbecue in Nevada was held on New Year's Day, 1853, in Dayton, a newly established town on the Carson River, where a few hundred prospectors were working gold and silver claims. One hundred fifty men and nine women attended the celebration.[47] Similar events were held in Utah and the Oregon and Washington Territories. By the time Oregon was admitted to statehood in 1859, barbecue had spread to the northwestern-most corner of the country.

It can be fairly said that up until the 1840s barbecue was primarily a southern tradition, but by the eve of the Civil War that was emphatically no longer the case. Whether for political rallies, civic celebrations, or just having a good time, barbecues were regular events in communities from the Atlantic Coast to the Pacific. Only in the northeast was the barbecue a relative stranger, and even there a few could be found now and again. Barbecue had become a national institution.

Barbecue and the Civil War

On May 19, 1856, Massachusetts senator Charles Sumner, a leader of the Radical Republican faction and one of the most bitter and outspoken opponents of slavery, took to the floor of the Senate to deliver a speech entitled "The Crime Against Kansas." The chamber was embroiled in the debate over the Kansas-Nebraska Act, which would allow settlers in the territories of Kansas and Nebraska to vote whether to accept or reject slavery. In his speech, Sumner declared that Senator Andrew Butler of South Carolina, one of the sponsors of the Kansas-Nebraska Act, was a Don Quixote who "believes himself a chivalrous knight" yet has chosen as a mistress "the harlot, Slavery." Butler had suffered a stroke that left him with speech problems and odd physical mannerisms, which Sumner mocked, claiming that Butler "with incoherent phrases, discharged the loose expectoration of his speech."[1]

Two days later, as Sumner sat writing at his desk on the floor of the nearly empty Senate chamber, Representative Preston Brooks of South Carolina entered, accompanied by Laurence Keitt, also of South Carolina, and Henry Edmundson of Virginia. Brooks was the nephew of Senator Butler, and he walked with a gold-headed cane due to a wound suffered during a duel. He approached the seated Sumner and declared, "Mr. Sumner, I have read your speech twice over carefully. It is a libel on South Carolina, and Mr. Butler, who is a relative of mine." As Sumner started to rise from his desk,

"Southern Chivalry—Argument versus Club's": an 1856 lithograph by John L. Magree depicting the caning of Charles Sumner by Preston Brooks in the U.S. Senate chamber. Following the incident, Brooks was welcomed home to Edgefield County with a barbecue attended by more than ten thousand South Carolinians.

Brooks began pounding him over the head with the cane, continuing until the cane broke and Sumner was left unconscious and bleeding on the floor.

The attack created a firestorm in the press, exposing the depth of the divisions within the country over the issue of slavery. Northern newspapers denounced the attack as an outrage against democracy and decency, while southern editors lauded Brooks as a noble defender of honor and chivalry. Brooks survived an expulsion vote from the House of Representatives, but resigned his seat in July 1856, unrepentant of his actions.

Upon returning home to South Carolina, Preston Brooks was welcomed with a massive barbecue in his honor at Ninety Six in the Abbeville District. Between eight to ten thousand people attended, and ten thousand pounds of beef, pork, and mutton were barbecued for the event. Six tables were constructed, each two hundred feet in length, along with a large platform for the speakers and temporary seats for the ladies. Brooks was met at his hotel at eleven o'clock in the morning by a parade of gentlemen, including the governor of South Carolina, and escorted to the celebration. A band played patriotic tunes and a series of orators took the platform to praise Brooks for his recent actions. One of these speakers, Dr. Cain, concluded that the barbecue's turnout "showed plainly that his constituents approved his conduct upon a late occasion, when he prostrated the traducer of his State in the Senate Chamber of the United States. The act was noble; it was daring; and possibly it might be the means of solving the problem whether the South should have an equality in the Union or a separate independence out of it."[2] Brooks was returned to the House of Representatives during the 1856 election, though he died of croup only a few months later.

The Brooks-Sumner Affair was one of the most dramatic incidents during the bitter sectionalist disputes that preceded the Civil War, but Brooks's homecoming welcome was only one of hundreds of barbecues that would be associated with partisan debates. It's not surprising that, being the key political issues of the day, slavery and secession dominated the rhetoric at political barbecues on the eve of the Civil War. In the border states, barbecues played an even more instrumental role, for it was at these events that the debate was played out to determine whether to secede or remain in the Union.

The Election of 1860

The presidential election of 1860 was a four-way race. The Republicans nominated Abraham Lincoln at their convention in Chicago. The Democratic Party, divided along sectional lines over the issue of slavery in the territories, split into two conventions, with the northern faction backing Senator Stephen A. Douglas of Illinois and the southern faction nominating John C. Breckenridge of Kentucky, the sitting vice president. A fourth party, the National Constitutional Union, was formed specifically for the election, with a platform based solely on preserving the Union. John Bell of Tennessee was its nominee.

Public barbecues and torchlight parades had been an inseparable part of national presidential elections since the Harrison and Van Buren race of 1840. Prior to 1860, though, the presidential nominees themselves did not attend such events, remaining instead at their homes in gentlemanly seclusion. Stephen Douglas broke from this tradition. The "Little Giant," a nickname earned by his short stature and political prominence, was a skillful and flamboyant orator, with a booming voice and dramatic gestures that enlivened his platform appearances. He traveled widely throughout the country, sometimes delivering as many as twenty speeches a day.

The other three candidates consciously sought to maintain the older tradition of seclusion from campaigning. John C. Breckinridge stayed at home in Lexington and declined requests for public speaking. He was, however, the subject of harsh criticism from Douglas during his many stump speeches as well as from other partisan campaigners, such as John J. Crittenden. Crittenden, the senior senator from Kentucky and an active supporter of John Bell of the Constitutional Union Party, spoke at a rally at Louisville and accused Breckinridge of leading the "disunion party." On August 18, fifteen of Breckinridge's friends and supporters urged him, in a public letter published in the *Lexington Standard,* to address the people of Kentucky at a barbecue "for the purpose of publicly vindicating yourself from the violent personal assaults made upon you since your nomination for the presidency at Baltimore."[3] Breckinridge accepted, and arrangements were begun for the massive public barbecue that would be his only campaign appearance.

John R. Viley, the chairman of the Committee of Arrangements, sought to secure the fairgrounds outside of Lexington, but its owners refused, saying they did not want the property used for partisan purposes. Viley turned next to Ashland, the former home of Henry Clay and the site of a famous barbecue that was given to the late Kentucky statesman back in 1837. Ashland was now owned by Henry Clay's son, James, a staunch Breckinridge supporter, who eagerly made his woodlands available. The choice of venue outraged old-time Whigs, who looked upon it as little short of a sacrilege to allow a Democratic gathering on a spot sacred to the memory of their great leader, but the Breckinridge event moved ahead as planned.[4]

Trenches were dug and the wood laid in for barbecuing five beeves, one hundred and thirty sheep, one hundred shoats, and sixty hams. Special trains brought attendees from Louisville and Covington, and the crowd was estimated to number between eight and fifteen thousand people. Breckinridge's arrival was hailed by a thirty-three-gun salute, and the candidate took to the stage for a vigorous three-hour defense of his political record, his platform, and his motives in pursuing the presidency. Above all, he defended himself and the Southern Democrats against the charge of advocating disunion, arguing that he sought to protect the rights of all states and that it was the Republican Party members who were the real sectionalists and disunionists for trying to deny the Constitutional rights of the southern states. The barbecue was hailed by the Washington *Constitution* as "the greatest political event of the present campaign."[5]

The Douglas camp was not to be outdone by its southern rivals. They took the daring step of bringing the campaign barbecue to New York City for the first time. The Douglas Central Campaign Club announced in early September that a "Monster Democratic Rally, Grand Political Carnival, and Ox Roast" would be held on September 12 at Jones's Wood, a wooded estate on the edge of Manhattan (stretching between present-day 66th and 75th Streets) that was commonly used for picnics, festivals, and sporting events. A great "Kentucky ox" was procured for the occasion, and the animal was paraded through the streets for two days before the event to generate interest. More than twenty thousand people turned out, many drawn not so much by the chance to hear Douglas as by the prospect of sampling the novelty of a barbecued ox. The *New York Herald* declared, "Nothing like it in politics ever occurred here before."[6]

Unfortunately, the city's first political barbecue turned into a fiasco. The ox, along with a hog, a heifer, and two sheep, were slaughtered and roasted for the occasion by Bryan Lawrence, a butcher from Centre Market. Lawrence was an Irish immigrant who had arrived in New York City in 1836 at the age of nineteen. While he would later go on to become a bank executive and philanthropist, it is unclear whether he had any prior experience supervising a barbecue pit.[7] One reporter declared that "the universal opinion was that the animals thus treated, when 'well done,' very much resembled the charred remains which are sometimes seen in this city after the destruction of an old tenement home."[8] The assembled crowd must not have been as choosy, for when "feeding time" was announced, they quickly degenerated into a mob. Bursting through the pine fences that had been set up around the serving area, they overturned tables, scattered the bread and crackers, and seized whatever bits of meat they could grab. Some three hundred policemen were required to restore order before Douglas could take to

A Description of New York's First Political Barbecue

On the lefthand side of the pathway a large piece of ground was enclosed with a wooden fence, and about three thousand persons were gathered around (two-thirds of whom were of the "rowdy" class) shouting, waving small flags, and cheering, their greatest anxiety being to get into a position where they could be near the carver, who was preparing to "cut up the bullock." At the centre of the enclosure were eight temporary tables, erected for the purpose of holding the portions of roasted carcass, large piles of crackers, and the heaps of loaves of bread, which were very bountifully provided for the [illegible], and were very temptingly displayed before the gaze of the hungry multitude. At about one o'clock the onslaught commenced, and the carver set to work with a will. One table, containing the crackers, fronted on the east side of the enclosed space, another, holding the large pieces of oily looking roasted fat pig, faced west; four others, on which the bread, mutton and beef were cut up, fronted on the south, and the remaining two, on one of which were the piles of loaves and on the other rested a whole quarter of the roasted ox, occupied a more central position. The pit at which the ox, the sheep and the hog were roasted occupied a place in the centre of the enclosure, and was about fifteen feet in length by six feet in width and four feet in depth.

DISTRIBUTION OF THE FOOD

As many of the surrounding individuals were anxious, as soon as the carving commenced, to be within the pine fence, the police were kept actively engaged, running about, driving the intruders out of the "sacred limits," as none but the press were allowed inside the same unless they were legally engaged in distributing the food. The bread, having been cut into huge slices, was handed around on trays, each borne by two boys; and occasionally, in the anxiety of the "famished mortals," to get at the staff of life, the tray would be upset and a scramble ensue. The meat being also cut up in "chunks," were likewise handed round, but as "first come first served" seemed to be the wish of the crowd, a struggle ensued directly any of the provisions were offered, and, as is always the case, the "weakest went to the wall," or rather to the background of the mob, for by their conduct this part of the meeting could scarcely be otherwise designated.

DESTRUCTION OF THE FENCE

At last the patience of the mob began to expire, and fearful that they might not be able to get any of the gratuitous supply of roast beef, they resorted to physical force, and tore down the pine fences and burst into the enclosure. The police were in too small a force to keep the crowd now back, and a

MOST DISGRACEFUL SCENE

Ensued. The shouting mob rushed to the not over-steady tables, on which were the provisions, and at once overturned them, with the exception of two, on one of which were large pieces of pork and

mutton, and this the police surrounded; and the other, being occupied by the principal carver, the crowd respected as long as he
could meet their demands. But at last he was obliged to give way
and leave his post, and an onslaught at once commenced. One man
attired in a puce colored shirt was very prominent, having secured
a hatchet with which he hacked into pieces the quarter of the bullock and the larger joints that had not until then been mutilated. A
scramble ensued to get from him portions of the several remains,
and as fast as he divided the same so were the pieces wrested from
him. At last, having secured a "small morsel" of about twenty pounds
weight, more or less, he "left the field" to his unruly neighbors. . . .
At one time about a hundred [crackers] were in the air together,
coming to the ground in a perfect shower. After the ammunition of
wheaten food had been exhausted, the bones and remaining joints
of meat were next thrown at one another, followed by portions of the
fence, and lastly by the flour or cracker barrels. . . . The police, beginning to see that the fun was likely to prove dangerous, as two or
three fights had already ensued, rushed in a body and took the barrels from the crowd and "cast them into the pit," which lay, as it were,
yawning to receive them. While they were engaged in this commendable work, the unruly host seized upon the only table that had
been preserved and began demolishing the provisions thereon,
and really the table itself.

Source: "The Douglas Barbecue," *New York Herald,* September 13, 1860, 3

the platform for his post-barbecue speech. (See page 87, "A Description of New York's First Political Barbecue").

It is unclear how much support the Jones's Wood barbecue gained Douglas among New York voters. This and other similar events did, however, earn him the same sort of criticism that had been heaped on backwoods campaigners three decades before, when the election barbecue was just becoming a part of frontier political life. The correspondent for the *Constitution* scoffed at "the public exhibition of candidates for the highest offices in the world before as motley a crowd from the purlieus of New York as any the sun ever shone on." Douglas, he charged, was placing the presidential race "on a level with mountebank performances" by wandering through the country "like a traveling circus, attending clam bakes, barbecues, and tight-rope performances."[9]

In the end, barbecues and tireless stump speeches were not enough to lift Douglas to victory. He outpolled Breckinridge and Bell in the popular vote, but he carried only a single state, Missouri. Breckinridge carried the Deep South cotton states while Bell captured the border states of Virginia, Kentucky, and Tennessee. Abraham Lincoln swept the free states, giving him a resounding majority in the electoral college, securing the presidency for the Republicans and pushing the country to the brink of war.

Secession and the Onset of War

As soon as Lincoln's election was apparent, the South turned its eyes toward secession. In 1860, a day-long debate on abandoning the Union was held in Langdon Hall, the chapel at the Auburn Female Academy in Auburn, Alabama (now Auburn University). In attendance were some of the most noted orators of the South, including Alexander Stephens and William G. Brownlow arguing against secession and Benjamin Harvey Hill and Robert Toombs arguing in favor. Howard M. Hamill, who was thirteen years old at the time, attended the debates, and recalled that people poured in from the towns and countryside within a hundred-mile radius of Auburn, and for two days and nights in advance there were rival parades with fife and drum bands. Hamill described the great barbecue prepared for the occasion, with "its long lines of parallel trenches in which under the unbroken vigilance of expert negro cooks, whole beeves and sheeps and hogs and innumerable turkeys were roasting." More than anything, Hamill recalled the emotion of the times, writing that "to the small boy there were meat and drink, sights and sounds illimitable, and a tenseness of excitement that thrilled him with a thousand thrills."[10]

On the day of the debate, the two sides alternated speakers. Robert Toombs, the Georgia senator, delivered a stirring pro-secession speech in the early afternoon, but then Brownlow, the fiercely pro-Union newspaperman from eastern Tennessee, took the platform, and the Union position seemed to gain the upper hand. William L. Yancey, the Alabama "Fire-Eater," was a fearsome debater and had been one of the most passionate supporters of slavery and Breckenridge during the 1860 presidential campaign, but he lay sick in bed sixty miles away in Montgomery. Seeing the tide of the debate turning toward the Unionists, Yancey's friends sent a special train to carry him from his home to Auburn, where he took to the platform and, despite looking pale and emaciated, made an impromptu, two-hour oration with a "singularly musical voice and an indefinable magnetism" that carried the day for the pro-secessionists.[11]

Led by firebrands such as Toombs and Yancey, secession swept quickly through the Deep South. Immediately following Lincoln's election, the South Carolina legislature summoned a convention, which voted on December 20, 1860, to secede from the Union. Five more states—Mississippi, Florida, Alabama, Georgia, and Louisiana—quickly followed.

Texas was a slaveholding, cotton-producing state with strong pro-secession leanings, but it was also home to many powerful Unionists, including Sam Houston, the sitting governor. Houston refused to call the legislature into special session and blocked a secession convention. He was able to delay until January, when it became apparent that secession advocates would establish their own extralegal convention if not allowed to convene under the existing laws. Houston relented, and the convention met on February 1 and voted to secede. Houston, however, was able to force a public referendum to be held to ratify the results, and the vote was scheduled for February 23.

Pro-secessionists rallied support for their cause through a series of barbecues and public gatherings. On the day of the referendum, the farmers of Port Sullivan, Texas, provided what the editor of the *Austin State Gazette* called "one of the best barbecues

I have ever had the pleasure of partaking of." Following two hours of orations, one of the speakers called upon all the ladies who were in favor of secession to rise to their feet. "To see who should be first on their feet was the greater struggle," the *Gazette* reported. "For in an instance every lady, even down to the girls of 8 to 10 years, were up; not one kept her seat."[12] Some two hundred miles to the east, near the Louisiana border, the people of San Augustine staged a "sumptuous barbecue" that followed the traditional pattern of a Fourth of July celebration, complete with a procession and orations. On the way to the barbecue grounds, the procession stopped off at the courthouse, where the eligible men deposited their votes in favor of secession.[13] This scene was repeated in one Texas town after another, and the results of the referendum were 46,153 votes in favor of secession and 14,747 against. Texas joined the six other seceding states at a meeting in Montgomery, Alabama, to form the Confederate States of America, electing Jefferson Davis as their president.

The middle southern states moved more slowly than the Deep South cotton states. In a referendum on February 9, 1861, the people of Tennessee rejected a secession convention by a vote of 68,000 to 59,000.[14] Secession was hotly debated in the Kentucky legislature during the months of February and March, too, with ardent support for the institution of slavery but strong opposition to leaving the Union.

Open military action began in Charleston, South Carolina, on April 12 with the bombardment of Fort Sumter, and Virginia, Arkansas, and North Carolina quickly voted to join the Confederacy. Unionist sentiment in Tennessee eroded rapidly, and a second referendum on secession was called. The voting was preceded by several weeks of passionate pro-Confederate barbecues and parades, and the state voted on June 8 to leave the Union, 104,913 to 47,238.[15] The barbecues continued after the referendum as a way to enlist recruits for the war. One notable such event took place at Shady Grove Church outside Saltillo in western Tennessee, where the orator called upon the crowd to devote themselves to "the Sunny South." Prior to the barbecue's being served, the men who had already enlisted paraded around the meeting with small stars-and-bars flags attached to the heads of their horses, then a call went out for more men to volunteer for the Confederate army. B. G. Brazelton, in his 1885 history of Hardin County, Tennessee, sadly noted that "few of those volunteers lived to see the war closed."[16]

Kentucky staked out a position of neutrality, refusing to join the South in secession but also refusing to send troops to the Federal army. Some pro-Union supporters in Kentucky reached out to their fellow states to the north. In June 1861, "a grand Union barbecue" was given by the citizens of Oldham County, Kentucky, for their neighbors across the Ohio River in Clark County, Indiana. Over five thousand people attended, including one thousand women, and the *New York Herald* reported, "The Union sentiment was strong, and the feeling exhibited against rebels and traitors was very bitter."[17] A few days later, the people of Woodford, Kentucky, held a large barbecue in honor of John J. Crittenden and the recent Union victory he helped lead, and Crittenden delivered a stirring speech in favor of neutrality and peace.[18]

The secessionist forces in Kentucky were not silent. After losing the presidential race, John C. Breckenridge had returned to the United States Senate. He spent the summer of 1861 in Washington for special sessions of Congress, where he did what he could to block legislative attempts to prosecute war against the rebellious southern states. After the session ended in August, Breckinridge returned to his home state and participated in a series of anti-Lincoln rallies. On September 5, the secessionists organized "a grand barbecue" in Owen County, about twelve miles from the state capitol of Frankfurt, where the legislature was about to convene to consider resolutions to more firmly bind Kentucky to the Union. The pro-secession State Guard was invited, and some ten thousand people turned out in support of the cause.

The meeting at Owen raised fears among the Unionists that an armed revolt was brewing, but the rallies were in fact the last gasp of the secession cause. After Confederate forces moved into the westernmost part of the state in early September, the legislature abandoned all pretense of neutrality and aligned itself with the federal government of the United States. At a barbecue in the woods owned by William Buford in Woodford County, Breckinridge and other secessionist leaders delivered farewell addresses to their supporters. On September 19, an armed Federal force from Camp Dick Robinson began moving toward Lexington with orders to arrest Breckinridge. Warned of the movement, Breckinridge fled on horseback during the night to eastern Kentucky, where he was joined by other states' rights supporters and proceeded onward to Richmond, Virginia, to cast his lot with the Confederacy.[19]

Barbecues during the War

As the Confederate states prepared for war, they naturally turned to barbecues to send off the troops. In the summer of 1861, from South Carolina all the way to Texas, companies of new volunteers were honored with barbecues by their communities. It was standard at these events for a young woman to present the company with a banner or flag and to make an impassioned speech in honor of the soldiers' gallantry. The captain of the company would accept the gift and, with equally florid words, express his men's thanks and reiterate their devotion to the cause. Often a minister would offer a prayer for the safe return of the soldiers to their homes once the fighting was over. There were even a few barbecues for Union troops. The Twenty-third Pennsylvania Volunteer Infantry, for example, was honored with a barbecue near Philadelphia. Flags and swords were presented to the regiment's officers and a whole ox and fifteen hogs were barbecued—as the reporter for the *Philadelphia Inquirer* pointed out—"in this favorite Southern style."[20]

These barbecues, and the mixture of gallantry and optimism displayed in the speeches, reflected the southern mood during the opening months of the conflict. At Bull Run (Manassas) in July, the first major land battle of the war, the Confederate troops turned back the first Union excursion into Virginia, and there was little additional fighting for the rest of the year. The Union blockade was not yet hurting the South, and it was not until the fall of 1862 and bloody battles like Antietam (Sharpsburg) that the full weight of the conflict began to be felt.

Barbecues took on a very different purpose and tone during the middle years of the war. Some were held to raise funds for war-related causes. In May 1863, a barbecue given at Courtney, Texas, raised $1,650 for the benefit of soldiers from the local volunteer regiment.[21] The proceeds from a barbecue and fair in Navasota, Texas, in August were used to establish a soldiers' home.[22] Others were held to welcome returning troops, such as the barbecue organized in Richmond, Arkansas, for the Confederate soldiers who had been captured following the four-month siege of Vicksburg and Port Hudson and then paroled by Union officers.[23] In all of these cases the barbecues were organized by the women of the community, though it is safe to assume that male slaves tended the pits. At the Richmond barbecue, the ladies themselves waited upon the guests—a remarkable reversal of what was normally a male-dominated tradition.

The Closing of the War

Barbecues had long been an important part of the life of slaves on southern plantations. Lincoln's Emancipation Proclamation radically changed the nature of these celebrations. The Proclamation actually consisted of two executive orders. The first, issued on September 22, 1862, declared that slaves would be emancipated in any of the Confederate States of America that did not return to Union control by January 1, 1863. The second order, issued on New Year's Day, put the emancipation into effect, naming the specific states where slaves were freed.

The arrival of January 1 was a momentous occasion for African Americans in the parts of the South that were under Federal occupation. At Camp Saxton outside Beaufort, South Carolina, a celebration was planned in a live oak grove adjoining the camp, to which several thousand black residents from the surrounding Sea Islands were invited. Ten oxen had been procured to barbecue for the event. Colonel Thomas Wentworth Higginson, a prominent author and abolitionist, was stationed at Camp Saxton as the leader of the First South Carolina Volunteers, the first Union regiment recruited from former slaves. Barbecue was something new for the Massachusetts native, and he described the preparation with interest in his diaries, noting, "Touching the length of time required to 'do' an ox, no two housekeepers appear to agree. Accounts vary from two hours to twenty four. We shall happily have enough to try all gradations of roasting, and suit all tastes." This was wartime, though, and by the time the skinny oxen were in place over the flames, Higginson noted that "the firelight gleams through their ribs, as if they were great lanterns."[24]

On New Year's Day, the people began to gather around 10:00 A.M., arriving by land and by special steamers sent by the camp commander. The band of the Eighth Maine played music for the ceremonies, and, following a prayer, Lincoln's Proclamation was read to the assembled multitude. The moment the speaker finished, the assembled freedmen spontaneously broke into singing, "My Country 'Tis of Thee." Following an oration and more patriotic songs, the assembly broke to eat. Apart from the barbecued ox, the provisions were pretty bare: just hard bread and, to drink, water sweetened with molasses and ginger. Susie King Taylor, a former slave who had become a schoolteacher on St. Simon's Island, recalled the feast as "a fitting close and the crowning event of this occasion . . . Although not served as tastily or correctly as it would have been at home, yet it was enjoyed with keen appetites and relish."[25]

The celebration at Camp Saxton was just one of many. Across the occupied South, Union officers read the Emancipation Proclamation to gathered slaves and announced that they were free. Although the Proclamation took effect on January 1, 1863, the measure could be enforced only in the territory controlled by Union troops, so it took several years for emancipation to reach all of the Confederacy. The last state was Texas. On June 18, 1865—some two months after General Robert E. Lee surrendered the Army of Northern Virginia at Appomattox Court House—General Gordon Granger of the Union army landed with Federal troops in Galveston, Texas. The next day he read Lincoln's Proclamation to an assembled crowd, putting into effect the emancipation of over 250,000 Texas slaves.

Southern whites greeted the end of the war with barbecues, too, though with quite a different tone. As Confederate soldiers returned home to resume their lives in the occupied South, they also returned to their traditional forms of recreation. Eliza Frances Andrews, the daughter of a prominent judge and planter in Washington, Georgia, noted in her journal in July 1865, "Barbecues, both public and private, are raging with a fury that seems determined to make amends for the four years intermission caused by the war."[26] Her brother Henry, a former Confederate soldier, got into a bit of a scrape following one such barbecue. Returning home with "more liquor aboard than they could hold," Henry and his friends passed by the hotel downtown where the officers from the occupying Federal garrison were lodged. Henry "cussed out" the gathering of officers, which led to an order for his arrest and, ultimately, a twenty-five-dollar fine.[27]

That year, the Federal troops in Washington, Georgia, staged a Fourth of July celebration in the traditional southern fashion, organizing a barbecue at the old Cool Spring picnic ground, which was heavily attended by the county's African Americans. White Washingtonians boycotted "this anniversary of our forefathers' folly," as Eliza Frances

Andrews phrased it, and instead shut themselves up at home. To show their contempt for the holiday, a group of white men organized a counter-celebration on July 6. Captain Cooley, the commander of the Federal garrison, threatened to send in a body of African American troops to halt any such "rebel 'cue," but the organizers were undeterred. The barbecue on the sixth came off without incident, though Andrews noted that "it was hot enough to roast a salamander, and nobody enjoyed it very much."[28]

The sentiments of the white residents of Washington, Georgia, against the Fourth of July were shared throughout the South. Independence Day—including the traditional barbecue feast—remained a key event in the social life of African Americans, but white southerners ceased celebrating the holiday. The traditional Fourth of July barbecue did not return to prominence in the white community for another thirty years, when the onset of the Spanish-American War rekindled the patriotic sentiments of the New South.

Barbecue, Reconstruction, and the Gilded Age

"Every year since the signing of that celebrated document," the editors of the *Atlanta Daily World* wrote in 1955 about the Emancipation Proclamation, "there has been staged among our group some sort of anniversary of grateful expression. Hardly any individual or specific organization can claim credit for the initiation of this practice, for it had its beginning among the early freedman in every state involved in the slavery question."[1] Emancipation celebrations played an important role in the civic life of African Americans during the Reconstruction era, and barbecue was front and center in those events.

The date for a community's Emancipation celebration varied from state to state. January 1 was the traditional date in Alabama, Georgia, North Carolina, South Carolina, and Virginia, while August 4 and 8 were the norm in Kentucky, north-central Tennessee, northeastern Arkansas, and central Oklahoma.[2] In Texas, June 19—the day General Granger read the Emancipation Proclamation in Galveston—became the date for that state's annual celebrations, and it was there that perhaps the most enduring Emancipation Day tradition was established.

The Texas festivities always included a big barbecue along with a reading of the Emancipation Proclamation followed by speeches, prayers, and entertainment like rodeos and baseball games. In the early years, these celebrations were frequently attended by members of the white community, too. Anderson Jones, a former slave, recalled late in his life, "I was jes a boy about nine years old w'en freedom cum's . . . w'en we commenced to have de nineteenth celebrations . . . an' everybody seem's like, w'ite an' black cum an' git some barbecue."[3] Prominent white citizens were frequently asked to deliver addresses, and they typically lectured—often condescendingly—on topics such as citizenship and self-improvement. Despite these visitors, the celebrations were clearly organized by and for the African American community. As more and more black Texans became landowners, they began to acquire tracts specifically for holding Emancipation Day and other celebrations. In Houston, for example, Jack Yates, a former slave and the pastor of Antioch Baptist Church, led an effort that raised one thousand dollars to purchase ten acres of open land that became Emancipation Park.[4]

The Emancipation Day holiday in Texas grew decade by decade. In 1893, the *Dallas Morning News* reported on the festivities not just in Dallas but in a dozen other cities ranging from Tyler to San Antonio. Many celebrations, like the one in Waco, were said to be "on a scale larger than any previous year."[5] Five years later, over five thousand people turned out for a barbecue at Stamps, near the Louisiana line, while fifty miles north in Texarkana a special excursion on the Cotton Belt railroad was chartered to take "almost every negro in town" to the local celebration.[6] The events that year were held on June 18, since the nineteenth fell on a Sunday. It was around this time that the holiday began to be known commonly as "Juneteenth."[7] As former slaves and their descendants began leaving the cotton farms and migrating outside the state, they started making an annual pilgrimage back to Galveston for Juneteenth, and the day took on an additional theme of homecoming. One constant was the barbecue pit, which always took the central place at the festivities.

The popularity of Juneteenth ebbed in the early twentieth century, as black Texans began to leave the farms and move into cities. July Fourth was already established as a civic holiday, and nonagricultural employers were less inclined than their rural counterparts to let employees take another day off on June 19. The civil rights movement of the 1960s sparked a revitalization of Juneteenth, as many activists began to look back to the civic traditions of the African American past. In 1980, the Texas legislature made June 19 an official state holiday, and it has since spread well beyond the borders of the Lone Star State as a time to commemorate freedom and civil rights.

Juneteenth has lasted the longest as a formal holiday, but Emancipation Day barbecues were held by African Americans throughout the country in the nineteenth century, even in states that had never permitted slaveholding. In Kansas, for example, the day of the celebration was August 4, following the traditions of Kentucky and Tennessee, where many black Kansans had family roots. Ella Boney grew up in Hill City in the 1870s and 1880s and, in a 1938 WPA interview, recalled that the Emancipation Proclamation Picnic was "one of the biggest events of the year for Negroes in Kansas." Held for four days in a large grove outside of Nicodemus, African Americans would travel in from all over the state to attend. "There are about twelve barbecue pits dug," Boney recalled, "and they are going all day barbecuing chickens, turkeys, ducks, pigs, sides of beef etc."[8]

The Fourth of July was also an important day for African Americans in the Reconstruction era. Most white southerners had abandoned the holiday during the Civil War, but black southerners embraced it as a special day of celebration. These events followed the traditional patterns of antebellum Independence Day celebrations, including grand processions, music, the reading of the Declaration of Independence, and orations, followed, of course, by a barbecue dinner in a shady grove.

In the years immediately following the Civil War, prominent white citizens were invited as guests to African American Independence Day barbecues—dining at a separate, specially reserved set of tables—and sometimes were asked to address the assembly. Self-improvement and civic responsibility were underlying themes in all of the addresses, by black and by white speakers. The speeches by the white guests, in fact, tended to be lecturing and highly condescending. J. A. Turner, for example, spoke at a freedman's Fourth of July barbecue in Eatonton, Georgia, in 1866, and urged his listeners "to cultivate friendly feelings toward the white people." Turner defended slavery as having been, at the time, in the best interest of African Americans, arguing, "Your forefathers were savages like the wild Indian when they were brought to this country. Now, you, their descendants are civilized, and intelligent, and all enjoy Church privileges. Had it not been for slavery you would now be savages in Africa."[9]

These events represented an attempt by the prewar white elite to reassert control over their communities, which they sought to do at first by winning over the hearts of the freedmen and minimizing the influence of the Reconstruction administrations. Reporting on the July Fourth speeches at Eatonton, the *Macon Telegraph* advised, "Other speakers should talk to the Negroes in the same way. The Southern people must have control of their education, and must win back, and hold the affection and esteem which were so nearly destroyed by Yankee emissaries."[10]

In 1868, the Democratic Party started hosting its own barbecues to try to win black voters away from the Republicans. These were, on the surface, old-fashioned campaign events, but in the past African Americans had been present only as cooks and not as the audience for the politicians' speeches. In Yalobusha County, Mississippi, where there were several hundred more black voters than white, the Democrats hosted a "grand barbecue" outside of the town of Grenada, "designed more particularly for the colored population, whose minds it was sought to enlighten with the gospel of Democracy."[11] The speakers lavished attacks on the current Republican-controlled state legislature and the recently enacted Constitution of 1868, which had instituted universal suffrage. The orations sought to convince the newly empowered voters that the Radical Republicans cared only about exploiting southern blacks for profit and that Democrats were actually the party most concerned with the welfare of black Mississippians—a theme that was omnipresent at Democratic barbecues aimed at African American voters that year.

The northern press responded to these efforts with a mix of amusement and outrage. Thomas Nast, the father of the American political cartoon, lampooned the Democratic barbecues in a full-page illustration for *Harper's Weekly* called "All the Difference in the World," which depicted two versions of Democrats' reactions to black voters. In the first, a black farmer is being courted by a Republican rally with banners offering, "Equal Rights to All," and an onlooking Democrat—standing in a pig sty—holds his nose in disgust against the offensive odor of the black man. The second image shows a grand party with a poster advertising "Democratic Balls and Barbecues Every Day & Night—Colored Voters Everywhere Are Invited." Far from being offended now, the Democrats are making every effort to cater to the black guests, and General Wade Hampton—the leader of the Conservative Democrats in South Carolina—is kneeling to shine the shoes of a black man in evening dress.[12]

In the end, the Democrats' barbecued pork and florid rhetoric did little to win African American votes. In Tennessee, despite extensive Democratic courting of freedmen's votes, the Republican governor William G. Brownlow was reelected in 1867 by an overwhelming majority, including all but forty-three of the state's forty thousand African American votes.[13] Similar results were seen in elections across the South during the late 1860s. Southern whites soon turned to harsher tactics, including intimidation and the systematic disenfranchisement of black voters through legal and extralegal means.

Barbecues remained one of the most important African American social events through the rest of the century. As black southerners began migrating to northern cities and to the West Coast, they took their barbecue tradition with them and helped carry it to new parts of the country. Today's barbecue cultures in cities such as Houston, Memphis, St. Louis, Kansas City, and Chicago have their roots in the Emancipation Day and July Fourth celebrations of the Reconstruction days.

The Broadening Footprint of Barbecue

In both white and black communities in the South and, in fact, in just about every part of the United States except New England, the occasions at which barbecue was served expanded during the second half of the nineteenth century. School celebrations, social club gatherings, estate sales, town-boosting land sales, and community betterment efforts were just a few of the events where it was common to find barbecue being served.

Barbecue was a prominent feature of Confederate veterans' reunions, which flourished in the southern states in the 1880s and 1890s. Most were held by veterans associations for a particular army unit, and they were a time for old soldiers to renew the bonds of military camaraderie as well as a chance for communities to honor the men who had served in the conflict—and, in the process, instill in the younger generations the ideology of the "Lost Cause." Local businesses closed for the reunions, and entire towns were decorated with flags and banners. Organizers canvassed the area for contributions of money and food, and massive amounts of meat were frequently donated for the pits. The 1887 reunion of the Seventh Georgia Infantry served five beef cattle,

Cooking meat, barbecue style.

Cooking barbecue in Southern Pines, North Carolina. (*Frank Leslie's Illustrated Weekly*, December 19, 1891.)

eight sheep, five hogs, and two thousand chickens, while the 1893 Third Georgia gathering required over one thousand feet of tables to hold the one hundred twenty-five pigs and sheep and one hundred gallons of hash served for the occasion. Old soldiers could talk all day about the exploits of their old regiment, one veteran observed, but they "can't talk against a barbecue."[14]

Some of these reunion barbecues took on themes of reconciliation. In 1888, the Sur-

The barbecue pits at a Masonic picnic, Kissimmee, Florida, 1886. (Courtesy State Library and Archives of Florida.)

vivors' Association of the Third Georgia Volunteers invited the surviving members of the Ninth Regiment of New York Volunteers, whom they had fought against at Antietam, to be their guests at their annual reunion in Fort Valley, Georgia, and "taste the sweets of peace with us in partaking of a Georgia Barbecue." A large delegation of New Yorkers traveled by steamer to Savannah and then by rail to Fort Valley, where the speeches following the barbecue focused on "fraternal greetings, sentiments of good will and patriotic utterances."[15]

Reunion barbecues were also used to raise money for veteran causes. The October 1885 Soldiers' Reunion in Union County, Kentucky, drew five thousand guests to the fairgrounds and raised $640.30 to aid disabled Confederate soldiers and the families of deceased comrades. Stella Guice, the president of the Barbour County, Alabama, chapter of the Daughters of the Confederacy, staged numerous barbecues at her family's home on the Chattahoochee River and raised over $3,000 to erect the thirty-five-foot-tall marble Confederate monument that still stands today at the corner of Broad and

Stereoview of a Florida barbecue, 1870s. (Courtesy State Library and Archives of Florida.)

While barbecue remained uncommon in northeastern cities, the New York political machines occasionally experimented with the types of rallies more common in the South and Midwest. This scene, entitled "A Democratic Barbecue," shows guests at a Harlem ox roast sponsored by Tammany Hall. (*Frank Leslie's Illustrated Newspaper,* October 18, 1884.)

Eufaula Streets in Eufaula, Alabama.[16] These were some of the first instances of barbecues being used for fundraising, a practice that would become more common and be extended to a wide variety of causes in the twentieth century.

Pitmasters also began selling barbecue to turn a profit, and barbecue stands were common fixtures at fairs, expositions, and other festivals. In August 1887, the Old Settlers Reunion in Perry, Iowa, featured a procession, music, and addresses along with roast beef and mutton at the barbecue stand.[17] Vendors at the 1900 "Reunion" in Mexia, Texas, included lemonade, candy, popcorn, peanuts, hot tamales, chili, watermelon, chewing gum, and a barbecue stand.[18] The *Springfield Republican* of Massachusetts noted that county fairs were much more popular in the South than in New England, and that barbecue so dominated events south of the Mason-Dixon Line that "the rates are generally arranged with the barbecue in view: so much for the entrance to the fairground and so much for the barbecue ticket." A ticket generally entitled its holder to all the barbecue he or she could eat, and since utensils were limited, foresighted fairgoers often equipped themselves with their own plates and knives.[19] These early enterprises were precursors of the barbecue restaurants that would appear upon the American scene after the First World War.

Barbecue Men

The late nineteenth century is notable as the era of "barbecue men," experienced cooks who became famous in their communities as masters of the pit. They became well known for their barbecuing skills and were in high demand to cook at public festivals and private functions.

Having a noted barbecue man lined up for an event was a big draw, and organizers regularly advertised who would be cooking the barbecue at their functions. As the national press took a renewed interest in life in the South, some barbecue men made the jump from local celebrity to national fame, earning recognition for their cooking skills above the Mason-Dixon line. Others remained known only in their local communities, but they had a significant effect on barbecue culture in their regions.

In South Carolina, one of the leading barbecue men was Hezekiah "Kiah" Dent. Born in 1832, Dent was a farmer and a Confederate veteran, and he made a name for himself in the 1890s preparing barbecue for functions ranging from political rallies, gatherings of fraternal organizations such as the Knights of Pythias, and Labor Day picnics. He was particularly fond of preparing barbecue for his old comrades at the county Confederate veterans' reunions. Upon Dent's death in 1908, the Columbia *State* newspaper noted that he was "jealous of his reputation as a cook and no one ever partook of a feast prepared by him who went away other than thoroughly satisfied."[20]

Joel Stowe of Floyd County, Georgia, was one of that state's noted barbecuers, and gained wide recognition for the meat he barbecued for the joint encampment of Confederate and Union veterans at Chickamauga in 1887. "Old Rozier," the leading barbecue man of Muscogee County was touted by his local newspaper to be able to "barbecue meats to the queen's taste, and his barbecued chickens cannot be equalled on earth."[21]

But, far and away, Georgia's most famous barbecue man was Sheriff John W. Callaway of Wilkes County. Callaway was born in 1847 in Washington, the seat of Wilkes County in eastern Georgia. As a teenager, he served in the Confederate army, and after the war became a deputy sheriff in Wilkes County. Within a few years he was elected sheriff. A tall man weighing almost three hundred pounds, Callaway became known throughout Georgia as the "Big Sheriff," but he achieved fame not as a law enforcement officer but as a barbecue man.

How Callaway began cooking barbecue is not clear, but by the 1880s he was frequently cooking a range of meats—including beef, hog, sheep, and chicken—over hand-dug trenches for community celebrations, private parties, and other special events. He also specialized in his own brand of stew, which he called "hash" but newspaper reporters persisted in calling Brunswick stew, reflecting perhaps the proximity of Wilkes County to the border of South Carolina, where hash was already a staple regional specialty. In 1889, the *Atlanta Constitution* reported that Callaway "knows more about barbecues than any man in the country."[22] On the side, Callaway did find time to pursue criminals. In 1890 the *Constitution* noted that the sheriff "has been very busy at barbe-

John W. Callaway (1847–1915), sheriff of Wilkes County, Georgia, and noted barbecue chef. (*Atlanta Constitution*, 1891.)

cues, public and private, but he has not been negligent in his proper business," having just arrested three men for murder.[23]

In 1895, the city of Atlanta staged the grand Cotton States and International Exposition at the Piedmont Driving Club just north of the city (the area now occupied by Piedmont Park). Intended to showcase the South to the rest of the world and encourage trade, the exposition ran from September 18 until the end of the year and hosted some 800,000 visitors, thousands of them from the North. Sheriff Callaway set up shop in a shed near the Manufactures and Liberal Arts Building, where he sold barbecue dinners along with pickles, bread and butter, and hash. The meals were served on thick ironstone china with forks, knives, and paper napkins at rough wooden tables. The meats included lamb and pork and were cooked in the back of the eating house over a large pit filled with hickory wood. Callaway's appearance at the Exposition gained him the notice of the national press, including a November 1895 article on Georgia barbecue in *Harper's Weekly* that identified him as "the patron saint of barbecue as it is known in Georgia."[24]

John W. Callaway at a barbecue in Washington, Georgia. (Courtesy Georgia Archives, Vanishing Georgia Collection, wlk138.)

Over the succeeding years, Callaway became a fixture at the Georgia State Fair in Atlanta, where each year he constructed a large stand just to the right of the main entrance to the grounds. His stand served barbecue dinners, hash, and beer to thousands of hungry visitors and was one of the event's most popular attractions. "The people of Georgia who visit the fair always ask among their first questions if Callaway is on hand," one of the fair managers told a reporter in 1901. "He is a host within himself, genial and hearty, with a cordial handshake and a dinner fit for a prince for everyone who comes."[25] A few years later he was invited to New York City to prepare a barbecue for newspapermen at the New York Press Association, taking with him a black assistant. The event was a great success, and Callaway soon found himself receiving invitations to prepare similar dinners for occasions across the country, only a few of which he could accept.

Callaway continued public service as both a politician and a barbecue man until well into the twentieth century, eventually relinquishing his sheriff's office to serve as com-

Tracing the Origins of Hash

IT WAS DURING THE era of the barbecue kings that hash, the classic South Carolina specialty, came into prominence. A thick gravy made from pork and various pig organ meats, hash is generally served over white rice (though sometimes grits or bread are used instead), and it is almost exclusively considered a side dish to accompany barbecue, not a meal unto itself.

Hash appears to have originated sometime prior to the Civil War in the counties on either side of the Savannah River, which forms the border between Georgia and South Carolina. Estrella Jones, a former slave who was born on Powers Pond Place near Augusta, Georgia, recalled that when she was a child, the slaves would sometimes steal hogs from other plantations and "cook hash and rice and serve barbecue." In 1861, at the opening of the Civil War, a barbecue was held to honor the Edgefield Riflemen, who hailed from the county in South Carolina just across the Savannah River from Augusta, as they prepared to leave for battle. The menu included "barbecued meats, and hash."

On one level, hash is a way to use all of the pig slaughtered for a barbecue. In nineteenth-century accounts, it is sometimes referred to as "giblet hash" or "liver and lights hash." In most early versions, the cook would start with a hog's head, the liver, and other organ meats and cook them with water in an iron stew pot over an open fire. Like the original Brunswick stew recipes from Virginia, this combination was slowly simmered for many hours—sometimes a full day—until the ingredients had all broken down into a thick, consistent gravy-like liquid.

Some cooks would add a few other ingredients—including red pepper, mustard, onion, and potatoes—but in general hash has always depended upon the slow-simmered meats for its rich, hearty flavor.

By the 1880s, hash was being served at barbecues as far north as Newberry, South Carolina, and as far south as Macon in central Georgia—much farther south than hash is found today. In fact, there seems to be a good bit of confusion in central Georgia between hash and Brunswick stew. Sheriff John W. Callaway for Washington, Georgia, always called his barbecue side dish "hash," but reporters frequently labeled it "Brunswick Stew." But it doesn't seem merely a renaming of a single recipe, for, according to a 1907 newspaper account, a Christmas barbecue Callaway cooked for Wilkes County convicts included "several gallons of hash and a like quantity of Brunswick Stew."

It is possible that what Georgians call Brunswick stew today actually evolved out of the hash tradition as a variant of the original recipe. Visiting the Cotton States and International Exposition in Atlanta in 1895, Maude Andrews of *Harper's Weekly* sampled Sheriff Wilkes's famous stew and claimed that it "for reasons not altogether clear even to its maker, bears the mysterious name of Brunswick." Andrews got the recipe from one of the black cooks, and its formula is remarkably similar to that of classic South Carolina hash, with a few additions: "[Y]er jest takes the meat, de hog's haid, an' de libbers, and an' all sorts er little nice parts, an' yer chops it up wid corn and permattuses, an' injuns an' green peppers, an' yer stews and stews tell hit all gits erlike, an' yer kain't tell what hit's made uv."

Hash remains an integral part of the Midlands South Carolina barbecue tradition today, where it is served over white rice at barbecue joints from Columbia down to Charleston. The hearty gravy is barely known beyond the borders of the Palmetto State, and visiting diners find it as puzzling as the region's signature mustard-based barbecue sauce. In Georgia, Brunswick stew reigns supreme as the standard barbecue side dish. A lot of hot air has been expended in the debate with Virginia over which state originated the stew—a pointless argument, since the Virginians clearly have the solid historical claim (see chapter 3). Georgians would be better off looking over the Savannah River to their neighbors in South Carolina, for hash and the Georgia version of Brunswick stew are likely distant cousins.

Source: Louise Oliphant, interview with Estrella Jones, Federal Writers' Project, Augusta, Georgia, Slave Narratives (online database), http://www.ancestry.com (accessed March 22, 2009). "The Barbecue at Moore's," *Edgefield Advertiser,* August 7, 1861, 2. "Wilkes Convicts Eat Barbecue Cooked by World's Best Chef," *Atlanta Constitution,* December 29, 1907, 29. Maude Andrews, "The Georgia Barbecue," *Harper's Weekly,* November 9, 1895, 1072. See also, "Treat for the Editors," *Columbia (SC) State,* May 25, 1897, 3, or "The Home of the Barbecue," *Macon Weekly Telegraph,* April 5, 1887, 2.

missioner of roads and revenues, a position he held until his death in February 1915. Callaway passed his pit knowledge on to Charlie Gerrard, Joe Hester, and Randall Denard, who themselves became legendary barbecue men in Wilkes County, Georgia.[26]

Frank T. Meacham was one of North Carolina's last great barbecue men before the rise of the restaurant era. He was born in Missouri in 1869, but his parents were both native North Carolinians, and they moved back to the state when Meacham was a small child. Meacham was raised in Wake County (near Raleigh), and he was part of the first graduating class from North Carolina A&M (now known as North Carolina State). In 1903 he accepted a position as the superintendent of the Piedmont Experimental Station in Statesville, where he presided over the experimental farm and assisted farmers throughout the state with agricultural improvement. It was at the Experimental Station that he first started serving barbecue to large numbers of guests, including thousands of diners at the annual Iredell County farmer's picnic. As Meacham's cooking reputation grew, he tended the pit for a wide range of public functions in and around Statesville, including barbecues for the Traveler's Protective Association, the Chamber of Commerce, the Patriotic Order of the Sons of America, the Kiwanis Club, the Boy Scouts, and church gatherings. By 1922 he was well known enough in the area for the *Statesville Landmark* to announce that a Farm Bureau barbecue would be "prepared a la Meacham style." During the 1920s he was traveling throughout the state to cook at big functions, such as the Fourth of July celebration in Taylorsville in 1922 and annual alumni reunions at North Carolina State in Raleigh. Meacham died in 1930.[27]

The Kentucky Burgoo Kings

Gustave (Gus) Jaubert was the undisputed king of Kentucky barbecue and also of burgoo, a thick stew that is the state's signature side dish. Jaubert was born in New York in 1840, the son of French immigrants, and moved to Louisville, Kentucky, when he was four years old. Jaubert's father was a confectioner and hoped his son would follow in his trade, but at age fourteen young Gus was hired by a pitmaster to help turn the spits at a Know-Nothing rally in Hopkinsville. He determined there and then to master the art of barbecue and follow "the call of the suet pot," a reference to the pots of melted lard that were kept next to the pits for basting the meat.

In April 1861, Jaubert enlisted as a private in the Confederate army. By his own account, he lent a hand "whenever there was any barbecuing to be done" in his regiment.[28] After the war, Jaubert returned to Kentucky, where he opened the Magnolia Saloon on Mill Street in Lexington. He soon became involved with a Captain Beard and Jake Hostetter, two veterans who had already established themselves before the war as respected Kentucky barbecue men. Little is known about Hostetter, a Lexington butcher who was born around 1817 and cooked barbecue for the big political rallies of the antebellum era, and even less is known about Captain Beard. Jaubert began cooking with them for stump speeches and inherited the mantel as the region's top barbecuer after they died. In 1866, Senator George H. Pendleton of Ohio traveled to Kentucky to make a speech in support of James B. Beck, a Lexington lawyer running for Congress. For the occasion, Gus Jaubert decided to serve not just the traditional barbecue but also a massive pot of burgoo—perhaps the first time the two dishes were served together at a Kentucky political event.

Popular legend has long credited Jaubert not only as being the first Kentucky Burgoo King but also with having invented the stew from whole cloth. Most accounts have Jaubert creating the first version of burgoo for John Hunt Morgan, the famous Confederate general who led a series of infamous raids behind Union lines in Indiana and Ohio. The more fanciful versions of the story have Jaubert making the stew from blackbirds, other meat being scarce, and the name of the dish has been attributed to either Jaubert's French accent or a harelip that caused "blackbird stew" to be pronounced "burgoo."[29]

These tales are merely legend. Jaubert served in the First Kentucky Infantry, not in Morgan's Second Kentucky Cavalry.[30] He was born in New York and raised in Kentucky, so he was unlikely to have had a French accent. And burgoo clearly predates the Civil War by several decades. R. Gerald Alvey has found references to burgoo in Lexington newspapers as far back as 1830.[31] In a newspaper interview, Jaubert himself explained that burgoo originated as a Welsh stew that gained popularity in the British

Gus Jaubert, Kentucky's first Burgoo King, at a barbecue at Woodland Park in Lexington, Kentucky, circa 1900.

maritime service, then was brought by sailors to Virginia and other southern states. As Jaubert tells it, burgoo was once made from a shank of beef, chickens, corn, tomatoes, onions, and bacon. In his version, he eliminated the bacon, increased the amount of beef and chicken, and added potatoes to thicken the stew.

Jaubert may not have invented burgoo, but he helped make it a Kentucky barbecue staple. Jaubert tended the pits at so many events for the state Democratic Party that he later bragged that he had "made more Democratic votes in the South than any other living man."[32] His career as a burgoo king was not limited to political events, either. In the decades around the turn of the century, he cooked frequently at gatherings of tobacco farmers and at public auctions and estate sales, too. Serving burgoo at public auctions had apparently been a common practice in Kentucky for many years. A 1904 article in the Lancaster, Kentucky, *Central Record* announced that a sale would be held "on the old time plan. That is, a sumptuous dinner will be spread, and everybody invited. Gus Jaubert, of Lexington, whose fame for making the celebrated Kentucky burgoo, has been engaged, and many gallons of this toothsome article will be served."[33]

Perhaps Jaubert's proudest moment came in 1895, when he presided over the barbecue pits at the National Encampment for the Grand Army of the Republic, the famed fraternal organization for veterans of the Union army. It was the twenty-ninth time the organization had held such an encampment, but this was a special one. Two years in the planning, it was the first time the gathering had been held below the Mason-Dixon line, and reconciliation was the theme. Civil War leaders from both sides came to be honored and to speak, and an estimated 150,000 veterans attended. To feed the assembled crowds, Jaubert had 350 cooks and 500 waiters under his direction. They roasted 45 beeves, 383 sheep, and 241 shoats. In addition to the barbecue, Jaubert's crew made 12,000 gallons of burgoo, with some 4,000 pounds of beef, 900 whole chickens, 4,500 ears of corn, 50 bushels of onions, and 100 pounds of pepper going into the pots. Enough tin plates and cups were on hand to feed 30,000 veterans at a time.[34] The Grand Army of the Republic event eclipsed even the national party conventions as the biggest gathering of the year, and it may well have been the largest barbecue ever in the United States.

With credentials like this, it would seem hard for any cook to compete with Jaubert for the title of Burgoo King, but some tried. In 1904, the *Frankfort Roundabout* announced that David Kirkpatrick, the manager of French's restaurant, had been awarded the contract to make the burgoo for the local Fourth of July celebration, contending that "Dave is an experienced hand at the business and can make as good burgoo as Gus Jaubert, 'or any other man.'"[35]

After Jaubert's death in the 1920s, the crown of Kentucky Burgoo King passed to James T. Looney. Looney, born around 1870, owned and operated a grocery store in downtown Lexington. He learned to cook burgoo around the turn of the century from Gus Jaubert himself, and he soon became a fixture at Bluegrass political meetings and horse races. Looney cooked his stew in a massive 500-gallon iron kettle that had been

The pits at the 1895 Grand Army of the Republic Barbecue in Louisville, Kentucky, which were presided over by Gus Jaubert and served some thirty thousand diners. (Courtesy Library of Congress, Prints & Photographs Division.)

used during the Civil War to make gunpowder.[36] In 1930, he served seven thousand people attending a charity horse race at the private track owned by Edward R. Bradley, one of the country's preeminent owners and breeders of Thoroughbred race horses. Bradley was so taken with Looney's work that he pledged to name a colt after him. Two years later, "Burgoo King" won the Kentucky Derby and Preakness Stakes, helping spread Looney's reputation nationwide.

In 1934, Looney cooked for ten thousand farmers at a tobacco festival in Carrollton, Kentucky. The event earned him a mention in *Time* magazine, which reported his recipe to be made from "800 lb. lean beef with no bones; 200 lb. fat hens; 900 lb. canned tomatoes; 240 lb. canned carrots; 180 lb. canned corn; 200 lb. cabbage; 60 lb. salt; 4 lb. pepper; 'my own seasoning.' Cook 18 to 20 hr. in iron kettle out of doors over a wood fire."[37] The seasoning for Looney's burgoo was supposedly a closely guarded secret, but an Associated Press reporter published the formula in 1948, listing red and black pepper, salt, Angostura bitters, Worcestershire sauce, curry powder, tomato catsup, and sherry.[38] Looney remained Kentucky's top barbecue man and burgoo maker well into his eighties, continuing to cater special events until just a few months before his death in 1954.

Burgoo King, the Kentucky Derby–winning race horse named after James T. Looney, the "Kentucky Burgoo King," May 1937. (Courtesy University of Kentucky Libraries, Special Collections and Digital Programs.)

An Aside on Barbecue Sauce

One of the great differentiators in regional barbecue styles today is the sauce. In eastern North Carolina it's thin, spicy, and vinegar-based while in Texas it's sweet, thick, and tomato-based. Some variations—like the bright yellow mustard-based sauce from the Midlands of South Carolina and the mayonnaise-based white sauce from Alabama— are specific to only a narrow region and not widely known in other states. This regional variety is a relatively recent development. In the nineteenth century, the sauces used for barbecue followed a consistent formula across the country.

A Kentucky Barbecue

IN 1905, THE REVEREND John H. Aughey captured his memories of a Kentucky barbecue and burgoo in *Tupelo,* his memoirs of life in the South just before and after the Civil War.

THE SOUTHERN BARBECUE.

In ordinary times Uncle Jake Hostetter may be an humble citizen in Lexington. Now, as master of the barbecuing, he rules supreme in the cooking lot, for the trenches are enclosed by a tight board fence, and it requires some persuasion to get past the guards. There are only a few favored persons within. The thousands who sniff the odors, and look longingly toward the incense arising from the fires, are wandering through the park wondering when dinner will be ready. The master of the barbecue moves among the trenches and his word is law. He served his apprenticeship away back when presidents came to these Kentucky festivities. Barbecues have not been so frequent of late years. But Uncle Jake feels safe in his experience, and he shows no uneasiness over the fact that 5,000 people are holding him responsible for their dinners, and some of them have gone breakfastless to stimulate appetite. Now and then two of the cooking corps bring up from the trenches to the table under the big tree a carcass to inspect. He cuts into it, slices off bits of the flesh, tastes, and looks knowing. Even the president of the day, Hon. W. C. P. Breckenridge, recognizes the authority. The speaking has commenced from a stand in the park, and somebody wants to know when the orators are going to stop for dinner. "Just when Uncle Jake Hostetter says the mutton is done to a turn," replies Mr. Breckenridge, and another statesman is let loose to say a great many pretty compliments about Kentucky, and a very few words about national politics.

The Blue Grass country has contributed to this occasion three great caldrons. Whatever useful purpose they may have subserved about hog killing time, they are now doing duty in the manufacture of 900 gallons of burgoo. Burgoo has a basis, as the chemist says. The basis on this occasion consists of 150 chickens and 225 pounds of beef in joints, and other forms best suited for soup. To this has been added a bushel or two of tomatoes. The heap of shaven roasting ears tells of another accessory before the fact. Cabbage and potatoes and probably other things in small quantities, but too numerous to mention, have gone into the pots. The fires were lighted under the vats before the roasting commenced on the trenches, and the burgoo has been steadily boiling ever since. This boiling necessitates steady stirring, and next to Uncle Jake's ministerial powers the old expert who presides over each kettle comes in for due respect and glorification. "You might not think it," says the old grey-headed Kentuckian whose eye is on the largest of the pots where 500 gallons of burgoo are bubbling, "but a piece of mutton suet as large as my hand thrown into the pot would spoil the whole mess. That shows you that there are some things you can't put in burgoo. Sometimes out in the woods we put in squirrels and turkeys, but we didn't have any this time. I think they've got a leetle too much pepper in that pot down there, so if you don't find what you get is just right come to me and I'll fix you up with some of this." As the meat boils from the bones the latter are raised from the bottom of the kettle by the paddle and thrown out. Gradually vegetables lose all distinctive form and appearance and the compound is reduced to a homogeneous liquid, about the consistency of molasses. "Burgoo ought to boil about 14 hours," says the old expert, "we've only had about 8 for this, but I think they'll be able to eat it."

Gradually the heap of barbecued meat accumulates before Uncle Jake. He goes over and looks at the burgoo, and consults with the old expert. Then he glances over the fence at the long tables, and finds that two wagon loads of bread have been hewn into rations and strewn along the pine boards. The tin cups, 3,000 of them, are hurriedly scattered with the bread. From all parts of the grounds there is a sudden but decorous movement toward the tables, and the orator on tap runs off a peroration and stops. Uncle Jake's corps of assistants bring out the carcasses still on the stretchers, and every rod of table length finds a smoking sheep and a shoat. Gus Jaubert and a dozen butchers, with their long, sharp knives, shave and cut and deal out with all the speed that long practice has given them. The burgoo, steaming hot in new wooden buckets, is brought in, and as the attendants pass along the lines the hungry people dip out cupfuls and sip it as it cools. There are no knives nor forks. Nobody asks for or expects them. Neither are there spoons for the burgoo. The great slices of bread serve as plates for the meat. There are 5,000 people eating together, and all busy at once. Not a basket has been brought. All types and classes of Blue Grass people are facing those tables, and handling their bread and meat and burgoo with manifestations of appetite which tell of the relish of the fare.

Source: John Hill Aughey, *Tupelo*, (Lincoln, NE: State Journal Company, 1888), 397–400

As early as 1700, colonists had been using a basting sauce when barbecuing, both to flavor the meat and to keep it moist. Edward Ward, the travel writer who chronicled a barbecue in Peckham, Jamaica, around 1706, noted that the cook basted the pigs with "a most admirable composition of Green Virginia Pepper and Maderia wine, with many other palatable ingredients" which he "plentifully dau'b on with a Fox's Tail ty'd to a long stick."[39] This sauce was used only during the cooking, for the pigs were simply removed from the fire, placed on a log, and chopped into quarters for serving. That seems to be the main way barbecue was prepared for the next two hundred years: basted during cooking and served dry.

The earliest instructions for pit-cooking barbecue can be found in Lettice Bryan's *The Kentucky Housewife* (1839), which calls for only the simplest of basting sauces: "nothing but a little salt-water and pepper, merely to season and moisten it a little." Once the meat was done, Bryan recommended the cook "squeeze over it a little lemon juice, and accompany it with melted butter."[40] Three decades later, Mrs. Annabella Hill, from La Grange, Georgia, published similar directions in *Mrs. Hill's New Cook Book* (1872), though her recipe incorporates butter and a little mustard into the basting liquid: "Melt half a pound of butter; stir into it a large tablespoon of mustard, half a teaspoonful of red pepper, one of black, salt to taste; add vinegar until the sauce has a strong acid taste." At the end of cooking, "pour over the meat any sauce that remains."[41]

This basic combination of butter or some other fat, vinegar, and pepper remained the standard throughout the nineteenth century. An 1860 account of a Virginia event described iron vessels positioned along the side of the pit, "some filled with salt, and water; others with melted butter, lard, etc. into which the attendants dipped linen cloths affixed to the ends of long, flexible wands, and delicately applied them with a certain air of dainty precision to different portions on the roasting meat."[42] *Harper's Weekly's* 1896 account of a Georgia barbecue noted that the meat was cooked for twelve hours and "basted with salt water . . . then, just before it is eaten, plentifully bedabbled with 'dipney'—a compound of sweet country lard and the strongest vinegar, made thick and hot with red and black pepper."[43] Barbecue sauces are very different today on the East Coast than they are in Texas, but *On a Mexican Mustang Through Texas,* an 1883 travelogue, described a barbecue outside San Antonio with a sauce almost identical to that

Preparing the barbecue at the Coon Dog Field Trials in Henderson, Tennessee, April 28, 1940. The nineteenth-century-style outdoor barbecue remained a characteristic of rural southern life well into the 1950s.

used in Virginia and Georgia: "Butter, with a mixture of pepper, salt, and vinegar, is poured on the meat as it is being cooked."[44] The famed regional variations in barbecue sauces do not seem to have developed until the twentieth century.

Barbecue Gains National Attention

In the closing decade of the nineteenth century, a curious phenomenon occurred. The tradition of barbecue had long before pushed its way westward, and since before the Civil War it had been a common part of social life not only in southern states but in the Midwest, the Southwest, and on the Pacific Coast, too. Yet, suddenly, four decades later, the press in the Northeast and Mid-Atlantic seemingly discovered barbecue for the first time.

"The barbecue is one of the institutions of the South," raved Maude Andrews of *Harper's Weekly*. "To have known it means happiness: not to have known it means that a link in the chain of life has been lost."[45] Another *Harper's Weekly* contributor, writing the year after Andrews, was equally superlative, claiming, "a barbecue appeals equally to the stomach and the understanding. Once you have tasted it in perfection, you have a realizing sense of how it smoothes and softens campaign asperities, and makes joint debate not only possible but pleasant."[46] Georgia barbecues even gained recognition in the British press, with John R. Watkins of London's *Strand Magazine* proclaiming, "No one who has had the good fortune to attend a barbecue will ever forget it. . . . England has its roast beef and plum-pudding dinners, Rhode Island its clambakes, Boston its pork and beans, but Georgia has its barbecue, which beats them all."[47]

Much of the northern and English attention to barbecue was tied in with a highly romanticized view of the old South. Maude Andrews wrote in *Harper's Weekly*, "The Georgia barbecue is one of the few remaining feasts of *antebellum* days left to the present generation—a feast typical, indeed, of that lavishness of living peculiar to the old South—a lavishness not elegant perhaps, often barbaric, indeed, but proffered with the generosity and magnificence of monarchs."[48] These sorts of journalistic depictions appeared at about the same time that romanticized fictional accounts of antebellum plantation life were reaching wide national audiences through Charles Chesnutt's *The Conjure Woman* (1899) and Joel Chandler Harris's Uncle Remus tales. While this literary genre helped reconcile the South with the rest of the Union, it was a key contributor to the overly sentimental and whitewashed "Moonlights and Magnolia" view of life in the antebellum South.

The romantic image of barbecues as an old South institution remained well into the twentieth century, as reflected in the famous barbecue scene that features prominently in Margaret Mitchell's novel *Gone With the Wind* (1936) and the 1939 MGM movie adaptation. But the antebellum version of the barbecue was truly gone with the wind. The social and economic forces revolutionizing American life were starting to transform the institution of barbecue as well.

The Rise of Barbecue Restaurants

The famed barbecue men of the late nineteenth century straddled the line between an old world of free public barbecues and a new world where barbecue was a commercial product. As private functions such as those held by schools, commercial organizations, and civic groups became more popular, barbecue men began charging to cook for the events. The commercialization continued as pitmasters such as John W. Callaway began selling barbecue dinners for twenty-five and fifty cents at state fairs and other gatherings.

By far the biggest factor in the commercialization of barbecue was the rise of barbecue restaurants, which first appeared on the American scene around the turn of the twentieth century. Some evolved out of casual backyard operations while others sprang up as stands on vacant city lots. Still others opened along the sides of the country's new automobile highways. A common pattern can be seen among all these early restaurants. They grew slowly from informal trade to permanent businesses, emerging wherever there were a lot of people who lacked their regular sources of food. Be they motorists on the road, farmers traveling to the county seat for court and market days, or urban workers without time to go home for lunch, people needed to eat, and barbecue restaurants arose to meet that need. In the process, they permanently changed the nature of the food and the way Americans ate it.

Barbecue Stands and Early Restaurants

As in the early nineteenth century, the changes in barbecue culture were reflections of the shifting social landscape of the United States. In the late nineteenth and early twentieth centuries, America's population steadily moved from the countryside into towns and cities. They were joined by waves of new immigrants, who concentrated primarily in urban centers. In 1860 some 80 percent of the country's citizens lived in rural areas; by 1900 that number had fallen to 60 percent. Twenty years later, the urban population of the country outnumbered the rural for the first time, 51.2 percent to 48.8 percent.[1]

In a rural environment, it took a special occasion such as a stump speech or a civic celebration to draw a large enough crowd to justify roasting a whole pig. Country barbecues were one-time events, with pits dug in the ground for the occasion and supplies provided by the general community. As America's towns and cities grew, they attracted enough people to serve as a stable clientele for daily operations, and it was in downtown areas that the first barbecue restaurants appeared. The term *restaurant* is used loosely here, for these operations were usually impromptu stands put up to sell food at public events or as a sideline to another trade, such as selling illegal whiskey. It took several decades for these informal ventures to evolve into full-service, sit-down restaurants.[2]

Unlike pizza and hamburger restaurants—for which there are no shortage of claimants for being the first in the field—not even the cockiest barbecue restaurateurs have claimed to have invented the trade. The evidence is murky, but Dallas, Texas, has a good claim of being the home of the nation's earliest barbecue restaurants. In 1897 and 1898, at least three grease fires were reported at three separate barbecue stands along Commerce Street in the city's main commercial district.[3] Several towns and cities in North Carolina have a good claim, too. An 1893 ordinance in Kinston, North Carolina, levied a five-dollar tax per stand on barbecue dealers and prohibited the sale of barbecue on Queen Street, too.[4] An 1899 notice in the *Charlotte Observer* announced that Mrs. Katie Nunn had rented a store on South Church Street, where she planned to run a grocery store and a barbecue stand, with her husband doing the cooking on a pit he had constructed behind the store.[5] Two weeks later, a classified ad in the paper

Clement Lamar Castleberry, Barbecue Entrepreneur

SOME BARBECUE MEN TOOK the commercialization of barbecue a step further. In Athens, Georgia, Clement Lamar Castleberry ran a grocery store on Broad Street in the early part of the century, and on the side he catered large club gatherings and civic events, specializing in barbecued pork, beef, and hash—the signature side dish of the region that stretched from the eastern counties of Georgia through the Midlands of South Carolina. In 1926 Castleberry's son, Clement, started canning his father's hash and Brunswick stew, and the next year the two men opened a small cannery in a shed on Fifteenth Street, where they produced six hundred cans a day. Within ten years they had moved to a modern brick factory, and their thirty-five employees were cranking out ten thousand pounds of food per day, achieving a nationwide distribution for the products. The business continued to grow as a private company, expanding into beef stew, chili, tamales, and clams, and it continues today (under the ownership of Bumble Bee Seafoods) as one of the country's largest canned meat producers.

Sources: Federal Writers' Project in Georgia, *Augusta* (Augusta, GA: City Council of Augusta, 1938), 158–159. "Food Canner Agrees to Sell," *Augusta Chronicle,* December 23, 2004.

announced, "CALL at the barbecue stand for good barbecued meats, beef, pork, and mutton. Well prepared by the only barbecuer in Charlotte."[6] Mr. Nunn appears to be the first restaurant pitmaster for whom a name is recorded, and it's notable that the first barbecue stand on record in North Carolina specialized not only in pork but beef and mutton as well—items not typically associated today with either of that state's two distinctive barbecue styles.

The first barbecue joints were not sophisticated places. Some of the earliest records of such businesses can be found not in newspapers or magazines but in court proceedings, usually for cases involving illegal whiskey and violence. In 1913, Walter Faucett was convicted of manslaughter for stabbing John Cox to death with a butcher knife after a fight at Faucett's barbecue stand in Tulsa, Oklahoma. In the court testimony, witnesses repeatedly refer to the restaurant as "the house," suggesting a residential home turned into a business. One witness testified that he went to the barbecue stand "for the purpose of taking a drink"—suggesting that whiskey sales were as much a part of Faucett's trade as selling barbecued meat. In the Southwest, in particular, liquor and barbecue seem to have gone hand in hand.[7] In 1914, two deputy sheriffs found a large number of empty whiskey bottles in J. W. Kintz's barbecue stand near Convention Hall in Muskogee, Oklahoma, along with three gallons of whiskey "in a trash pile three or four steps from the back door" with "a well defined path from the back door to the trash pile."[8] In April 1915, Phil Gibson got himself into similar trouble when he resold unlicensed liquor from a barbecue stand at the corner of Thirteenth and Monroe Streets in Fort Worth, Texas.[9] Apart from passing references in court records, no information survives about any of these early ventures. By World War I, though, barbecue stands seem to have been common if informal businesses within the larger cities of the South and Southwest.

The first permanent barbecue restaurants evolved out of these sorts of improvised stands as their owners expanded operations, adding brick and cinderblock pits, enclosing dining areas, and offering all the amenities of full-service restaurants. But it wasn't just a matter of a few entrepreneurs starting to sell an item that was formerly available only at large public gatherings. In order to become a commercial product, barbecue itself had to change, and it changed differently in each part of the country. Early bar-

A Small Fire.

The grease which was on the furnace of the barbecue stand at No. 382 Commerce street caught fire at 12:05 this morning, and the fire department was called out. There was no damage.

Newspaper report of a fire at a Dallas barbecue stand. (*Dallas Morning News*, May 24, 1897.)

Barbecue Stand.

Mrs. Katie Nunn has rented No. 1 of the new row of stores on the rear of The Observer lot, and will run, in connection with a grocery store, a barbecue stand. Mr. Nunn will do the barbecuing. He has built a large pit in rear of the store, for this purpose. He will be ready for business Saturday morning.

Notice of the opening of Nunn's barbecue stand in downtown Charlotte, North Carolina. (*Charlotte Observer*, March 30, 1899.)

becue restaurants were the single greatest influence on the regionalization of barbecue, which created the multitude of local styles that we know today.

At old-style outdoor public barbecues, diners had a wide choice of meats because local farmers would donate to the cause whatever livestock they had on hand. It is common to see lists like the following in descriptions of such events: "beef, mutton, pork, and fowls were provided in superabundance and barbecued in an excellent manner."[10] As barbecue became a business, things became more standardized. In the days before mechanical refrigeration a proprietor could not keep much meat on hand for very long. Many restaurants began as weekend operations, with the proprietor barbecuing a whole hog or a side of beef on Thursday and selling it through the weekend until the supply was exhausted.[11] It made sense for early businessmen to settle on one or two standard

Kansas City's Streetcar Barbecue Palaces

IN KANSAS CITY, EARLY entrepreneurs converted old retired cable cars into barbecue stands, which dotted the city's streets in the early part of the century. Such improvised structures didn't last long. In 1919, the *Kansas City Star* noted the following:

> *The old cable car on Vine Street near Eighteenth Street is a cheerful reminder that there have been street cars in Kansas City with a shorter wheel base, a more erratic jerk, and a more limited speed range than the present "kiddie cars."*

> *With many other street cars of its generation, [this one] became the "palace" of a barbecue "king." The dynasty of barbecue kings now has more pretentious quarters; either from a newly acquired dignity, or because the Kansas City Railways company never retires cars. Most of the once familiar street car "palaces" have now disappeared. This one is vacant now.*

Source: "A Street Car 'Palace' Is Vacant," *Kansas City Star,* December 5, 1919, 12.

products to serve, and most chose the meat most readily available in the area—hence the prevalence of pork in North Carolina and beef in Texas.

Side dishes needed to be standardized, too. When barbecues were large, community-organized affairs, the side dishes consisted of food that was easy to carry in bulk and without refrigeration. Martha McCulloch-Williams, remembering her experiences of antebellum barbecues as a child, adamantly stated, "The proper accompaniments to barbecue are sliced cucumbers in strong vinegar, sliced tomatoes, a great plenty of salt-rising light bread—and a greater plenty of cool ripe watermelons."[12] This list is typical of the descriptions found in newspaper accounts of old barbecues.

As cooks began establishing regular barbecue businesses, they generally chose a different (but reasonably small) set of side dishes to carry. Many reflected local specialties or preferences; others were simply recipes that the particular proprietor knew well and felt would be an economical item to sell. "Back in the old days," recalls Wayne Monk of Lexington Barbecue in Lexington, North Carolina, "you was trying to have something you could handle in the hot weather but didn't cost an arm and a leg—what is locally available and what's cheap."[13] Initially, sides tended toward items like bread, pickles, and onions. Coleslaw was an early favorite in North Carolina because locally grown cabbage was abundant and cheap and, if you didn't add mayonnaise, it wasn't very perishable. As mechanical refrigeration, air conditioning, and electric deep fryers became more common, new items such as potato salad and French fries began to appear on barbecue restaurant menus, too.

Another factor in the regionalization of barbecue was the informal apprenticeship system that shaped the trade. Young people would go to work for an established local pitmaster, learn the craft, and then go out and open their own places. In city after city, key mentors can be identified who taught an entire generation of restaurateurs, who in turn passed on their knowledge to the next generation. Sometimes this apprenticeship occurred within a single family, with parents teaching their children, who then passed the business on to the grandchildren. In other cases it was simply a casual friendship or pure business relationship.

Beyond simply teaching the skills of tending a pit and managing a business, the mentorship system helped codify the style of barbecue served in a particular region. The identifying characteristics of a particular region's style include the cuts of meat used, the equipment and technique used to cook it, and how the meat is chopped, sliced, or otherwise prepared for serving. A region's style also includes the type of sauce to be served (assuming, that is, that sauce is served at all) as well as the side items that accompany the meat. Over the course of a half century, the menus and styles within particular areas began to coalesce into the unique regional variations that are so treasured by today's barbecue lovers. This trend can best be seen by looking at the evolution of restaurants in different parts of the country between 1920 and the Second World War.

North Carolina Barbecue

It is no accident that almost all of the legendary eastern North Carolina barbecue restaurants can be found in just three towns—Goldsboro, Rocky Mount, and Wilson—for these were some of the region's most important centers of commerce. Goldsboro, originally known as Goldsborough Junction, grew up at the intersection of the Atlantic and North Carolina Railroad and the Wilmington and Weldon Railroad. Rocky Mount was a stop on the Wilmington and Weldon, too, and the establishment of a tobacco market there in the late 1880s and the rising popularity of cigarettes (and, therefore, demand for the region's bright-leaf tobacco) made it a commercial hub. Tobacco also made the fortunes of Wilson, North Carolina. The town's first tobacco market was established in 1890, and by 1920 it was recognized as the largest market in the world.

As people began coming into these towns to trade, a group of men started cooking barbecue to feed them. One of the first was Adam Scott of Goldsboro, who got into the barbecue business just after World War I. A janitor and elevator operator, Scott cooked barbecue on the side and catered parties and receptions. The business caught on, and he began selling smoked meats from his backyard every weekend. In 1933, he enclosed the back porch of his house to create a dining room, and he enlarged the restaurant three times as business grew. Scott was a preacher in the Holiness Church, and he claimed the ingredients for his sauce came to him in a dream. The sauce is a classic

Preparing a tray at Scott's Barbecue, 1944. (Courtesy North Carolina Office of Archives and History, Raleigh, North Carolina.)

Bob Melton's barbecue restaurant in Rocky Mount, North Carolina, during a flood of the Tar River.

eastern North Carolina blend, with vinegar, salt, and red and black pepper along with other spices, and it is still sold today both at Scott's Barbecue in Goldsboro as well as in grocery stores throughout the Carolinas.

Some fifty miles to the north in Rocky Mount, Bob Melton's barbecue business grew in a similar fashion. Melton, a merchant and horse trader, started cooking barbecue as a hobby in 1919. In the early 1920s he bought fifty acres of bottomland along the Tar River and started a truck farm, selling vegetables and pecans to neighbors in Rocky Mount. His barbecue business was casual at first—just a pit in the ground where he occasionally cooked pigs for friends. Soon, he was barbecuing by request and selling the meat by the pound, and it wasn't long before townspeople would come down to the river on Saturday to buy lunch. This spurred Melton to build a shed with rough tables, and he screened it in to keep out flies. Two years later he replaced the structure with a permanent restaurant with room for forty people, and he expanded the dining room several more times over the succeeding decades.

Though Adam Scott was probably selling barbecue earlier, Melton created his enclosed dining room first, making his establishment likely to be North Carolina's first sit-down barbecue restaurant. A menu board from 1929 hung in the restaurant until it closed in 2005, and it showed that in the early days a plate of barbecue and boiled potatoes went for forty-five cents, barbecue sandwiches for fifteen, and a soda for a nickel. Melton's trade was helped by nearby U.S. Highway 301, which, before Interstate 95 was built, was a main thoroughfare for travelers from northern states to Florida, and the restaurant became well known outside of the state. When Bob Melton died in 1958 he was declared by *Life* magazine to be the "king of Southern barbecue."[14] The business changed hands several times over the years, but it remained in the same spot on the Tar River until 1999, when the flooding following Hurricane Floyd forced it to move to a new location in a strip mall. The restaurant closed its doors for good in 2005.

Both Melton and Scott served a similar kind of barbecue, the type now known as the Eastern North Carolina style. They cooked whole hogs laid out on metal rods over a pit of oak and hickory coals. Once cooked, the meat was finely chopped (almost minced) and served with a hot, salty sauce that contained only vinegar, salt, black and red pepper, and not a trace of tomato or sugar—a formula that is essentially the same as that used nationwide during the nineteenth century. Though many eastern North Carolina restaurants today have moved from oak and hickory pits to gas cookers, finely chopped whole hog and vinegar-based sauce remain the characteristic style of the region. Brunswick stew is a common menu item, too. The North Carolina version is thick, sweet, and orange and is made with chicken, tomatoes, potatoes, onions, corn, and lima beans. As early as 1929 Bob Melton was serving boiled white potatoes with his barbecue, and these along with coleslaw and corn sticks (corn bread baked into long fingers then deep fried) remain the classic side dishes of the region.

The birth of Piedmont North Carolina barbecue restaurants followed a pattern similar to that of their eastern cousins. The undisputed capital of Piedmont North Carolina barbecue is Lexington, the Davidson County seat. In the early part of the century farm-

Eastern North Carolina-Style Barbecue

Meats: Whole hog, finely chopped

Wood: Hickory, oak

Sauce: Vinegar-based

    Vinegar, water, salt, black pepper, red pepper, crushed red pepper. No tomato, no sugar.

Side Dishes:

- Brunswick Stew: A thick, reddish orange stew. Standard ingredients include chicken, tomatoes, corn, onions, potatoes, and lima beans, usually sweetened with sugar. Sometimes shredded pork or beef is added
- Barbecued Potatoes: Boiled white potatoes, cut into chunks
- Hushpuppies: Deep-fried cornmeal batter
- Corn Sticks: Corn bread fingers, baked in a mold then deep fried
- Coleslaw: Shredded cabbage with mayonnaise or mayo/mustard mixture. Often includes sweet pickles, celery seed

Classic Examples:

- Wilber's (Goldsboro)
- Skylight Inn (Ayden)
- B's (Greenville)

Sid Weaver *(left)* at his barbecue stand in downtown Lexington, North Carolina. (Courtesy Davidson County Historical Museum, Lexington, North Carolina.)

ers would pour into town for "court week," many staying for several days to transact business. In 1919, Sid Weaver and George Ridenhour began selling barbecue from a tent on a corner across from the courthouse. Soon after, Jess Swicegood erected a tent nearby and began competing for the farmers' business. At first they cooked barbecue only during court week, but by the mid-1920s farmers were coming into town every Saturday, and the two businesses began regular weekend operations. The tents were soon replaced by more permanent structures with wooden sides and tin roofs.

Weaver and Swicegood perfected the "Lexington style" of barbecuing. Rather than the whole hogs of eastern North Carolina, the Lexington pitmasters used pork shoulders. Shoulders have a higher fat content than the hams and loins, so Piedmont North

Jess Swicegood at his Lexington, North Carolina, barbecue stand. (Courtesy Davidson County Historical Museum, Lexington, North Carolina.)

Carolina barbecue tends to be juicier and more tender than the eastern variety. It is also more coarsely chopped or even sliced. Gary Freeze has attributed the popularity of pork shoulders in the region to a German American influence. Many of the pioneers of Piedmont North Carolina barbecue, he points out, including Weaver, Stamey, Swicegood, and Ridenhour, were descended from German immigrants who arrived in the American colonies in the eighteenth century and whose families migrated from Pennsylvania and Virginia down into the Carolinas. Smoked pork plays an important role in German cookery, and smoked pork shoulder was a particularly favored cut. John and Dale Reed also attribute the popularity of coleslaw as a side dish to this German influence, cabbage and slaw having a long history with the German American immigrants.[15]

Warner Stamey *(right)* tending the pits.

Sid Weaver and Jess Swicegood influenced the commercial landscape not just in Lexington but throughout the western part of the state. Swicegood trained Carlton Everhardt, who went on to found Lexington Barbecue Number 1, and Weaver trained Alton Beck and J. B. Tarleton, both of whom opened their own restaurants. And then there was Warner Stamey. In 1927, while still in high school, Stamey began working for Jess Swicegood in Lexington. Three years later he moved to Shelby, North Carolina, and (like his mentor) began selling barbecue from a tent with a sawdust floor. Stamey passed his knowledge on to two Shelby residents, Alston Bridges and Red Bridges (no relation), who opened Alston Bridges Barbecue and Bridges Barbecue Lodge, respectively. Stamey returned to Lexington in 1938 and bought out Swicegood's operation for three hundred dollars. There he taught the style to Wayne Monk, another legendary North Carolina barbecue man, who would go on to open Lexington Barbecue.

Piedmont North Carolina-Style Barbecue

Meats: Pork shoulders, chopped

Wood: Hickory, oak

Sauce: Vinegar-based (with tomato)

Side Dishes:

- Hushpuppies: Deep-fried cornmeal batter
- Coleslaw: Cabbage chopped to tiny bits, seasoned with barbecue sauce (not mayo or mustard)

Classic Examples:

- Stamey's (Greensboro)
- Lexington Barbecue (Lexington)
- Barbecue Center (Lexington)
- Bridges Barbecue Lodge (Shelby)

Whatever Happened to Virginia Barbecue?

THE COLONY OF VIRGINIA was the birthplace of barbecue, the soil where the seed was planted and from which it spread throughout the country. As Virginians left their home state and migrated southwestward through the Carolinas into Georgia, Tennessee, and Alabama, they took their barbecue traditions with them, and it is common to see references in nineteenth-century newspapers to "old-fashioned Virginia barbecues." In the 1920s and 1930s, Virginia had as many "good old-fashioned" election and church-picnic barbecues as anywhere else. Yet somehow no legendary barbecue restaurants developed in Virginia that could rival the likes of Arthur Bryant's or Gates's in Kansas City, the Rendevouz in Memphis, or any of the two dozen joints in Lexington, North Carolina.

So what is "Virginia-style" barbecue? You can find some good barbecue in Virginia these days, particularly in the Tidewater region, but many of the restaurants there unabashedly advertise "North Carolina–style" barbecue. The Silver Pig Barbeque Restaurant in Lynchburg claims to have "the most authentic Carolina barbeque this side of the North Carolina state line." Three Li'l Pigs in Daleville (just north of Roanoke) boasts "the tastiest, slow-cooked, hickory-smoked North Carolina–style barbeque anywhere in the valley." Residents of Richmond sometimes refer to the thick reddish barbecue sauce that adorns their restaurants' tables as "Virginia style" sauce, but that seems mostly to distinguish it from the spicy, vinegar-based version that is always there alongside the red stuff and is clearly Eastern North Carolina style. Most commentators who have tried to document America's divergent regional styles either omit Virginia altogether or lump it in the same category as North Carolina.

People in Virginia still love to eat barbecue, but it just doesn't seem to have taken on much of a distinct regional identity.

BARBECUE TOMORROW, SEPTEMBER 6,
at Waverley Methodist Church Grove,

312 Gervais Street, End of Waverley Car Line

This will be the biggest and best cue we have had
yet. We are sorry that we could not serve all our
friends on July 4, but ample provision has been made
for tomorrow.

1000 Pounds of Meat and 500 Pounds of Hash

Buckets will be served at 11:15. Dinner served
from 12:00 to 2:30.

Advertisement for Labor Day barbecue,
Columbia, South Carolina (*Columbia [SC]
State*, September 5, 1920.)

Stamey ended his journeys in Greensboro, where he opened Stamey's on High Point
Road in 1953. In addition to spreading the Lexington method of smoking pork shoulders, Stamey is credited with introducing hushpuppies to the North Carolina scene,
and they are now one of the standard side dishes at barbecue restaurants throughout
the state.[16]

South Carolina Barbecue

A hundred miles to the south, barbecue in the Midlands of South Carolina entered
the commercial world by way of cooks who offered up their wares to the general public
around key holidays—particularly the Fourth of July and Labor Day. As early as 1897,
Columbia's barbecue men started running advertisements in the *State* newspaper offering barbecue meat sold by the pound. Their trade was aimed at holiday picnickers,
many of whom apparently carried it home in buckets. On July 4, 1923, no fewer than
six vendors posted announcements. S. E. Perry offered "Bucket Barbecue" with meat at
sixty cents a pound and hash at thirty. The Lakeview Tea Room was hosting a barbecue
from 10:00 A.M. until 4:00 P.M., while J. C. Dreher on Broad River Road promised pork
"cooked by one with 25 years experience." At McConnell's market you could get sauce
free with your order of pork, lamb, or hash, and J. D. Perry's market advised "bring your
own bucket." Down at the Waverly Church Grove, E. B. Lever was the chairman and

South Carolina-Style Barbecue (Midlands)

Meats: Pork

Wood: Hickory, oak

Sauce: Mustard-based

Side Dishes:

- Hash: A cross between a meat stew and a gravy, generally served over white rice. Recipes for hash vary greatly from restaurant to restaurant, but it generally consists of the leftover parts of a hog—including fine bits of pork along with some innards—and vegetables such as onions and potatoes that are highly spiced and cooked till the ingredients are almost dissolved into a thin, spicy stew.
- White Rice
- Coleslaw

Classic Examples:

- Maurice's (Columbia)
- Duke's (Orangeburg)
- Sweatman's (Holly Hill)
- Bessinger's (Charleston)

pitmaster for the church's annual fundraiser, which offered "Bucket Que" starting at 10:00 A.M., and, at 11:45 A.M., a "Real Barbecue Dinner" for seventy-five cents in the church basement.[17] Notably, all these advertisements featured both pork and lamb. Barbecue in the Carolinas is dominated today by pork, and lamb or mutton is something associated usually with Kentucky. As late as the 1940s, however, it was regularly served at barbecues in South Carolina.

E. B. Lever would prove to be a lasting figure on the Midlands barbecue scene. He continued cooking for the church through most of the 1920s, but by the end of the decade set out on a more commercial path. On July Fourth and Labor Day he set up his own stand on Pendleton Street in downtown Columbia, selling smoked pork, lamb, and hash. In 1930 he advertised, "Why do so many demand my barbecue? Because I select the best meat and cook to suit."[18] By 1935 he had moved to River Drive in the northern part of town, and he eventually ended up running a restaurant out on Broad River Road. E. B.'s operations were continued by his family after his death. Ray Lever ran a restaurant between Columbia and Blythewood that remained in operation until the 1990s.

Georgia, Alabama, and Mississippi Barbecue

The city of Atlanta had barbecue stands as early as 1900, and these flourished during the early part of the century. By 1924, Jones' Barbecue Café at 136 Highland Avenue was selling "barbecue lunches" and smoked pork for sixty cents a pound.[19] Savannah had its own barbecue joints, too, including that of Johnny Harris, who opened a white clapboard stand with black shutters and a sawdust floor at the corner of Bee Road and Estill Drive (now named Victory Drive) just outside of the city. Estill Drive was still a dirt road at the time, and the restaurant catered to those traveling from Savannah out to the village of Thunderbolt (home of the Savannah Yacht Club) or to the resorts at Tybee Island. In North and South Carolina, barbecue restaurants tended to be simple places that focused on food only, with no alcohol served and no entertainment. This wasn't necessarily the case in Georgia and the states to the west. Johnny Harris's business was a nightspot, and patrons could dine on barbecue and fried chicken, drink beer

A 1960 postcard for Johnny Harris Restaurant, Savannah, Georgia. Harris's operation began as a barbecue stand selling bootleg liquor during Prohibition and evolved into an elegant nightspot by the 1940s.

and bootleg liquor, and play slot machines. A small zoo out back displayed Harris's collection of monkeys and birds, captured during various hunting expeditions.

In 1936 Harris and his partner, Red Donaldson, moved the business to a grander building at its present-day location at 1651 East Victory Drive, and it soon became one of the city's leading nightclubs. In the 1940s, patrons dressed in tuxedos and ball gowns danced in its circular "starlight" dining hall, which had tiny light bulbs embedded in the ceiling and a revolving bandstand at the center of the floor where leading big band stars such as Harry James performed. Johnny Harris Restaurant is still in business, and it hosts live music once a month, though most nights it is more of a family-dining restaurant than the nightclub of its heydey. Harris features a rarity in Georgia barbecue: a lamb sandwich, which is served on toasted white bread with sliced dill pickle.

Georgia-Style Barbecue

Meats: Pork

Wood: Oak, hickory

Sauce: Ketchup and molasses base

Side Dishes:

- Brunswick Stew: While the version of Brunswick stew served in North Carolina and Virginia is almost always made with chicken, the Georgia version is often made with pork, beef, or chicken, or any combination of the three, along with corn, potatoes, lima beans, and tomatoes. In his book *Searching for the Dixie Barbecue,* Wilber W. Caldwell made a further distinction between "Virginia-style" and "Georgia-style" Brunswick stew. In the former, the chicken and other meats are boiled first in the main pot along with the vegetables, removed to be boned, and the picked meat returned to the stew. In the Georgia variety, the meats are cooked separately and chopped or ground and added to the stew pot.
- Barbecued Beans

Classic Examples:

- Sprayberry's (Newnan)
- Fresh Air (Jackson)
- Harold's (Atlanta)

Big Bob Gibson's Bar-B-Q, Decatur, Alabama.

Commercial barbecue was not limited to cities. The smaller towns of Georgia, Alabama, and Mississippi began adding barbecue businesses to sell to the growing number of townspeople as well as the residents of outlying rural areas who traveled into town to conduct business. Some of the region's oldest barbecue restaurants date from this period. In 1929, Dr. Joel Watkins opened the Fresh Air Barbecue stand on Highway 42 just outside of Jackson, Georgia. It was later leased by G. W. "Toots" Caston, who bought it outright in 1945 after Watkins died. The stand is still in operation today in the same structure, which has changed little since it first opened. The Fresh Air specializes in the two classic items of Georgia barbecue: finely chopped pork, which is served relatively dry, and Brunswick stew, which, in the Georgia version, is a thick red stew made from pork or beef, potatoes, tomato, and corn.

In Alabama, a unique regional twist was developed in the 1920s: white barbecue sauce. Its creator was Bob Gibson, a railroad worker for the L&M railway who started cooking and selling barbecue on weekends at his house outside of Decatur, Alabama.

Alabama-Style Barbecue

Meats: Pork ribs, pork shoulder (served chopped or sliced)

Wood: Hickory, pecan

Sauce:

- Tomato-based, spicy
- "White barbecue sauce": mayonnaise and vinegar base

Side Dishes:

- Potato Salad
- Mustard Slaw
- Beans

Classic Examples:

- Big Bob Gibson's (Decatur)
- Dreamland (Tuscaloosa)
- Golden Rule (Irondale)

Gibson started with a pit dug in the ground and some makeshift tables supported by boards nailed into the side of trees. As business grew, Gibson replaced the dirt trench with a raised brick pit with a flat iron grate. The menu remained simple: pork shoulders and chickens with coleslaw and potato chips. Between 1930 and 1940 Gibson moved his restaurant to a succession of increasingly larger buildings before settling in 1952 at a location that was more permanent and is next door to where the Big Bob Gibson Bar-B-Q still operates today.[20] Gibson created his signature white sauce to accompany his barbecue chickens, which he would pull from the pit and dunk in sauce before serving. "White barbecue sauce" can now be found in restaurants throughout northern Alabama.

About the same time that Gibson was setting up shop, James Ollie McClung opened a barbecue stand on Green Springs Highway on the south side of Birmingham. A year later, in 1927, McClung moved his restaurant to Seventh Avenue where it would thrive for the next seventy years. Ollie's had both pork and beef on the menu and was known for its homemade pies. (Ollie's was also the subject of a landmark Supreme Court desegregation case, as detailed in chapter 8.)

Abe's Barbecue in Clarksdale, Mississippi, was founded in 1924, by Abraham Davis, a twenty-one-year-old immigrant who had arrived in the United States from Lebanon eight years before. Originally a snack stand on Fourth Street, the business moved in 1937 to a building at the corner of Highways 61 and 49. Davis cooked Boston butt over pecan wood, then cooled the meat overnight and sliced it. When a customer ordered a sandwich, the pork slices were heated on a griddle, chopped into pieces, and served on a bun with the thick, dark-red barbecue sauce that is characteristic of Mississippi barbecue. Abe's featured another Delta specialty on its menu: tamales, which began being sold by street vendors in Mississippi towns sometime around the turn of the century. Davis, following a recipe learned from a local vendor, made his tamales from ground pork shoulder, spreading the meat mixture over a corn shuck that had been lined with cornmeal, then rolling, tying, and boiling it. You can still get a pork sandwich and tamales from Abe's Barbecue today, which is run by his son, Pat, at the same crossroads location in Clarksdale.[21]

Tennessee Barbecue

While most barbecue styles are defined by state, two American cities—Kansas City, Missouri, and Memphis, Tennessee—have distinct enough barbecue to have their own styles. Memphis developed its local version in the early twentieth century, when smoked ribs and pork sandwiches became both a lunch staple and, due to Memphis's lively nightlife scene, a late-night delicacy, too. In the decades following the Civil War, the city was an economic magnet that drew people from the surrounding countryside. The great proportion of these immigrants were African Americans looking for new opportunities. Memphis's black population grew from 3,800 at the time of the Civil War to over 50,000 at the turn of the twentieth century, comprising more than half of the city's total population of 100,000. The city also drew crowds of weekend visitors. Memphis was the world's largest timber market, and laborers from lumber and turpentine camps in the bottomlands of Mississippi would pour into town on leave, looking for places to spend their hard-earned wages. They were joined by waiters, cooks, porters, and deckhands from docked riverboats along with the more than 1,000 men who worked in the city's booming railroad yards.

All of these people constituted a huge market for entertainment, and a vibrant nightlife developed with its center on Beale Street. By day, Beale was the heart of black commerce in the city, home to a range of African American businesses including banks, dentist offices, dry good stores, bakeries, and restaurants. By night, it was a thriving entertainment center, with saloons, theaters, and the music halls that gave birth to the Memphis blues. Beale Street was also home to late-night barbecue joints. The most famous belonged to Johnny Mills, an African American who opened a barbecue restaurant on Fourth Street between Beale Street and Gayoso Avenue in the 1920s. The restaurant had two dining rooms, one for white patrons and one for black, and its barbecue was cooked in a large pit in the alley behind the building.

Even more barbecue action could be found about two miles to the southeast in the area around McLemore Avenue. In 1922 Leonard Heuberger opened Leonard's Barbecue at the corner of Trigg and Latham, four blocks south of McLemore. According to legend, Heuberger acquired the seven-stool sandwich stand as a barter for a Model-T Ford. Ten years later he moved half a mile down McLemore to the corner of South Bellevue and created a drive-in restaurant. Heuberger was from a German Jewish family, and his restaurant served only white patrons until segregation ended in the 1960s. The cooks, however, were all black, and they slow-roasted pork shoulders and ribs over hickory charcoal in a brick pit. They cooked overnight, barbecuing up to thirty-two shoulders at a time. James Willis, who started as a "tray picker" in 1938

Memphis-Style Barbecue

Meats: Pork ribs, pulled pork sandwiches

Sauce: Tomato and molasses base, dark and sweet

Side Dishes:

- Barbecue Spaghetti: Also known as "side spaghetti": spaghetti noodles boiled till soft, then tossed with bits of chopped pork shoulder and barbecue sauce
- Barbecued Bologna: Rolls of bologna barbecued on the pit, scored with a knife, served in inch-thick hunks, topped with barbecue sauce

Classic Examples:

- Leonard's
- Jim Neely's Interstate Barbecue
- Charlie Vergos' Rendezvous

at age fifteen and learned to cook from pitmaster Tom Tillman, recalled keeping the fire going under the meat and turning the shoulders every hour and a half. In between turns, he had to "open that pit every five or six minutes and see whether it's caught a fire or not. You cooking it on an open pit. That grease gets hot and starts a fire." Leonard's crew would salt the shoulders and cook them a full seven hours, the first four dry and the last three with a mop of basting sauce applied.[22]

Leonard's did a brisk business on weekends, and their busiest time was on Sunday evenings, when families out for a drive would stop by for barbecue. Leonard's claims to have invented the Memphis-style barbecue pork sandwich, which is made from chopped pork shoulder on a bun with finely diced coleslaw and a red, tomato-based sauce.[23] These sold two for a quarter in the 1930s. At its peak in the 1940s and 1950s, Leonard's had twenty carhops working under the canopies, making it one of the largest drive-in restaurants in the country. Although the Bellevue restaurant closed in 1991, Leonard's is still going strong today at locations on Fox Plaza and downtown on Main Street.

Many of the early barbecue businesses in Memphis were more beer joints than restaurants. They catered to late-night crowds, with jukeboxes and beer and sometimes areas for dancing. The owners would cook ten or twelve slabs of ribs on small pits in the back, slow cooking and mopping them all day to prepare for the night's crowd. A popular menu item in the 1940s and 1950s was a rib sandwich, which consisted of three or four ribs served between slices of bread with slaw and a little barbecue sauce. Served with the bones in, the sandwich was meant to be pulled apart with the fingers and eaten.

Barbecue restaurants flourished in Memphis, but before World War II they do not appear to have been very common in the eastern parts of Tennessee. Charlie Nickens, originally a meat wholesaler, opened a barbecue restaurant at Third and Jefferson in downtown Nashville in the 1930s, where one could get a "Charlie Special"—a pulled pork sandwich served on corn bread—for twenty-five cents and a barbecue plate for forty cents. Chattanooga had the Busy Bee Barbecue, but it was more a downtown café than a barbecue stand, featuring hamburgers, waffles, and the "best coffee in the city" in addition to pork sandwiches. Barbecue restaurants would not become widespread east of Memphis until well after the Second World War.

Kansas City Barbecue

Both as an economic center and as an American barbecue capital, Kansas City, Missouri, has many parallels to Memphis. Each was a river city that grew explosively in the latter half of the nineteenth century, and both developed large African American

Busy Bee Barbecue, Chattanooga, Tennessee, circa 1926.

communities and an active nightlife that included music, dancing, and dining. While Memphis made its fortunes on lumber and turpentine, Kansas City made its on beef and grain. In 1867, the town had only twelve thousand people. Two years later, the Hannibal Bridge became the first permanent span over the Missouri River, and Kansas City became a way station for watering and feeding cattle being transported on the railroad lines that linked Abilene, Kansas, to Chicago. Stockyards, grain elevators, and meat packing soon followed. By 1910, with over a quarter of a million people, it had become a major American city.[24]

"Exodusters"—black families fleeing the economically shattered South—started coming to Kansas City in the 1870s, where many found work in the new packinghouses. The Great Migration, which began around the time of World War I, increased the size of the African American community to over thirty thousand by 1920.[25] Kansas City was strictly segregated, with most black residents isolated in a few neighbor-

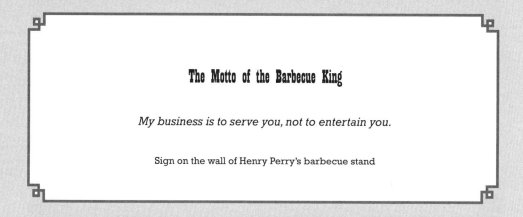

The Motto of the Barbecue King

My business is to serve you, not to entertain you.

Sign on the wall of Henry Perry's barbecue stand

hoods such as Hick's Hollow, Belvidere, and Quality Hill. The latter sat atop high bluffs overlooking the Missouri River and was once home to the stately mansions of the city's founders. By the 1890s, affluent white residents began moving southward to fashionable homes in newly developed areas, and their old mansions were divided into multitenant rooming houses. It was in these predominantly black neighborhoods that Kansas City's famous barbecue tradition got its start.

The grandfather of Kansas City barbecue is widely acknowledged to be Henry Perry. Perry was a southern transplant, born near Memphis, Tennessee, in 1875. He bounced around the Mississippi area for a while, working as a steamboat cook and kitchen hand, before settling in Kansas City in 1907. He found work as a porter at a Quality Hill saloon and on the side operated a barbecue stand in an alley off Bank Street in the heart of downtown, where he cooked ribs over a wood-filled pit dug into the ground and sold them wrapped in newspaper for twenty-five cents a slab. As his operation grew, Perry moved several times, first to a location at 1514 East Nineteenth Street and then to an old trolley barn two blocks east at Nineteenth and Highland.[26] Both locations were located in the African American neighborhood known as "The Bowery," but Perry's clientele, the *Kansas City Call* noted in 1932, was about equally divided between black and white, and "swanky limousines, gleaming with nickel and glossy backs rub shoulders along the curb outside the Perry stand with pre-historic Model T Fords." Perry cooked short ribs, long ribs, ham, and pork over hickory and oak coals, and he was adamant about his technique. "There is only one way to cook barbecue," he insisted, "and that is the way I am doing it, over a wood fire, with properly constructed oven and pit."[27] It was this technique that earned him the title of "The Barbecue King" of Kansas City.

Like Sid Weaver and Jess Swicegood in North Carolina, Henry Perry not only cooked barbecue but also trained an entire generation of Kansas City barbecue men. Charlie Bryant served his apprenticeship at Perry's stand before setting out on his own and opening a restaurant at Fourteenth and Woodland.[28] He borrowed Perry's cooking method, but created his own formula for sauce and soon gained his own reputation as a barbecue man. Charlie Bryant moved his restaurant to Eighteenth and Euclid in 1929, and ran it until 1946, when he retired for health reasons. His brother Arthur took over the restaurant, renaming it Arthur Bryant's, covering the sawdust floors, and replacing the wooden tables with Formica-topped ones. He also toned down the spiciness of the barbecue sauce, since he thought "Old Man Perry and my brother used to make the sauce way too hot."[29] Arthur Bryant was dedicated to his restaurant, arriving at dawn each day and making his own pickles and cutting the potatoes for his fries by hand. Over time the reputation of Bryant's grew, helped by a parade of famous diners that included Count Basie, Harry Truman, and many Hollywood stars. In the 1970s, Calvin Trillin declared Bryant's "the best single restaurant in the world." Today, it remains the most famous barbecue joint in Kansas City, if not the entire country.

The Bryants weren't the only barbecue men who learned their craft from Henry Perry. Arthur Pinkard began working for Perry in the 1930s, then later moved to a rundown joint called Ol' Kentuck Bar-B-Q, which had just been bought by George and Arzelia Gates. Pinkard taught George Gates the Perry method of barbecuing, which involved slow-cooking the meats directly over a wood fire so that the juice dropped down onto the coals. Gates transformed the Ol' Kentuck into a prosperous restaurant, and he later passed his knowledge on to his son, Ollie, who now runs Gates & Son Barbecue at

Barbecue King

Henry Perry, Kansas City barbecue pioneer. (*Kansas City Call*, 1932.)

Forty-seventh and Prospect—one of the legends of the Kansas City barbecue scene—as well as a growing chain of other Gates's restaurants in the Kansas City area.[30]

One last classic Kansas City barbecue joint deserves mention: Rosedale Bar-B-Q. During the depth of the Depression, Anthony Rieke was scraping by selling vegetables from his truck at the city market. In 1932 he rented a small plywood stand and started selling hot dogs and beer. By 1936 he'd moved to a new location and renamed his stand The Bucket Shop, since he sold customers buckets of beer for twenty-five cents (customers had to bring their own buckets). When Rieke decided to branch out and sell smoked ribs alongside the beer, Rosedale Bar-B-Q was born. The restaurant still operates today in the same location, which is just over the Kansas state line on Southwest Boulevard, just a few blocks from Rosedale Park. Rieke ran the restaurant until he died at age ninety-two in 1997, and in the process became—like Henry Perry before him—

Kansas City-Style Barbecue

If it moves, we cook it.

Carolyn Wells, executive director of the Kansas City Barbeque Society

Meats: Beef brisket, ribs, burnt ends, pulled pork, chicken, ham, turkey (generally sliced)

Woods: Hickory, oak, pecan

Sauce: Tomato-based, sweet

Side Dishes:

- French Fries
- Baked Beans
- Coleslaw
- Potato Salad
- Pickles

Classic Examples:

- Arthur Bryant's
- Gates's
- Rosedale

one of the city's great barbecue mentors. Rosedale employees went on to found a string of restaurants that include Quick's 7th Street Bar-B-Q, Wyandot Barbeque, Porky's Pit Bar-B-Q, and Johnny's Bar-B-Q.[31]

Entrepreneurs like Henry Perry, Arthur Bryant, and Anthony Rieke helped originate the Kansas City style. The selection of meats is broad, including pork, pork ribs, beef brisket, smoked ham and turkey, and smoked sausage, too. "Burnt ends" are one the city's signature offerings. These are the small, crispy bits of meat cut off the ends of a smoked beef brisket, and they're often served alone with a side of sauce or on a sandwich. Most restaurants serve a sweet, tangy sauce made with tomato and lots of sugar, a style that—in the 1950s—was imitated by large food processors like Heinz and Kraft and spread nationwide.

Texas Barbecue

Robb Walsh has observed, "Southern barbecue is a proud Thoroughbred whose bloodlines are easily traced. Texas barbecue is a feisty mutt with a whole lot of crazy relatives."[32] The state has at least four distinct barbecue styles: East Texas, Central Texas, Cowboy Style (West Texas), and Mexican *barbacoa*. The East Texas style was brought by migrants from other parts of the Deep South and, with its pork shoulder and ribs and thick tomato-based sauce, is similar to that found in Mississippi and Alabama. In central Texas, the emphasis is on slow-smoked beef and sausage, while west Texas is known for its "Cowboy Style" of beef barbecue cooked over open mesquite fires. *Barbacoa* developed along the Mexican border, where cooks adapted the traditional *barbacoa* of central Mexico (lamb or goat roasted in maguey leaves) to the ingredients they had on hand, creating a specialty of cowheads wrapped in maguey leaves and roasted in a pit dug in the ground. All four of these styles can be found in Texas restaurants today, but the East Texas and Central Texas styles were the two that became the most commercialized before the Second World War.

During the cotton boom of the 1850s, thousands of new planters migrated to east Texas from the Carolinas, Georgia, Alabama, and Mississippi, bringing with them large numbers of African American slaves and a deep-rooted barbecue culture. Following emancipation, many rural workers moved into the large east Texas cities such as Houston and Dallas, and it was in these cities' downtown districts that the first East Texas style barbecue restaurants developed.

Houston's Third and Fourth Wards, which include much of downtown and the area to the southeast and southwest, were the center of the city's African American life during the first half of the twentieth century. Houston was heavily segregated, and the Third and Fourth Wards functioned much as separate cities. Dowling Street was the main thoroughfare of the Third Ward, and it was lined with black-owned businesses, theaters, and restaurants. The area's nightclubs included the El Dorado Ballroom, built in the 1930s on Elgin Street, a high-class venue that hosted the likes of Cab Calloway during the 1940s and B. B. King and Ray Charles in the 1950s.

The 1917 Houston City Directory lists two men whose trade was "barbecue," Charles Lemuel at 1701 Nelson Street and Andrew White at 1919 Dowling. Both men were black and lived in the Third Ward.[33] Matt Garner moved from Beaumont, Texas (near the Louisiana state line), to the Fourth Ward in the 1920s. He opened Matt's Barbecue on West Dallas, which he later moved to West Gray Street. Garner taught barbecuing to Joe Burney, who opened Burney's Barbecue and Avalon Barbecue on Dowling Street. Burney, in turn, taught Harry Green, who went on to open three of his own restaurants and became a legend of Houston barbecue.

Looking back on old-style Houston barbecue, Green recalled, "Nobody cooked briskets in the old days. I used to go down to the packing house and buy a front quarter of a steer. I'd cut it up myself. And I served mutton, too. But ribs and beef were the biggest sellers."[34] Green also sold "juicy links," sausage made with fatty ground beef and seasoned with garlic and paprika, a recipe he learned from Burney and Garner that is a classic part of the East Texas barbecue style. Burney's influence wasn't limited to recipes, either. Many of the early barbecue stand operators in Houston cooked over pits dug in the ground, a method carried over from the outdoor barbecues of the nineteenth century. Before long they began to run afoul of city health inspectors as restaurants began to be more tightly regulated. Burney taught his fellow barbecue men to construct pits out of cinder blocks that would pass city inspection, and their barbecue restaurants

BEFORE

Fine quality meat properly cooked and a touch of Red's famous sauce, is the answer to why the "SMOKEHOUSE" always serves delicious, flavorsome barbecue.

We hope the food you are about to enjoy is the best you have ever ...
If it isn't, please tell us; we will do our utmost to make it the best

AFTER

Illustration from the back of the menu at Red Bryan's Smokehouse, showing the restaurant's evolution from an old converted streetcar in 1930 to a large, stone-sided building in 1947.

East Texas-Style Barbecue

Meats: Pork shoulder, pork ribs

Wood: Hickory

Sauce: Tomato-based, sweet and thick

Side Dishes:

- Pinto Beans
- Potato Salad
- Coleslaw
- Texas Toast

Classic Examples:

- Sam's (Austin)
- Drexler's (Houston)

thrived in the black neighborhoods until the 1970s, when desegregation started breaking down the old geographic boundaries.[35]

Over in Dallas, one of the city's first barbecue restaurants was founded by Elias Bryan, who moved from Cincinnati, Ohio, to the town of Oak Cliff, just outside Dallas. Bryan opened a smokehouse on Centre Street in 1910, where he barbecued untrimmed beef cuts and developed a thick, spicy sauce recipe. Elias's son William Jennings Bryan, known as "Red," opened his own smokehouse on Jefferson Street in 1930 in an old converted streetcar with a sawdust floor, where he sold barbecue sandwiches for a dime and hamburgers for a nickel. In 1947, Red moved from the "tin shack" to a grand building with a stone exterior and calf-skin booths where he eventually had eighty-five employees and a flourishing drive-in business and later expanded to four other locations. "Sonny" Bryan followed in his father Red's footsteps and founded his own restaurant in 1958, which now has fourteen locations throughout north Texas.

In central Texas, the barbecue business evolved out of meat markets and grocery stores. The tradition there was strongly influenced by the large number of German and Czech immigrants who came to the state in the latter part of the nineteenth century. These immigrants brought with them Old World sausage-making and meat-smoking traditions, and many opened meat markets and groceries in central Texas towns. Prior to World War II, ice provided the only form of refrigeration, and most customers wanted steaks and roasts, since ground beef was not yet widely used. To prevent the less popular cuts from spoiling, butchers would smoke the meatier pieces to make beef barbecue and use the rest in sausage. This barbecue and sausage found a ready market as a take-out lunch. It was sold wrapped in butcher paper, with no sauce, and the customer would often buy a few items from the grocery to go along with it, such as crackers, pickles, and onion.

Some of central Texas's most famous barbecue restaurants got their start in just this way. Kreuz Market in Lockhart was opened by Charles Kreuz in 1900 as a meat market and grocery store. From early on the market sold take-out meats wrapped in paper as a supplement to the butcher and grocery business. In 1948, Edgar Schmidt, a longtime employee, purchased the market. By 1960 the barbecue trade had developed into a full restaurant business, and Schmidt closed the grocery side. He retained some of the more popular take-out items as side dishes, including crackers, bread, pickles, onion, and cheese, which remain on the menu today. Black's Barbecue, also in Lockhart, grew in a similar way to its crosstown rival. In 1932 the Black family gave up farming to take over running a meat market, to which they added a small grocery section and started selling take-out meat. In 1949 they moved the restaurant into an adjacent building and built a new double-walled pit to handle the volume. Black's and Kreuz's are today considered two of the legendary central Texas barbecue joints.

In Texas, as in other states, the barbecue business was driven by a need to feed hungry people. In Texas's case, it was hungry cotton pickers. The cotton industry had surged in the state during the last decades of the nineteenth century, as thousands of immigrants from the Deep South and Europe moved into the Blackland Prairie section of central Texas and started cotton farms. The industry peaked in the 1920s, but remained a key part of economic life in the region for many more decades. Until the widespread introduction of mechanical pickers in the 1960s, most Texas cotton was picked by hand by migrant workers. An estimated 600,000 workers were needed for the 1938 crop, and they moved from farms in the Lower Rio Grande Valley in June to Lubbock in September.[36] These cotton pickers needed to eat, and many went to local grocery stores and meat markets for take-out barbecue and sausages.

In 1918, William Harris Smolik, the son of a Bohemian Czech farmer and sausage maker, opened Smolik's Meat Market in Karnes City, Texas, about fifty miles southeast of San Antonio. Smolik's did a brisk trade during cotton season. "The pickers ate barbecue at our place for breakfast, lunch, and dinner in those days," his son Bill Smolik recalls. "I remember one Saturday we made a thousand dollars in one day, selling barbecue at fifty cents a pound."[37] Edgar Black Jr. of Black's Barbecue in Lockhart remembers that during summers at his father's meat market, the pickers "started coming in the minute we opened at 7 a.m., and they kept coming until we closed. We served nothing but beef and sausage on butcher paper with crackers on the side. That was it. We didn't have time for anything else."[38] At many establishments, cotton workers—most of whom were black or Hispanic—were not allowed inside the stores and restaurants. Instead, they bought the meat from the back door and ate it sitting on the ground in the store parking lot.

It wasn't just the meat markets that got into the trade. Gas stations, grocery stores, and beer halls all made and sold barbecue during the harvest season, and many of these businesses later grew into full-time restaurants. In Taylor, Texas, Louis Mueller added a barbecue shed in the parking lot of his Complete Food Store, and the business became such a hit that in 1959 he moved it across the street into a former indoor gymnasium, installing a brick barbecue pit in the center. The grocery closed in 1974, but Louie Mueller's is still selling brisket with a black-pepper rub in butcher paper.[39] Two blocks away, the Taylor Café got its start as a beer joint, but proprietor Vencil Mares,

Central Texas-Style Barbecue

Meats: Beef brisket, sausage, pork ribs

Wood: Oak, pecan

Sauce: Often none at all, or a thin tomato and vinegar base

Side Dishes:

- Pinto Beans
- Potato Salad
- Coleslaw
- Texas Toast

Classic Examples:

- Kreuz Market (Lockhart)
- Black's Barbecue (Lockhart)
- Smolik's Market Bar-B-Que and Fresh Meats (Karnes City)
- Louie Mueller Barbeque (Taylor)
- Taylor Café (Taylor)

who learned to make sausage at the South Side Market in Elgin, soon added brisket and smoked sausage to the offering, and the café became a classic central Texas barbecue joint.

The barbecue of east Texas and central Texas was based on the traditional styles brought by immigrants from the southeastern United States and adapted to local circumstances. The *barbacoa* of the Lower Rio Grande Valley was created through a similar evolution, only the style was brought to the region by immigrants from central Mexico. The original *barbacoa* was lamb or goat wrapped in maguey leaves and roasted in a covered pit dug into the ground. In Texas, Mexican Americans substituted widely available (and inexpensive) cow heads and, eventually, replaced the maguey leaves with burlap sacks. *Barbacoa* was originally cooked at home for large celebrations, but in the 1930s and 1940s, grocery stores and butcher shops in the Lower Rio Grande Valley started preparing and selling *barbacoa* to the public. Families frequently would purchase the meat on the way home from church to eat for Sunday dinner.

Making *barbacoa* was often a family affair, and the grocers' children were enlisted to perform many of the simpler tasks. First, the cow heads were split in half, and the brains and inedible parts of the jaw were removed. The brains, which would be cooked separately, had to be rinsed thoroughly to remove any blood clots or bone chips left over from slaughtering, and the heads were thoroughly scrubbed with wire brushes. Then, the heads were packed along with garlic and salt into metal containers (frequently aluminum lard buckets) and wrapped with wet burlap sacks.

Classic *barbacoa* was cooked in a pit that was dug into the ground and lined with firebrick. The pit was filled with wood—including lots of aromatic mesquite—which was set ablaze and allowed to burn for hours until reduced to coals, thoroughly heating the brick walls in the process. The metal containers were then placed on the bed of coals and the pits covered with metal and more wet burlap sacks, then the whole thing was covered with dirt to seal it tight. Early the next morning, the pit was uncovered and the containers removed. The eyes, tongue, sweetbreads, and cheek meat—now tender and falling from the bone—were separated, cleaned of any inedible portions, and packaged for sale, typically wrapped in white butcher paper.[40]

Restaurants specializing in *barbacoa* did not appear until well after World War II, but the tradition established by local butchers and grocers added another flavorful variety to the Texas barbecue tradition.

Barbecue and Independence

Meeting the market demand for a filling, inexpensive meal was one driving force behind the growth of barbecue restaurants in America's towns and cities, but it was not the only one. For black entrepreneurs in particular, an additional motivation for opening a restaurant was that such businesses were a route toward self-sufficiency and independence in a society that offered few other opportunities. In interview after interview, black barbecue restaurateurs cite the desire to not have to answer to anyone as a key reason why they went into the business—and why they stay in it despite long, physically demanding work weeks.

George and Arzelia Gates, the heads of the legendary Kansas City barbecue family, are prime examples. In the 1920s and 1930s, George Gates worked as a waiter on the Rock Island Line railroad. Over the years he worked his way up in seniority and aspired to be a steward—a position that oversaw all the operations of the dining car, including managing the staff, ordering provisions, and managing the cash receipts. At the time, that job was reserved only for white men, and a frustrated Gates eventually quit the railroad. He worked for a while in the post office and in other jobs before deciding to open his own restaurant. When he and his wife, Arzelia, bought the Ol' Kentuck Bar-B-Q at Nineteenth and Vine, it was little more than a speakeasy, selling more bootleg whiskey than it did food. The Gateses stopped the whiskey sales and turned it into a legitimate operation. "It was hard work," Arzelia Gates recalled, "but I didn't mind. I knew that working for yourself is easier than working for someone else. I had worked for somebody else since I was 11 years old. It was a chance to do what I thought was best, not what somebody else told me."[41]

A similar sentiment was expressed in a 1939 interview conducted by a WPA writer as part of the Federal Writers Project. Bill and Geraldine Long, two black residents of Athens, Georgia, had both worked as domestic servants for much of their early lives—Bill as a houseboy, butler, chauffeur, and fraternity house attendant, Geraldine as a maid and cook. Bill lost his butler's job in the early years of the Depression when the white family for whom he worked could no longer afford to keep him on. Tired of "house work," he moved to Atlanta and took a job at a barbecue stand. He worked at several different places around the city, learning to barbecue meat and cook hash and Brunswick stew, all the while saving money so he could open his own stand. After two years in Atlanta, Bill Long moved back to Athens, where he married Geraldine. Together they opened their first barbecue stand at their house in downtown Athens. "We dug our first barbecue pit in our own back yard," Bill recalled, "and that good old meat was barbecued in the real Southern style. We done so much business that first summer that we decided to keep our stand going through the winter with home barbecued meat. We already had it screened but when winter come we boarded our pit up."[42]

The Longs ran their backyard stand for two more years until increased business forced them to look for a bigger place. They bought a corner lot on Church Street in downtown Athens and moved their stand to the new location. Bill Long printed five hundred circulars and distributed them around the area within a ten-block radius, and over time built up a regular clientele that included both black and white customers. The Longs cooked their meat in an outdoor pit behind the stand, and they sold barbecue sandwiches for a dime. Side dishes included Brunswick stew, corn bread, liver, and bottled beer. Later, they expanded their business to include a small store where they sold fresh meats, groceries, beer, soft drinks, cakes, cigars, and cigarettes. The couple put in long hours, and the restaurant was busy for most of the day, but they felt the hard work was worth it, both for the money it provided and, perhaps more important, for the independence. Bill Long drove "a shining new car of a popular make" (as the WPA interviewer described it), and Geraldine Long concluded "we are making enough to live on, and we don't have to call on nobody for nothing."[43]

Roadside Barbecue Stands

Downtown street corners were not the only places where barbecue was being sold. Beginning in the 1920s, when millions of Americans took to the road in newly affordable automobiles, barbecue took to the roadways as well. The introduction of Ford's Model-T and the founding of General Motors (both in 1908) helped make automobiles available to the general public, and by 1921, eight million cars were registered in the United States; by 1931 that number had almost tripled to twenty-three million.[44] During the 1920s new automobile owners ventured out across the country not just for transportation but also for entertainment and sport.

In the early days of automobile touring, there were almost no restaurants outside of towns' downtown business districts, and no hotels, either. "Gypsying" motorists would camp out overnight along the roadside, sleeping in tents and cooking their meals over

Roadside barbecue stand made of galvanized tin, Corpus Christi, Texas, 1939. (Courtesy Library of Congress, Prints & Photographs Division.)

campfires. After a few years, the novelty of roadside camping began to wear off, and tourist campgrounds became popular. Though bare-bones operations at first, these campgrounds started to offer increased amenities, including running water, electricity, and bathhouses. It wasn't long before other entrepreneurs saw a chance to make a few bucks feeding the hundreds of thousands of new motorists who were taking to the road each year.

The first roadside food stands were flimsy wooden structures, often homemade, that were thrown up quickly to capitalize on the auto boom. Unlike the more elegant tearooms, which had flourished in the previous decade and catered to an earlier wave of wealthy automobile tourists, the roadside stands of the 1920s targeted the growing number of middle- and lower-class car owners. The menu was similar to that found at

Postcard for Hamby's Famous Pit Barbecue Place in South Baxley, Georgia. Many barbecue restaurants got their start as add-ons to gas stations and tourist cottage businesses.

county fairs: hamburgers, hot dogs, ice cream, and sandwiches. And, particularly in the South, one menu item reigned supreme: barbecue.

Barbecue was an ideal food for roadside stands. It did not require expensive equipment, just a pit dug in the ground and filled with glowing wood coals. Wrapped in brown paper or placed between slices of bread, barbecue was easy to serve and easy to take away. As *Collier's Magazine* noted, the smoke from a barbecue pit was often the only advertising needed: "Down South, the mingled savor of pork and hickory wood rising from the pit sets the traveler's nose to twitching half a mile away … small wonder that barbecue stands have grown as thick as filling stations, especially as we cross the Mason and Dixon Line."[45] In the early days, most roadside barbecue stands were seasonal operations, with the exception of Florida and California, where the warm climate allowed for a year-round auto trade. Cecil Roberts, a British travel writer who toured Florida in the 1930s, noted, "Everywhere one sees 'Joe's Barbecue' or 'Tom's Barbecue.' It may be an elaborate pseudo-Spanish bar, with gay awnings and aluminum stools, a soda fountain, or a mere wooden shanty on the roadside."[46] By 1934, *Fortune* magazine estimated the total annual revenue from roadside restaurants to be $630 million.[47]

Many barbecue restaurants were started by proprietors of other roadside businesses who began to serve barbecue on the side and then found the sideline pursuit more profitable than the original enterprise. In 1928, for example, Alex and Gladys McClard, the owners of the Westside Tourist Court in Hot Springs, Arkansas, added a barbecue pit and started selling slow-cooked beef, ham, and goat to their guests. The barbecue business took off, and soon they were selling to non-lodgers, too. In 1942 they moved the restaurant into the whitewashed stucco building that it still occupies today, which evolved into a drive-in with carhops and a jukebox that broadcast music over an AM band for diners to hear in their cars. Today the carhops are gone, but the restaurant remains in the same building as a sit-down establishment and is a landmark of Arkansas barbecue. Owens' Bar-B-Q in Lake City, South Carolina, followed a similar evolution. In 1946 Mellon Owens opened a grocery store and filling station in the small South Carolina town. Six years later he started cooking barbecue and selling it in the store. Before long the Owenses abandoned the grocery store altogether and focused on a barbecue restaurant, which was in operation until the 1990s. Other legendary barbecue restaurants that evolved out of roadside businesses include the Golden Rule in Irondale, Alabama, which started off as a pit stop for travelers on US 78, the main highway from Birmingham to Atlanta; and Sprayberry's in Newnan, Georgia, which began as a gas station on Highway 29, just north of Newnan, and closed its pumps in 1925 to focus on barbecue.

A few of these restaurants, like McClard's and Sprayberry's, thrived and became long-standing institutions, but most were short-lived. Barbecue was a natural adjunct to the gasoline trade, and many filling stations throughout the South and Midwest added barbecue pits and sold smoked meats to their patrons. Burlington, North Carolina, a medium-sized town midway between Greensboro and Durham, provides a good illustration. Burlington in 1930 had some twenty thousand residents, and several Main Street restaurants—including the Barbecue Lunch and the Community Shoppe—featured barbecued pork on their menus. On the outskirts of town, a succession of filling station owners offered up barbecue to the automobile trade. Eat the Pig Barbecue at

Sprayberry's Bar-B-Q, 1143 North Park Street, Carrollton, Georgia. This second Sprayberry's location—the original opened in Newnan, Georgia, in the 1920s—was sold to the Moore brothers in 1959. (Courtesy University of West Georgia Special Collections.)

W. S. Oakley's gas station between Burlington and nearby Graham sold meals to travelers on NC Highway 10, which was the original Central Highway that connected the mountainous western part of the state with the coast. In July 1930, Oakley sold his barbecue stand and filling station to Henry M. Johnson, a transplant from New Orleans, who renamed it Henry's Place. On the other side of town, at the intersection of Alamance Road and Highway 10, Bobby's Café offered two kinds of service twenty-four hours a day: gas and oil for cars and "all pork barbecue" curb service for drivers. In 1932, C. W. Harper placed a want ad in the paper offering for sale his "Barbecue Café, Filling Station, and Grocery Store" at the corner of Highways 62 and 54, explaining he "must devote time to other business."[48] Burlington was typical of small towns on main highways, and by the 1930s barbecue could be found at tens of thousands of roadside stands throughout the country. Many of these stands were in business for only a few years before changing hands or fading away altogether, and only a small number lasted past the 1950s. For the moment, though, barbecue was king of the American highway.

Barbecue and Early Restaurant Chains

Today, hamburger chains like McDonald's and Burger King dominate the take-out market, but the country's first drive-in restaurant chain was devoted not to hamburgers or hot dogs but rather to barbecue pork and beef sandwiches. The first Pig Stand opened in Dallas in September 1921 at the corner of Chalk Hill Road and the Dallas–Fort Worth Turnpike. Its founders were Jesse G. Kirby, a candy and tobacco wholesaler, and Reuben W. Jackson, a local physician. The Pig Stand was an unassuming operation—a small, white wooden stand on a corner lot—but it had one revolutionary feature. Jesse Kirby was alleged to have said, "People with cars are so lazy they don't want to get out of them to eat!" and his restaurant was likely the first in the country to offer curb service for motorists.[49] Customers could pull up to the curb in their automobiles and be served by carhops, young men in white shirts and black bow ties who would hop up on the running boards of arriving cars and take passengers' orders even before the car had come to a stop. The carhops worked for tips only, and the competition was fierce to get to each car first and return with the sandwiches as quickly as possible.

The menu was simple—a pork or beef sandwich wrapped in paper and served with a bottled soft drink—but the curb service was a hit. There was a traffic jam at the grand opening, and Kirby and Jackson opened five more Pig Stands in the Dallas–Fort Worth area by 1925. Their first restaurants had curbside service only, and customers had to either stop in their cars along the street or walk up to the stand on foot. By the late 1920s, the newer Pig Stand restaurants had evolved into pagoda-like buildings that were set back from the street and allowed motorists to pull in head-first and park, making them true "drive-in" restaurants. The chain began franchising and continued to grow, and by 1934 over 120 Pig Stands were in operation, stretching from Florida along the Gulf Coast through Texas and also in Southern California.

Other operators soon adopted the drive-in concept. A&W Root Beer, whose roadside stands had been around since 1919, added curb service to its parking lots, with carhops bringing heavy glass mugs of root beer and food straight to customers' automobiles. Other pioneers included Carpenter's in Los Angeles, whose octagonal restaurant at the corner of Sunset and Vine in Hollywood, California, was a dressed-up version of the

Curbside service at the Pig Stand #2, Dallas, Texas, 1920s.

Pig Stand. J. D. and Louise Sivils, owners of a sit-down restaurant in Houston, opened a "Drive-Inn" branch on the outskirts of the city in 1938 and became probably the first business to use the term that would become universal for restaurants that served diners in their cars. Many early drive-ins ran a basic operation along the Pig Stand model, serving sandwiches wrapped in waxed paper and drinks in glass bottles. Others adopted innovations such as window-mounted serving trays and, later, long serving boards that diners would stretch from door to door inside the car, making it possible for meals to be served on china plates with glasses and silverware. Menus remained varied, too, with barbecue one of the leading items. Once found only at large rural gatherings, barbecue was now being eaten daily in cars from the East Coast to the West.

Roadside barbecue stand near Fort Benning, Georgia, December 1940. (Courtesy Library of Congress, Prints & Photographs Division.)

The Expansion of Barbecue

By World War II, barbecue was a standard restaurant offering in towns and cities from eastern North Carolina all the way to the West Coast. Many of these establishments were sit-down restaurants, where barbecued pork or beef was listed on the menu alongside steaks and chops. Others were much more informal—wooden stands erected on street corners that sold smoked meat that had been cooked in a hole in the ground and wrapped in brown paper. Still other early joints were nightspots, where the barbecue was a sideline to beer and liquor sales and provided late-night fuel for dancers and revelers. These many different forms of restaurants had one thing in common: they created stable, fixed locations where barbecue was sold on a regular basis.

As the restaurant industry matured, the equipment used to make barbecue matured, too. The "pit" evolved from a trench dug in the ground into permanent structures that reduced much of the intensive labor of lifting and basting meat. A typical barbecue pit by midcentury was elevated above the ground, with brick or cinderblock sides supporting a metal rack or grill at about waist level. Glowing hardwood coals were shoveled below the grill, and the meat placed on top, some two feet or so above the coals, where it would be loosely covered and cooked for hours until tender. In some pits, a sheet of tin was also placed above the meat so that coals could be shoveled on top to provide heat from both sides.[50]

Barbecue restaurants today tend to be specialized operations, with barbecue as the prime attraction and the other menu items being mostly side dishes like rice, beans, French fries, or coleslaw. In the 1930s and 1940s, however, countless full-menu restaurants added barbecue pits out back for cooking pork, ribs, and chicken. The South and the Midwest were dotted with signs advertising "Steaks - Chops - Barbecue," and many drive-in restaurants included barbecue sandwiches along with their offering of hamburgers, hot dogs, and fried chicken. Original barbecue joints like Bob Melton's and Arthur Bryant's continued to cater to those seeking out the best slow-smoked pork shoulders and ribs, but barbecue had entered the mainstream of American restaurant dining.

Barbecue Finds the Backyard

About the same time that barbecue began dotting the sides of America's roadways, it also became a fixture of the American backyard. Commonly called "grilling out" or "cooking out," the backyard barbecue differed greatly from the outdoor community tradition, but it had its roots in the days of pit-cooked barbecue. Over time, new ingredients, equipment, fuel, and commercial sauces helped take the backyard version further and further away from its original ancestor, and it acquired its own set of conventions. Between 1930 and 1960, "barbecuing" became a routine part of the suburban family experience and an iconic image of the good life in America.

In the 1920s, general interest magazines started publishing travel narratives from the Southwest that described outdoor barbecues as a curious regional experience. "An unusual way to entertain informally during the late summer or fall is to give a barbecue," a 1924 article in *Woman's Home Companion* opened. The writer provided instructions for staging an event for up to thirty people, including digging a pit in the backyard, and she depicted the barbecue as a very western kind of thing, complete with a recipe for "Cowboy Sauce" that she learned from "a Colorado cowboy, famed years ago on the plains for his expert skill in barbecuing meats."[1] These sort of western-inspired parties became popular during the 1930s as suburban residents adapted the pit-cooking tradition from the South and West and turned it into a small backyard event for family and friends.

Backyard barbecuing took hold initially on the West Coast, where the warm climate made possible year-round outdoor cooking. In 1936, *American Home* magazine noted that *barbecue* was "a word dear to the heart of a Californian, and in almost any sheltered garden one may find an outdoor grill, and on most any rancho, a barbecue pit."[2] In 1939, the editors of *Sunset Magazine*—a California publication dedicated to "Life in the West"—created *Sunset's Barbecue Book,* the first full-length book on the topic of barbecue. The volume opened by asking, "Why is it that practically everybody in the West has a barbecue, is planning to have a barbecue, or wishes he had one?"[3] *Sunset* defined a barbecue as not just a social gathering but also the fireplace or stove used for outdoor cooking, and the majority of the book focuses on instructions for building a backyard pit or fireplace.

To explain the appeal of backyard barbecues to Californians, *Sunset*'s editors pointed to the element of escape inherent in outdoor cookery. "The barbecue satisfies our desire to get away from hectic daily routine," they noted, awakening "impulses that hark back to pioneer days and put us 'right with the world.'"[4] The barbecue became an important part of the image of California that West Coast "lifestyle" magazines like *Sunset* promoted to eastern readers during a period of great economic hardship. "*Sunset* fought the Depression by ignoring it," the California historian Kevin Starr has observed, "by holding before the middle class an image of the good life as it was surviving even in dire times."[5]

This image of the California "rancho" life was linked to a highly romanticized view of the Mexican influence in early California. A 1933 article in *Touring Topics* claimed that history was responsible for the growing popularity of outdoor barbecue fireplaces and grills, which dated "back from the days when a caballero rode from hacienda to hacienda summoning the Señors and Señoritas to gather for the great fiesta."[6] Wealthy Californians (including part-time Californians from back East) purchased ranch-estates in places like Carmel Valley and the Santa Ynez Valley, where they constructed houses with adobe walls and red-tiled roofs. No rancho would be complete without a brick barbecue fireplace, and the more elaborate versions were equipped with iron spits, utensils, and other decorations intended to evoke Old Mexico.

THIS CURVED-TOP brick barbecue is at the W. P. Botkin home, Hillsborough, Calif. Note the raised platform, side work shelves and chains at either side that regulate the grill.

A RAISED CORNER PIT in Napa, Calif., built of light-weight concrete units. It's part of a garden wall. The wing walls form ample counters for pushing things around.

HERE'S A SIMPLE brick unit built against a wall at the Z. E. Page home, Lindsay, Calif. The step back construction is both decorative and useful for cooking equipment or ornaments.

A VARIATION on the outdoor fireplace shown on *Page 30* (Plan 9) is this brick and stone structure in the garden of Landscape Architect Charles Gibbs Adams, Los Angeles.

Sunset's Barbecue Book (1939) provided readers with dozens of examples of brick barbecue pits from California backyards, complete with plans for constructing them.

Before long, upper-middle-class Americans in other parts of the country began imitating the trappings of the relaxed, easygoing California lifestyle. Hosting a barbecue for family and friends around an outdoor fireplace was an enjoyable way to escape the pressures of the business world. By 1941, Genevieve Callahan could write in *Better Homes and Gardens,* "Indoors, outdoors, and year-round barbecues have the whole country's mouth watering."[7]

With the onset of World War II, the interest in outdoor cooking spread beyond the professional classes. "With the entire nation seeking simpler means of entertainment because of wartime requirements," noted a 1942 article in New Mexico's *Deming Headlight,* "backyard barbecues are becoming quite the style from California to Maine."[8] An article on new types of outdoor grills in the *New York Herald Tribune* strongly recommended such devices "in these harsh times" because they "afford an economical means of entertainment al fresco; good food, fresh air and the kind of relaxation that goes deep; i.e., a momentary return to primitive modes."[9] The focus on economy was essential not only because of high wartime prices but also because of rationing. With gas limited to only three gallons a week, picnics in the country became an inaccessible luxury, and Americans turned to their backyards for entertainment. Buying steak required twelve ration points per pound, but ground beef needed only seven, so the foods of choice for barbecuing were often hamburgers and frankfurters.[10]

Backyard Barbecues in Postwar America

After World War II, permanent home barbecue pits continued to grow in popularity among the upper-middle class, who proceeded to take it one step further. Magazines such as *House and Garden* and *House Beautiful* ran articles offering plans not only for permanent brick barbecue pits but also for entire "barbecue rooms," extensions to a house's patio or porch that provide a covered dining area built around a large brick fireplace. In 1947, Herbert Coggins in the *Atlantic Monthly* satirized the temptation of a homeowner building a barbecue pit to add more and more features to it. Starting with a simple outdoor fireplace, Coggins's narrator added rustic chairs and tables, a motorized rotating spit, then enclosed the fireplace in a glass room. Gradually adding one gadget

Dining in a suburban barbecue room. (*Better Homes & Gardens,* May 1941.)

after another, he ultimately migrated the entire kitchen—sink, refrigerator, and all—
"outdoors," then turned the old kitchen into a sunroom with wide French doors opening outside. Now the family could take the food cooked "outdoors" in the enclosed barbecue room and eat it "indoors" in the open-air kitchen.[11]

The menu for backyard barbecues was much broader than at the traditional pit-
cooked events. The recipe section of *Sunset's Barbecue Book* begins with steaks, veal sati,
chops, hamburgers, and shish kebab along with a range of potato, corn, and bean recipes
for sides.[12] In California, the backyard barbecue was not just for grilling dinner: "If
you've never used your barbecue for outdoor breakfasts," the *Sunset* editors insisted,
"you've missed a good part of its charm." Recommended menus included grilled ham
and sausage along with eggs and pancakes, which could be cooked in skillets placed directly on the grill.[13]

Grilling burgers on a backyard grill, of course, is quite a different thing from the
old-fashioned barbecue pit, and calling this backyard pastime "barbecuing" drew the
ire of traditional barbecue fans. "Many Georgia epicures insist that this is an insult to
the honorable name of barbecue," Rufus Jarman wrote in the *Saturday Evening Post*

Mr. and Mrs. Fred Hammond of Nashville, Tennessee, grilling in their backyard over a permanent brick barbecue, 1952. (Courtesy Tennessee State Library and Archives.)

in 1954. "You cannot barbecue hamburgers, roasting ears, potatoes, onions, tomatoes, wieners, or salami, and it is a shame and disgrace to mention barbecuing in connection with such foolishness."[14] For an increasing number of Americans, though, this was the definition of barbecuing, and they couldn't get enough of it.

Barbecue Equipment

The first commercial barbecue equipment for backyard chefs appeared on the market in the 1930s. By the 1940s, a wide array of barbecue grills could be found for sale in hardware, sporting goods, and heating supply stores. Many of these were dual purpose devices that could be used both as a grate within a living room fireplace and as a portable barbecue grill for picnics and other outings. Most were simple in design—a metal tray for holding wood or charcoal with a gridiron above it for holding the meat—though a few more sophisticated models featured accessories such as adjustable grill levels and spits for turning meat. Early grills tended to be small, so that they could be packed up and easily taken on outdoor picnics.

In 1952, George Stephen, a backyard barbecuer from Mount Prospect, Illinois, grew frustrated with battling wind and uneven, hard-to-control flames when cooking with his brazier grill. Stephen was an employee of the Weber Brothers Metal Works, and he fashioned a grill from metal parts that were being used to make buoys. He cut a spherical buoy in half to create a bottom, then added a dome-shaped lid and a three-legged stand to support the whole thing. The design worked, and Stephen soon launched a "barbecue division" at his company. Selling at close to fifty dollars (at a time when a brazier-style grill could be had for a fifth of the price), the Weber grill was a premium product. It gained popularity first in the Midwest then throughout the country and inspired numerous imitators of its "kettle grill" design. In the late 1950s Stephen bought Weber Brothers Metal Works, renamed it Weber-Stephen Products, and over the next two decades transformed it into one of the leading producers of equipment for the home barbecue market.[15]

Along with new types of grills, new fuel sources were introduced to make cooking easier. At first, most barbecuers fired their grills with wood or lump charcoal. The latter product was made by piling wood in a large mound, covering it with dirt, and setting it afire. It would burn slowly with little oxygen present, losing all its water and gradually decomposing over the course of three or four weeks until virtually nothing but pure carbon was left. Barbecuers generally found lump charcoal to be superior to wood, for it burned hotly and more cleanly, but it also tended to crumble in a bag, leaving behind lots of powder and small chips rather than large lumps.

In the early part of the twentieth century, Orin F. Stafford, a professor at the University of Oregon, patented a new way to create charcoal. His "retort" method involved passing wood continuously through a series of ovens until it had become lump charcoal, then grinding it into powder, mixing it with starch, and compressing it into a briquette shape.[16] Stafford's method was popularized by Henry Ford, who started producing them as a way of achieving economy in his manufacturing operations. During the 1920s Ford undertook an extensive effort to reclaim waste from automobile manufacturing and sell it for additional revenue. These products included Portland cement made from blast furnace slag, benzol and ammonium sulfate by-products from coke production, and—most important for America's backyard chefs—charcoal briquettes made using Stafford's retort method, which allowed Ford to use up the hardwood scraps from auto body manufacturing. By 1925, Ford was generating nearly $4 million in sales from these recaptured by-products.[17]

At first, Ford's charcoal was used for firing ovens and stoves in railroad dining cars and hotel kitchens. In the late 1920s the company started selling to household consumers through coal and ice dealers, who encouraged customers to use the briquettes for starting furnaces and grate fires. It took another decade before Ford found his true market for the product. In the 1930s, coal dealers started adding blurbs to their newspaper ads suggesting, "On that week-end camping trip use Ford's Charcoal Briquettes for steaks and bratwurst roasts" and "Ford Charcoal Briquets in convenient paper sacks. Ideal for picnic roasts."[18]

Within a few years, the briquettes were being sold through Ford's network of automobile dealerships. "Going riding" was a popular form of evening and weekend rec-

A 1940 newspaper advertisement for Ford Charcoal Briquets and Grills.
(*Valparaiso[IN] Vidette Messenger,* August 13, 1940.)

reation for entire families, and the automobile retained strong connotations of out-door adventure and escape. Automobile dealers in the years just before and after World War II sold not just automobiles but the camping and cooking equipment that would be needed for weekend rambling. Ford's charcoal fit perfectly into this mix, and it was common in the 1940s for a Ford dealer to sell a portable grill for two dollars and a five-pound bag of charcoal for twenty-five cents. Through the 1950s, automobile dealerships would be the primary sales outlet for the charcoal.

Ford's charcoal was produced near Iron Mountain, Michigan, at the site of the com-pany's body part works. A company town grew up nearby and was named Kingsford after E. G. Kingsford, a relative of Ford's who helped found the charcoal works and later managed them. In 1951, Ford Motors sold the charcoal operations to a group of local investors, who renamed it the "Kingsford Chemical Company." The company later moved to Louisville, Kentucky, and began placing its products for sale in supermarkets. Acquired by Clorox in 1973, Kingsford remains the largest-selling brand of charcoal in the country.[19]

In the early 1960s, the first gas-fired barbecue grills were introduced, promising "the ultimate in cooking convenience for the backyard chef."[20] The initial models were built of aluminum with ceramic briquettes that were heated by gas burners, and they were meant to be installed permanently in backyards or on patios. The grills were sold by lo-cal gas companies, who were eager to find new ways to sell natural gas, and barbecue grills joined a line that already included gas lamps for permanent outdoor lighting and gas-powered air conditioners. One of the first models of gas grills was manufac-tured by the Arkla Air Conditioning Company, a subsidiary of the Arkansas Louisiana Gas Company, which sold natural gas to customers in a region that included Arkan-sas, Louisiana, Oklahoma, and Texas.[21] Around the same time, competing models were brought out by CharmGlow Products of Antioch, Ohio, Char Glo by Waste King Uni-versal of Los Angeles, and Falcon Manufacturing of Dallas.

Gas grill manufacturers touted their products as being easier and cleaner than char-coal models. With a three-position burner, the advertisements promised, controlling the heat was a snap, and the ceramic briquettes minimized flare-ups from dripping grease.

Best outdoor
flavor
ever!

revolutionary new
ARKLA GASGRILL
nothing down,
$2.60 monthly

Here's Space Age barbecuing! Gasgrill gives
you tasty outdoor flavor and complete heat
control! Permanent ceramic briquets glow
clean — fast, flexible gas starts them ra-
diating instantly! No more messy charcoal
to handle — grubby ashes to take out.
Smoke meats easily by closing the hinged
dome cover. Made of heavy-duty cast aluminum, Gasgrill is weatherproof . . . can't rust
. . . outlasts a dozen old-fashioned grills. In-
stalls easily in your yard . . . free up to 50-
ft. Get your Arkla Gasgrill (by the makers
of famous Arkla Gaslites and Gas Air Conditioning) now! Makes a great gift, too!

ONLY
$78.00
plus tax

LONE STAR
GAS
COMPANY

*Hear
PEGLER
speak out!
Nov. 8   Statler-
8 p.m.   Hilton

A 1966 newspaper advertisement for the Arkla Gasgrill. (*Dallas Morning News,* November 6, 1963.)

For $0 down and 30 payments of just $2.60 a month, Lone Star Gas Company customers could have either an Arkla or a Falcon gas grill installed in their yards. Within a few years, Char Glo and CharmGlow introduced portable models that could be moved around the yard. Charcoal grill pioneer Weber introduced its own gas-powered version, the Gas Barbecue Kettle in 1971, and fifteen years later brought out its Genesis line, which promised cooks more precise heat control. The popularity of gas-fired models continued to grow over the years. In 1985, 3.1 million gas grills were sold in the United States, compared to 7.8 million charcoal models. Today, gas grills outsell charcoal, with 10.1 million gas models sold in 2006 versus 6.8 million charcoal.[22]

Barbecue Sauce

Just as postwar manufacturers started producing new grills and fuels aimed at the backyard barbecue chef, the food industry also noticed the huge potential market being created by outdoor cooking. Barbecue sauce was one of the first products to which they turned their attention.

It took barbecue sauce a long time to become a commercially manufactured product. By the 1870s dozens of prepared sauces such as ketchup and Worcestershire were being sold, but barbecue sauce was not among them. Early barbecue cooks helped define regional sauce variations at their restaurants and barbecue stands, but few had shown any interest in bottling and marketing their secret recipes. The handful of early entrepreneurs who did try to enter the bottled sauce business found only limited success. The first of these, the Atlanta-based Georgia Barbecue Sauce Company, began advertising in the *Atlanta Constitution* in 1909, promising "the finest dressing known to culinary science for Beef, Pork, Mutton, Fish, Oysters, and Game of every kind."[23] The company's ads disappeared after only a few months. Two decades later, Eddy's Strictly Pure Barbecue Sauce began being carried in grocery stores nationwide, and Bayles and Topsy brands appeared in the Midwest around the same time. None of these brands was long lived.

At first, most backyard barbecue cooks made their own sauce, and the cookbooks and magazines of the 1920s and 1930s offered a steady flow of recipes for them to try.

Advertisement for Georgia Barbecue Sauce. (*Atlanta Constitution*, January 31, 1909.)

In the days of rural barbecues, sauces had been very basic, prepared in bulk, and relied on only a few staples such as vinegar, salt, and pepper for ingredients. Sugar was usually absent from the list. That began to change as mass-circulation magazines popularized the backyard barbecue, and in the 1920s sugar began steadily creeping into recipes along with commercially prepared products such as ketchup and Worcestershire sauce.

Mrs. S. R. Dull, the editor of the *Atlanta Journal*'s Home Economics page, included the following recipe for barbecue sauce in her 1928 volume *Southern Cooking:*

2 ½ lbs of butter
2 quarts of apple vinegar
1 pint of water
1 tablespoon dry mustard
½ cup minced onion
1 bottle of Worcestershire sauce
1 pint of tomato catsup
1 pint chili sauce (medium size)
2 lemons, juice only
½ lemon put in whole (seed removed)
3 cloves of garlic chopped fine and tied in bag
2 teaspoons of sugar[24]

The two teaspoons of sugar is a relatively small amount. Two decades later, Dorothy Malone tripled the amount in her barbecue sauce recipe in the 1947 *Cookbook for Brides*, which calls for two tablespoons of brown sugar along with onion, butter, vinegar, lemon juice, catsup, Worcestershire sauce, prepared mustard, parsley, salt, and pepper.[25] By World War II, recipes such as these had become standard, and homemade barbecue sauce had evolved from a thin, peppery basting liquid to a sweet, cooked product with a mix of many flavors.

Around this time the large commercial food producers entered the scene. Heinz was the first major company to put a brand on grocery store shelves, introducing Heinz Barbecue Sauce in 1940, and General Foods soon followed with its "Open Pit" brand. Kraft entered the market much later—around 1960—but it advertised widely, using full-page color spreads in women's magazines, and its brand quickly became the leading bottled barbecue sauce—a position that it maintains today. Ads from the 1960s show sauce being poured on top of steaks, hamburger patties, and hot dogs—often while they are still sitting on the grill. Kraft's advertisements advised cooks to brush on its sauce throughout the grilling process, claiming, "Kraft Barbecue Sauce simmers real

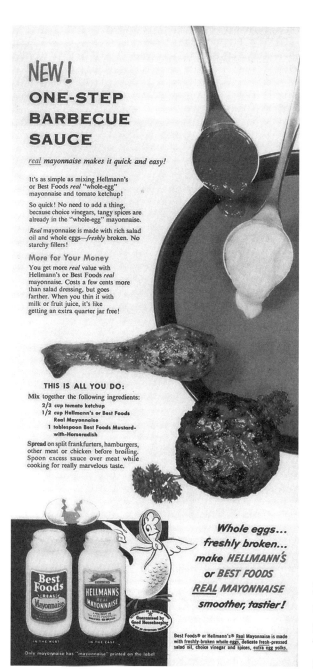

During the 1950s, food manufacturers sought to capitalize on the popularity of backyard barbecues. This example from Best Foods is from 1954.

Get new Kraft Barbecue Sauce
FREE just for trying it! (Wonderful on chicken!)

Simmers real cook-out flavor right into the chicken!

Here's the barbecue sauce that gives you the flavor you cook outdoors to get. Take us up on this offer and feast on the best chicken you've ever eaten!

Here's how to get your bottle of Kraft Barbecue Sauce FREE!

Buy your first bottle of the new Kraft Barbecue Sauce and use it to barbecue chicken. (When you taste what this new barbecue sauce does for chicken, you'll never be without it!) Or try it with ribs—hamburgers—your favorite cook-out specialty. Just *taste* the difference it makes! Then mail the neck band from the bottle of Kraft Barbecue Sauce with this order blank to: Kraft Barbecue Sauce Offer, Box 7795, Chicago 77, Illinois. We'll promptly send you a coupon good for one regular-size (18 oz.) bottle FREE!

NAME_____
(Please print)

ADDRESS_____

CITY_____ZONE____STATE____

Limit—one coupon to a family. Offer good in USA only. Void where prohibited, taxed or restricted. Offer expires December 31, 1961

Magazine advertisement for Kraft's new barbecue sauce. (*Woman's Day*, June 1961.)

cook-out flavor right into the meat!" All of these bottled sauces were similar in style and borrowed heavily from the traditional Kansas City variety. Tomato-based with lots of sugar and molasses, the thick, orange-brown concoctions continued the century's trend of increasing sweetness, and their mass marketing helped them gain acceptance nationwide.

By the 1960s, charcoal grills were almost universal on America's backyard patios, and bottled barbecue sauces could be found in kitchen pantries across the country. While "barbecuing"—used in the sense of cooking on a charcoal or gas grill—resulted in a very different type of food than its hickory-pit forebears, the backyard version continued barbecue's centuries-old tradition of bringing people together for relaxation and community, though on a much smaller and more personal scale. In only a few short decades, "grilling" or "cooking out" had become an entrenched part of daily American home life. More than just a favorite meal, the backyard barbecue was synonymous with "the good life," one of the favorite forms of entertaining in the postwar suburbs, and it remains so today.

The Golden Age of Barbecue

The two decades following the end of the Second World War may well be considered the Golden Age of American barbecue, for during that period barbecue was not a regional or artisanal specialty but rather one of the primary dishes in the American culinary repertoire. It could be found at fancy steak and chop houses, at drive-ins and cafés, and at countless backyard events throughout the country. All the while, the number of restaurants specializing in barbecue continued to grow. A typical medium-sized American city had just a handful of barbecue stands or cafés in the 1920s; by 1950 the same city had several dozen.

Nick Vergos, the son of Charlie Vergos and owner of the legendary Memphis rib joint Rendezvous, has observed that many of the people who took barbecue mainstream were not old-time barbecue men who decided to open restaurants but rather restaurateurs who decided to branch out into barbecue.[1] These restaurateurs often enlisted the help of an employee or friend who knew the old-time barbecue traditions from the pre-commercial days. The Rendezvous itself, which many credit with inventing Memphis-style barbecued ribs, is a perfect example.

Charlie Vergos's family immigrated from Greece to the United States in the early 1900s. His father, John Vergos, tried many trades before ending up selling hot dogs in Memphis, Tennessee. Charlie followed in his father's footsteps, running a meat-and-three restaurant called Wimpy's with his brother-in-law. In the late 1940s he set out on

"BBQ Pete" Petroff's Circle Room Restaurant in Inglewood, California. Opened in 1947 and specializing in barbecued chicken and spare ribs, the Circle Room is an example of barbecue's becoming a staple of mainstream, high-end restaurant menus nationwide.

his own and opened a snack bar in the basement of the building that housed Wimpy's. There was an old, unused elevator shaft in the corner of the basement, and Vergos decided to convert it into a smoker. His original plan was not to make barbecue but rather to smoke hams and use them in ham sandwiches. Vergos had learned from his father to keep the business simple: sell ham and cheese sandwiches on rye bread along with beer and little else. The Rendezvous was located in what was then the main downtown shopping district, and Vergos figured that in a city with so many one-car families he would find a captive clientele among men who would stop in for a sandwich and beer while their wives went shopping. The sandwiches themselves weren't the real money-maker: they were sold almost at cost and Vergos would make his profit off the beer.

The sandwich shop was only a moderate success, and over time Vergos started experimenting with other items in his smoker. He added salami first, which sold well, then tried chickens and oysters, both of which flopped. Then, in the late 1950s, the Rendezvous's meat distributor suggested he try pork ribs. Vergos didn't know anything about barbecuing, but one of his employees, a man named "Little John," did, and together they created a Memphis classic. Most barbecue joints slow cook their ribs, but the Rendezvous cooked theirs eighteen inches over a hot fire for only an hour and fifteen minutes. Little John suggested basting the meat in water and vinegar to keep it moist, and Vergos came up with a spice rub based on the combination his father once used for Greek chili: salt, pepper, bay leaf, cumin, chili powder, and oregano. To give the ribs more color, he added paprika, and the Memphis dry rib style was born.[2]

The members of the Vergos family weren't the only Greek Americans to get into the barbecue trade. Operating restaurants was an accessible way for recent immigrants to go into business on their own, and, while they may not have grown up eating barbecue, it was only natural that these new restaurateurs would try their hand at one of America's most popular foods. Birmingham, Alabama, was home to a large number of Greek American restaurateurs, and many of them—such as Angelo Serandos of Eli's Bar-B-Q and Aleck Choraitis of Andrew's Bar-B-Q—learned the southern art of pit-smoked barbecue. John and Dale Reed have identified a strong Greek American barbecue trend in North Carolina, too, including Simos Barbecue Inn in Winston-Salem (founded by Apostolos "Pete" Simos in 1939), the Red Pig Café in Concord (founded in 1945), and Mr. Barbecue, also in Winston-Salem (founded by Tom Gallos in 1952).[3]

These entrepreneurs joined a booming barbecue restaurant industry. In fact, it was in the postwar decades that the majority of the restaurants that are today considered classic American barbecue joints were founded. Of the twenty-four restaurants named on the North Carolina Barbecue Society's "Historic Barbecue Trail"—which were chosen by the NCBS board as "representative of the distinctive methods and barbecue cooking styles" of North Carolina—fourteen opened between 1945 and 1965. (Two others, Richard's in Salisbury and Stamey's in Greensboro, opened during the 1930s.)[4] The story is the same in other states. The list of famous restaurants opening during this period include, to name just a very few, Harold's in Atlanta (1947); the Ridgewood in Bluff City, Tennessee (1948); Boyd 'N' Son in Kansas City (1949); Starnes in Paducah, Kentucky (1954); Sconyers in Augusta, Georgia (1956); Dreamland in Tuscaloosa, Alabama (1958); and the Moonlite Bar-B-Q Inn in Owensboro, Kentucky (1963).

Gable's Motel and Restaurant, Florence, South Carolina.

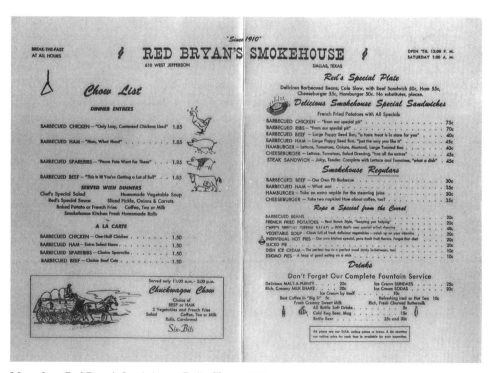

Menu from Red Bryan's Smokehouse, Dallas Texas, 1950s.

The Continuity of Barbecue

Barbecue had become firmly established in the world of commerce and in the suburban backyard, becoming transformed in the process, but that did not necessarily mean that the older barbecue tradition had ended. Through the 1950s and into the 1960s, the old-fashioned al fresco pit barbecue remained as strong a part of the social life of rural America—and particularly of the rural South—as it had in the nineteenth century, and the same methods and conventions largely remained.

"The traditional time for a Georgia barbecue," Rufus Jarman reported in the *Saturday Evening Post* in 1954, "is when crops are 'laid by,' when cultivation is finished and the farmer has only to wait for the harvest."[5] Throughout the rural South, barbecues remained a popular way for farmers to reward the hands that worked their fields. Ed Mitchell, one of North Carolina's most famous pitmasters, remembers, "In the hard days of putting in the tobacco or picking the cotton, everybody came together. . . . It didn't make any difference who owned the crop, but the one purpose in mind was to finish it and to do an excellent job. And when you finished, the farmer rewarded you by throwing a barbecue."[6]

Roy G. Taylor grew up in rural eastern North Carolina, and he described his memories of late-August tobacco farm barbecues in one of his columns for the *Wilson Daily Times*. Though the events took place well into the twentieth century, the details could easily have come from a century earlier. The preparations began late on a Friday afternoon, when the men killed a pig and prepared it for the pit, which was usually dug under "a backer barn shelter" and filled with coals from green oak. The meat was basted with "vinegar with red pepper cut up in it," and it was served not with coleslaw or corn bread but rather with fresh cucumbers, deviled eggs, and hoecakes along with a big wooden tub of lemonade. "It's just too good to be true," Taylor recalls himself thinking. "All that good food and no more backer to 'put in' either. Everybody's in a good mood with clean clothes and washed hair and looking good except for the hands that still carry the stain gathered over the barning period. And Saturday night and Sunday coming up too. What a great world!"[7]

As textile manufacturing spread across the South in the early twentieth century, the barbecue was extended to millworkers, too. In 1907 such barbecues were unusual

Tenant farmers and their families dining at the annual barbecue at Braswell Plantation, North Carolina, 1944. (Courtesy North Carolina Office of Archives and History, Raleigh, North Carolina.)

enough that the South Carolina Department of Agriculture said of the Middleburg Mills in Batesburg, "This company makes an innovation by giving its help an annual barbecue."[8] Within a few years, the mill barbecue was a regular management practice. In 1933, O. Max Gardner, the owner of the Cleveland Cloth Mill and a former governor of North Carolina, staged a "barbecue, dance, and love feast" for his workers to head off a drive for unionization.[9] Barbecues could work the other side of the labor struggle, too, and they became potent tools for union organizers. In 1919, more than one thousand unionized textile workers from mill towns across the Piedmont of North Carolina assembled in Charlotte's Electric Park for a "jubilee" to celebrate the end of a sixteen-week strike at the Highland Park and Johnson Mills.[10]

Employees Picnic, American Thread Company, Tallapoosa, Georgia, 1944. (Courtesy Special Collections Department & Archives, Georgia State University Library.)

Barbecues were soon adopted by workers in other industries, and they became an iconic feature of Labor Day celebrations. The Labor Day holiday originated out of the labor movement of the late nineteenth century. The first celebrations and gatherings were organized by various unions and other labor organizations starting in the 1880s, and it was made a federal holiday in 1894. In the early years, Labor Day was specifically linked to unionism and usually included massive parades with pro-labor banners and music, as well as lots of American flags and other patriotic symbols. During the conservative 1920s, the celebrations were gradually stripped of their more radical trappings, and marches were replaced by more general gatherings, festivals, and speeches, and, particularly in the Midwest and the South, barbecue was frequently served at the event.[11]

Over time, Labor Day became a more general public holiday. During the 1950s, the

Men cooking Brunswick stew for the Employees' Picnic, American Thread Company, Tallapoosa, Georgia, 1944. (Courtesy Special Collections Department & Archives, Georgia State University Library.)

American Federation of Labor and Congress of Industrial Organizations still hosted massive barbecues on Labor Day. In 1955, for example, the organizations hosted a Labor Day rally at Denison Dam that drew union members from all over the state of Texas and was capped by a keynote address by Speaker of the U.S. House of Represen tatives Sam Rayburn.[12] By this time, however, the Labor Day barbecue had lost many of its connotations of unionism and was treated more as a long weekend of relaxation, and the barbecue gradually shifted from the pit-cooked to the backyard variety. In 1956, the *Dallas Morning News* reported that members of the city's country clubs were "preparing for a gala and final summer fling over Labor Day weekend," with events including dances, swim meets, and barbecues.[13] Newspapers and magazines in the 1950s

Labor Relations and Barbecue Jurisprudence

IN 1914, HENRY M. WILLIAMS, a weaver at the Cotton Mills Company in Columbia, South Carolina, asked to be excused from work for two days because he wanted to prepare and give a barbecue. The request was denied, but Williams left work to barbecue anyway. When he returned to the mill a few days later, he was told that his loom had been given to someone else. Williams was offered another position at a lower wage, which he declined, and he was subsequently evicted from his company-owned house in the mill village.

Williams brought suit against the mill company for wrongful eviction and won. The mill company appealed and the case made it to the South Carolina Supreme Court. One of the key issues was whether Williams should have been allowed to testify about the reason he missed two days of work. The mill's lawyers had objected, apparently recognizing that—in South Carolina, at least—knowing that a man skipped work to barbecue would likely bias any jury in his favor. Williams won the appeal.

Source: "Williams et ux. v. Columbia Mills Co. et al.," *Southeastern Reporter* 85 (St. Paul, MN: West, 1915): 160.

and 1960s were filled with advertisements for charcoal, grills, and meat for Labor Day barbecues, and cooking out in the backyard remains a core part of the Labor Day tradition today.

Barbecue had been used by churches and other organizations to raise funds during the late nineteenth century, and that practice only picked up steam in the twentieth century. The Poplar Tent Presbyterian Church near Concord, North Carolina, held its first fundraiser in 1946, starting with a ditch in the ground and five hogs, from which it netted eighty dollars.[14] Sixty years later, the annual event is still going strong. The Episcopal Church of St. Hubert the Hunter in Bondurant, Wyoming, held its first Bondurant Barbecue in 1941. Beef is donated by local ranchers, and the church members cook baked beans, homemade cakes, and potato salad for the event, which raises money to maintain the church building as well as support area charities.

Perhaps the largest and most famous church barbecue is the annual October affair held by the Mallard Creek Presbyterian Church outside of Charlotte, North Carolina. The event began in 1929 after the congregation had borrowed money to build their first Sunday School classrooms but, after the stock market collapse, was in danger of defaulting. J. W. "Will" Oehler, a longtime member, offered to barbecue three whole hogs and a goat, which the congregation sold to the public for fifty cents a plate. The event raised $89.50, and it became an annual fundraiser. From the start, it was always held on the fourth Thursday in October, apparently because that was the day that Charlotte's maids had the afternoon off.

In the early days, the pigs for the barbecue were donated by farmers who were members of the congregation, and they were slaughtered and dressed by H. Y. Galloway at his house. The meat was cooked in open pits dug in the ground over coals from hickory wood that was also donated by church members. Things evolved over time. In 1946 the organizers started taking the pigs to an abattoir for slaughter, and a screened-in cookhouse with cement block pits was built.[15] After Oehler died in 1944, his son J. W. Oehler Jr. took over the pitmaster duties, and he in turn passed them on to his son Donnie, who still oversees the cooking today.

The Mallard Creek barbecue now draws more than twenty thousand people each year. They serve some fourteen thousand pounds of pulled pork (at $9 a plate) along with twenty-five hundred gallons of Brunswick stew, which is still cooked in a row of iron kettles stirred by volunteers with big wooden paddles. The money raised goes to support the church's local and international mission projects. Over the years, North Carolina politicians discovered that the Mallard Creek gathering was an ideal place to meet and talk with voters, and—in a merging of the political and religious traditions— the barbecue has become an obligatory campaign stop for anyone aspiring to a local or statewide office. As the political traffic increased, the church began corralling hopeful office seekers to a separate area roped off with colored flags, but walking the line and shaking politicians' hands remains an essential part of the Mallard Creek experience.[16]

"Barbecue men"—pitmasters who had gained fame in their region and even beyond— continued to play a key role in traditional outdoor barbecues, and they remained in demand for all of these sorts of events. As the century progressed, some of these barbecue men opened their own restaurants, but many remained freelancers who traveled around a region cooking for large gatherings and public events. A. B. "Bud" Foster, the sheriff of Fulton County, was considered the top barbecuer in the Atlanta area, keeping alive the Georgia tradition of barbecue-cooking sheriffs that had been started by Sheriff John W. Callaway of Wilkes County back in the 1880s.

In part, the strength of the barbecue tradition in rural areas reflected the sharp divide that still existed between urban America—which had changed remarkably in only a half century—and rural America, which in many places had seen minimal progress since Reconstruction days. Newspaper and magazine accounts from the middle of the twentieth century play up this distinction, depicting rural barbecues as quaint events out of an earlier age. Describing a barbecue held by the Euharlee Farmers Club of Euharlee, Georgia, for example, the *Saturday Evening Post* commented, "In such an atmosphere one almost expected to see Uncle Remus, Br'er Rabbit, Br'er Fox and 'de yudder critters' emerge through the early-morning haze out of a blackjack thicket across the cotton patch."[17]

Barbecue and Twentieth-Century Politics

Through much of the twentieth century, the barbecue remained an important part of American political life. The automobile helped accelerate things. The 1930s and 1940s saw the rise of the "political caravan," a convoy of cars and buses filled with candidates for statewide office that would crisscross the countryside, stopping at one town after another along the way for speeches, handshaking, and a big barbecue. In the 1950s, Herbert O'Keefe, a former editor of the *Raleigh Times* warned, "No man has been elected governor of North Carolina without eating more barbecue than was good for him."[18]

Barbecues also became important means of celebrating political victories, sometimes on a massive scale. John C. "Jack" Walton, the mayor of Oklahoma City who ran for governor of Oklahoma in 1922, was a lively and colorful platform speaker. Though a Democrat, he ran on a populist platform with enough progressive planks to draw support from the Farm-Labor Party, the Socialists, and even some Republicans. As he campaigned across the state, Walton promised that if he were elected there would be no "pink tea party" for his inauguration but rather an old-fashioned barbecue to which the whole state would be invited. Walton won the election and kept his word.

The two-day celebration was set for January 10 and 11, 1923. Dan V. Lackey, a prize-fight promoter, served as chairman of the committee of arrangements, and the Central Barbecue Committee included Major Gordon W. Lillie (Pawnee Bill) and Colonel George Miller Jr., both producers of famous Wild West shows. The center of a half-mile racetrack was floored in to be used for dancing, but Walton announced that no waltzes or other "citified" dances would be permitted. Instead, there would be square dancing, Virginia reels, and cowboy hoe-downs, and the Democratic headquarters in each county were asked to recruit "old fashioned fiddlers who know how to play 'Turkey in the Straw.'"[19] A thousand Indians from various Oklahoma tribes were enlisted to perform war dances.

Just before Christmas, Walton sent out a call to Oklahoma farmers for enough meat to serve 200,000 people. In addition to thousands of beeves, hogs, sheep, and chickens, the list of donations included 103 turkeys, 1,363 rabbits, 26 squirrels, 134 opossums, 113 geese, 15 deer, two buffalo, and two reindeer, which had been "shipped in from the North."[20] A man from Sayre, Oklahoma, captured a live bear and donated him to the cause. The bear won the sympathy of Oklahoma City schoolchildren, who pooled their pocket change, bought him for $119.66, and donated him to the Wheeler Park Zoo, where he was a crowd favorite for more than a decade.[21]

For the less fortunate creatures, six parallel trenches were dug at the Oklahoma state fairgrounds, stretching in total almost a mile. An estimated five hundred butchers, slicers, and pitmen were recruited to cook and serve the barbecue. Six giant coffee percolators the size of railroad boxcars were constructed for the event, each with a capacity of 10,000 gallons, and the rest of the provisions secured for the crowds, according to the *San Antonio Express,* read like "an emergency ration order to furnish food for the American expeditionary force": 339,000 buns, 55,000 pounds of sugar, 450 barrels of salt, 450 barrels of pepper, and 3,000 pounds of onions.[22]

By the night before the barbecue, it was estimated that some 50,000 people had arrived in Oklahoma City, traveling in cars and on railroad trains from even the most remote parts of the state. The *Dallas Morning News* considered 100,000 to be "a conservative estimate" of the crowd that showed up at the fairgrounds on the morning of January 9.[23] The official inauguration ceremonies, which had been performed the day before in the capitol, were repeated for the crowds, and, following a few short speeches, fiddlers began to play over a novel electrical amplification system. The feeding continued through the afternoon. From the leftover meat, 22,000 gallons of soup were made, which was distributed along with the remaining bread to the poor of Oklahoma City. The Walton barbecue was the largest political barbecue of the twentieth century, and it competes with the 1895 Encampment of the Grand Army of the Republic as the largest public barbecue in American history.

In the decades that followed, large inaugural barbecues became commonplace in the capitals of southern and southwestern states. The Louisiana gubernatorial race of 1940 marked the end of the twelve-year hold on the office by Huey P. Long's political machine.[24] Long's brother Earl was defeated in the 1940 Democratic primary by Sam Houston Jones, a reform-minded attorney who promised to roll back the excesses of the Kingfish era. Jones's inauguration on May 12, 1940, was celebrated with "the greatest barbecue ever seen in storied Louisiana." Held in the football stadium at Louisiana State University, the barbecue featured some 1,000 beef cattle cooked over the pits.[25] A year later, Governor Wilbert "Pappy" O'Daniel of Texas, stumped across the state, closing his reelection campaign speeches by imploring Texans to "come down to dinner at the Governor's mansion some time." Twenty-five thousand of them arrived in January 1941 for the inaugural celebration. A fifty-foot pit was dug in the yard of the gover-

Pappy O'Daniel's inauguration barbecue, Austin, Texas, January 1941. (Courtesy of Texas State Library & Archives Commission.)

nor's mansion, and 17,000 pounds of beef barbecue were served along with half a ton of potato chips, 6,000 pickles, and lemonade made from 24,000 lemons.[26]

The political barbecue was an inherently populist institution. Politicians who mastered the art of the campaign barbecue could use it to propel themselves to great heights. One such master was Eugene Talmadge, who served four terms as Georgia's governor in the 1930s and 1940s. Talmadge had a minimal political organization (one biographer called it "primitive by almost anyone's standards"[27]), but, unlike most Georgian politicians, he was able to sidestep the "courthouse gangs" that dominated the state's political machinery. He did so by appealing directly to the people, and there was no better way to do that than with free barbecue.

Eugene Talmadge addressing political rally, Gainesville, Georgia, July 4, 1946. (Courtesy Special Collections Department & Archives, Georgia State University Library.)

In 1932 Talmadge kicked off his first gubernatorial campaign with a massive Fourth of July barbecue in his hometown of McRae. Norman Graham, the "Barbecue King" of Telfair County, was recruited to oversee the pits, and letters were sent out to area farmers asking them to contribute pigs, goats, cows, and chickens. Three days before the meeting, farmers began arriving with donations, which were taken to City Park in downtown McRae for slaughter and cleaning. Graham started cooking early in the morning on the day before the event, with over ten thousand pounds of meat smoking over the shallow pits and one thousand gallons of Brunswick stew bubbling in iron kettles. He kept the fires going overnight, illuminated by a string of bare light bulbs, which, according to the local paper, drew so many insects into the stew pots that Graham didn't need to add any pepper, since "Bugs was good spice."[28]

An estimated ten thousand people turned out for the barbecue. They cheered wildly throughout Talmadge's speech and carried him from the platform on their shoulders at its conclusion. Talmadge repeated the performance on a two-month campaign tour through most of the rural Georgia counties. Nine other candidates were competing in the Democratic primary that year, the winner of which, in the Solid South, was guaranteed victory in the general election. Talmadge swept them all and won the nomination without even requiring a run-off.

The barbecue became the centerpiece of Talmadge's campaigns for the rest of his political career. Along the way, he attracted a band of regular followers, including the "Tree-Climbing Haggards of Danielsville." For rallies, the elder Haggard and his eight sons dressed like Gene Talmadge in black suits with wide-brimmed hats and red suspenders and climbed to the top of tall pine trees around the grove where the barbecue was being held. From these high perches they shouted down scripted cues for their candidate, like "Tell us about the schoolteachers, Gene!" or "Tell us about the old folks!" prompting Talmadge to launch into his canned remarks on the topic. One afternoon, the story goes, one of the Haggard boys, having eaten too much barbecue at the previous campaign stop up the road, fell asleep in his tree and tumbled to the ground amid the onlookers, bringing Talmadge's speech to a crashing halt and illustrating the dangers of too much political barbecue.[29]

The political barbecue reached its height of national and international attention with the presidency of Lyndon Baines Johnson. Johnson bought his LBJ Ranch in 1951, two years after being sworn in to the United States Senate, and he held his first barbecue there in 1953. After a few years, Johnson settled on a grove of trees along the bank of the Pedernales River as his favorite barbecue location. For Johnson, barbecues were not just social events but political tools, allowing him to project an image of himself as an ordinary man. The LBJ Ranch offered national and, later, international visitors a mythologized version of rural America, one that put suspicious urban politicians at ease and allowed Johnson to work his personal charm on them.[30] Johnson consciously styled his barbecues with western instead of southern imagery. Richard "Cactus" Pryor, the Texas broadcaster and humorist who was a frequent emcee at LBJ Ranch barbecues, recalled that they "had the look and feel of a chuck wagon dinner."[31] Guests dined at

Barbecue guests along the bank of the Pedernales River at the LBJ Ranch, April 1, 1967. (Courtesy Lyndon Baines Johnson Library and Museum.)

round tables with checkered tablecloths and coal-oil lanterns. Servers wore western gear, and Stetson hats were frequently given away to out-of-state guests. Such images helped Johnson brand himself as a "western" politician and distance himself from the poverty and racial strife then associated with the South.

Johnson's caterer of choice was Walter Jetton, a man the Texas barbecue historian Robb Walsh calls "the last of the open pit barbecuers and probably the single most influential pit boss in Texas barbecue history."[32] Jetton started in the barbecue business in 1930 as a sideline to his meat market, cooking for church picnics and other civic functions.[33] By the early 1950s, even before his association with Lyndon Johnson, Jetton had established himself as the Fort Worth "barbecue king." In 1951 and again in 1952, he took his catering rig—a motorized chuck wagon—all the way to Washington, D.C., to serve pit-cooked beef, ranch-style beans, potato salad, and coleslaw to eight hundred members of the Texas State Society.[34]

Walter Jetton's Barbecue Menu

IN **WALTER JETTON'S LBJ** *Barbecue Cook Book,* the pitmaster recorded President Johnson's favorite barbecue menu:

Texas Beef Barbecue with Natural Gravy

Smoked Ranch Beans

Cooked Country Corn

Country Potato Salad

Texas Cole Slaw

Sliced Dill Pickle Spears

Spanish Sweet Onions

Modern Day Sourdough Biscuits

Fried Apple Pies

Six-Shooter Coffee

Soft Drinks

Source: Walter Jetton with Arthur Whitman, *Walter Jetton's LBJ Barbecue Cook Book* (New York: Pocket, 1965).

Jetton's highly publicized barbecues at the LBJ Ranch gained him a national reputa-tion, but he remained an unrepentant devotee of the open pit and hardwood coals, even for casual backyard cooking. "To barbecue, you need a pit," he wrote in his 1965 *LBJ Barbecue Cookbook,* "and it definitely shouldn't be one of those backyard creations with a chimney. You want your smoke, you don't want to draw it off."[35] Jetton advocated a por-table pit made out of four pieces of sheet metal, with the fire built right on the ground inside the pit and a big metal grill laid over the top. He initially cooked whole steers for large gatherings, though—like most Texas pitmasters—he eventually switched to briskets.

As Jetton's fame grew, he expanded his catering business and opened two cafete-rias in Fort Worth. He continued to travel widely to cater barbecues, including serving pork ribs, beef brisket, chickens, and fried pies at Gracie Mansion, the official residence of the mayor of New York City, for a Young Citizens for Johnson campaign event.[36] By the time of his death in 1968, Jetton had a fleet of eighteen catering trucks that al-lowed him to provide barbecues for up to ten thousand people, and he estimated he was serving 1.5 million dinners each year.[37] But, the barbecues at the LBJ Ranch remain his overwhelming legacy. Over the course of his presidency, Lyndon Johnson hosted nearly one hundred barbecues at the ranch. Heads of state treated to Texas hospitality included Chancellor Ludwig Erhard of West Germany, President Gustavo Diaz Ordaz of Mexico, and Prime Minister Levi Eshkol of Israel. Barbecue had achieved interna-tional stature, being served at state dinners by the President of the United States.

Barbecue and Racial Politics in the South

The legacy of barbecue and race relations is a mixed one. In some ways, barbecue was an institution that brought blacks and whites together. The tradition was shared by everyone in the South, and many public events were attended by all of a community's residents regardless of skin color. Some barbecue joints, such as Red Bryan's Smoke-house in Dallas and Abe's in Clarksdale, Mississippi, were among the few restaurants in the South that served an integrated clientele prior to the civil rights movement, and whites would frequently seek out joints in black neighborhoods to find great barbecue.

More often, though, the same social divide that existed in the larger southern society was reflected in the world of barbecue, too. Black pitmasters earned respect in their regions and were invited to preside over massive events for the white community, but they and their families were usually excluded from dining at the main tables. At countless restaurants, like Leonard's in Memphis and Ollie's in Birmingham, black men did the hard work of cooking over the pits but were not allowed into the dining rooms. Some black-owned joints, like Scott's in Goldsboro, North Carolina, served both blacks and whites, but in segregated dining rooms.

The civil rights movement changed all that, and barbecue restaurants took center stage for some of the key legal battles for desegregation. The Civil Rights Act of 1964 was signed into law by President Lyndon Johnson on July 2. Title II of the act prohibited discrimination in hotels, restaurants, theaters, and other places of public accommodation that engaged in interstate commerce. In the case of a restaurant, that meant "it serves or offers to serve interstate travelers or a substantial portion of the food which it serves, or gasoline or other products which it sells, has moved in commerce."[38]

It wasn't by accident that barbecue restaurants were at the center of several landmark rulings about the act's public accommodation provisions. Not only was barbecue a food that had a long history in both the black and white communities, but by its very nature it challenged assumptions about regional culture and interstate commerce. In Alabama, the Birmingham Restaurant Association started planning to challenge the Civil Rights Act months before Johnson's signature. They saw the act's interstate commerce provisions to be its most vulnerable aspect, but most of the association's members could not volunteer for test cases because they clearly served interstate travelers.

So, they turned to Ollie's Barbecue, a white-owned barbecue joint located on the predominantly black south side of Birmingham. Owned by forty-eight-year-old Ollie McClung and his twenty-four-year-old son Ollie Jr., the restaurant did not advertise and was located well away from any interstate highway, railroad, bus station, or other avenues of interstate commerce. Two-thirds of Ollie's thirty-six employees were African American, but they served only white patrons in the dining room, requiring African American customers to use a take-out window.[39] The federal government had not yet taken any action to desegregate Ollie's, but Ollie McClung   at the urging of the

Birmingham Restaurant Association—brought suit in federal court, seeking an injunction to prevent Title II from being enforced against them in the future.

McClung won the initial case in the district court, but it was appealed to the United States Supreme Court, which delivered its landmark *Katzenbach v. McClung* ruling on December 14, 1964. Ollie's, it was determined, had purchased 46 percent of its food—mostly meat—from a local wholesaler who in turn had purchased it from Hormel meat-packing plants outside the state, which meant that "a substantial portion of the food served in the restaurant had moved in interstate commerce."[40] Discrimination at the restaurant, the Court ruled, indeed affected interstate commerce, since the fewer customers Ollie's served the less food it purchased from suppliers outside the state. In addition, it determined that discrimination made it difficult for African Americans to purchase prepared food while on trips, which discouraged travel and obstructed interstate commerce in a significant manner.

Ollie McClung peacefully desegregated his business two days after the Supreme Court handed down its decision. "As law-abiding Americans," McClung stated, "we feel we must bow to this edict."[41] Ollie's Barbecue, with both black and white customers eating in the dining room, remained a Birmingham institution until it closed in 2001.

A second test case of the Civil Rights Act involved barbecue restaurants in Columbia, South Carolina. A few days after the act was signed, J. W. Mungin, an African American minister, filed a complaint with the FBI after being refused service at one of the Columbia barbecue restaurants owned by L. Maurice Bessinger. Bessinger at the time operated Little Joe's Sandwich Shop on Main Street in downtown Columbia as well as five Piggy Park drive-ins, and he was the chairman of the South Carolina campaign committee for the segregationist presidential candidate George Wallace. It took almost two years for the case to come before U.S. District Court judge Charles Simons, who began hearing arguments in April 1966.

Bessinger argued that his restaurants were not engaged in interstate commerce in any form. He testified before Judge Simons that his barbecue was "made exclusively for the taste of central South Carolinians," and that his business was never meant for interstate travelers because "people from New York or North Carolina or Georgia have entirely different tastes for barbecue." Mrs. Merle Brigman, Bessinger's bookkeeper and food buyer, testified that Piggy Park Enterprises purchased all its meat from South Carolina processing plants, that items such as paper plates that originated from outside the state were not sold but given away with the food, and that the drive-ins refused to serve cars bearing out-of-state license plates.[42] Perhaps most sensational was Bessinger's claim that the Civil Rights Act "contravenes the will of God" and violated his constitutional right for free exercise of religion.

The district court gave little credence to Bessinger's religious arguments, and disagreed with him on the interstate commerce points, too, ruling that Little Joe's Sandwich Shop, which was a traditional sit-down restaurant, violated the Civil Rights Act by refusing to serve African Americans. The five drive-ins, however, were ruled to not be covered by the act because they were not "principally engaged in selling food for consumption on the premises." The Piggy Park drive-ins had no tables, chairs, counters, or stools, and Bessinger had testified that about half the customers ate their barbecue in their cars while parked on the premises, while the other half took it away. A year later, the decision on the drive-ins was overturned on appeal by the Fourth Circuit Court of Appeals, which ruled that Congress had not intended the Civil Rights Act to depend upon a headcount of people eating onsite but rather had crafted the language of "selling food for consumption on the premises" to differentiate restaurants from other businesses such as grocery stores or bars. A technical ruling about whether the prevailing party could be awarded attorney's fees made it all the way to the Supreme Court, which decided in 1968 that such fees should indeed be rewarded and were, in fact, an important means to ensure that people who had been discriminated against could seek redress in the court system.

Maurice Bessinger remains a divisive figure in the world of barbecue today. In 2000, when the South Carolina legislature voted to remove the Confederate flag that flew above the statehouse dome in Columbia, Bessinger responded by hoisting the Stars and Bars over each of his nine area restaurants. This action led to a boycott by the NAACP and prompted several large grocery and retail chains to remove Bessinger's bottled barbecue sauces from their shelves.

But, such divisiveness is the exception and not the rule in barbecue. Following the Civil Rights Act and the subsequent court rulings of the 1960s, barbecue restaurants have helped lead the way in removing the color barriers of a formerly segregated society. Barbecue restaurants were some of the first black-owned enterprises to establish significant white customer bases, and today it is common to see both white and black patrons eating side by side at the tables of barbecue joints across the country.

The Decline and Rebirth of American Barbecue

The Fate of Barbecue in a Fast-Food Era

In the 1950s, barbecue was a dominant player on the American restaurant scene, but changes were brewing that threatened its popularity. The American restaurant industry was continuing to expand and becoming more standardized, but it wasn't clear what the future held. Early burger franchises, such as McDonald's and Burger King, were just getting started. McDonald's grew from one restaurant in 1955 to one hundred in 1959, while Burger King still had only five outlets by the end of the decade, all in the metropolitan Miami area. Chains and franchises were increasing their share of the restaurant market, but the types and styles of food that lent themselves to franchising were still being sorted out, and hamburgers were by no means the dominant menu item.

Early in his restaurant career, Dave Thomas, who would later found the Wendy's hamburger chain, experimented with selling barbecue at the Hobby Ranch House, a restaurant he managed in Fort Wayne, Indiana. In the mid-1950s, he and the restaurant's owner, Phil Clauss, visited Mac McKenny's operation in Evansville and were impressed by what they saw. Mac's Barbecue seated two hundred people and had a limited menu: ribs, chicken, and potato salad, all served on paper plates and accompanied by rye bread, pickles, and onions. They cooked a hundred chickens and 150 pounds of ribs at a time over hickory coals in enclosed pits. Thomas noted that even with the limited menu, McKenney was doing more that $2,000 a night in carryout orders alone, and he felt barbecue was a promising trend.[1]

So, Thomas and Clauss became franchisees of Mac's Barbecue. In an informal arrangement typical of early restaurant franchising, they paid no royalties and didn't even use the Mac's Barbecue name. All they did was buy their sauce from McKenney—or, more accurately, the flavoring for the sauce, since they received dry powder from Mac's and added ketchup, vinegar, and water to it. Thomas spent a few months in Evansville learning the business, then returned to Fort Wayne to open the franchise, which was called (unmelodiously) the Hobby Ranch House with Barbecue. Like Mac's, the Hobby Ranch House had a simple menu of chicken and ribs on paper plates, though they added baked beans alongside the potato salad.

Barbecue did not turn out to be the moneymaker that Thomas had hoped. In retrospect, he blamed their deviation from Mac's bare-bones operating formula. "When customers complained about the paper plates we switched to china," Thomas recalled. "But china and silver ran our costs up. When customers said they would prefer rolls to rye bread, we gave them rolls and butter. . . . The variety killed our focus and made the business much harder to manage."[2] The lessons Thomas learned from his barbecue experience—and later from working with Colonel Harlan Sanders during the early days of the Kentucky Fried Chicken chain—were put into practice in 1969, when he founded the first of his Wendy's Hamburgers restaurants, which today is an eleven-billion-dollar corporation with over nine thousand restaurants, none of which serves barbecue.

Dave Thomas wasn't the first restaurateur to see the inherent problems with barbecue as a low-cost menu item. Perhaps no story is more emblematic of the fate of barbecue as a roadside food than that of Richard and Maurice McDonald, whose drive-in in San Bernardino, California, launched the fast-food revolution in America. The brothers' original drive-in was typical of the era: an octagonal wooden building with carhops serving motorists a broad, twenty-five-item menu that included ham, chili, and tamales in addition to hamburgers and French fries. Like many drive-ins of the era, the

Dave Thomas *(back)* preparing barbecued chicken at his Hobby Ranch House restaurant in Fort Wayne, Indiana.

menu also featured barbecue beef, ham, and pork sandwiches, and the meat was cooked behind the restaurant over a hickory-chip pit.

The restaurant was making money, but just barely, and in the late 1940s the McDonalds took a hard look at their operations. The carhops were a problem: service was too slow, and the carhops were easily distracted by other customers. Groups of teenage boys used the drive-in as a hangout, driving off many families. Operational costs were high, too, especially because of broken china and trays and flatware that disappeared on a regular basis.

In the fall of 1948 the McDonalds closed down their restaurant for three full months. When it reopened, the carhops were gone and the windows where they used to pick up their orders had been converted to self-service portals. Also gone were the china and silver, replaced by paper wrappers and cardboard cups. Most important were the changes to the menu. Slow-cooked barbecue was too time- and labor-intensive, so the

A 1943 menu for McDonald's Famous Bar-B-Q, prior to the restaurant's conversion to a fast-food hamburger stand. (Courtesy Ray Quiel.)

hickory pit was extinguished. The only sandwiches remaining were hamburgers and cheeseburgers, with the toppings limited to ketchup, mustard, onion, and two pickle slices. Side items were equally limited: French fries, coffee, milkshakes, and sodas. The patties had been reduced from 8 to the pound down to 10 to the pound, but the prices had been reduced even more: from thirty-five cents for a hamburger down to fifteen cents.

The principles of the McDonalds' "Speedy Service System" were simple: focus on a basic, low-cost menu, sell convenience and low price, and make money through volume. It was a flop at first. Their old customers missed the drive-in features to which they were accustomed. But, within a few months McDonald's began to attract a new

Richard and Maurice McDonald in the midst of converting their drive-in from barbecue stand to hamburger bar, 1948. (Courtesy Ray Quiel.)

customer base made up of commuters, workers, and families who wanted a cheap, fast meal without having to deal with the annoyances of a teen hangout.

It also gained the attention of Ray Kroc, the distributor of a new five-spindled milk-shake mixer called the Multimixer. In 1954, Kroc learned the McDonalds' hamburger stand had purchased eight of these mixers, and he paid them a visit to see what was driving such volume. Fascinated by the speed of service and customer volume, he convinced the McDonald brothers to start franchising, and he signed himself up to be their agent. The first franchise opened in Des Plaines, Illinois, in 1956.[3]

What was a big success for the McDonalds and for the hamburger was the beginning of the end of barbecue as a fast food. As fast-food chains grew in the 1950s and 1960s, they focused on speed, standardization, and low labor costs, which meant the ability to use low-skilled labor. Barbecue scored poorly in all of these areas. Hamburgers were pretty much the same from one state to the next, but barbecue differed greatly from location to location, with each region having its own style of cooking and its own favorite type of sauce. Not only did the meat take hours to cook, but it required a skilled pitmaster, too. Barbecuing was usually learned through an apprenticeship system over the course of months, if not years. You couldn't hire a sixteen-year-old off the street, give him an afternoon tutorial, and turn him loose on the pit.

The same pains that led the McDonald brothers to discard the carhops and limit their menu were being felt throughout the restaurant industry. During the late 1950s drive-in operators looked for new ways to improve their businesses, trying to attract more customers, serve them more efficiently, and sell bigger orders. Innovations included adding metal canopies to provide shade for diners (particularly in the South) and electronic ordering systems that reduced the number of carhop trips per customer and allowed operators to shrink their workforce. In the end, such improvements could not offset the inherent inefficiencies of the drive-in model. By the 1960s, catering to the automobile trade had become a liability. Rising land prices in cities made large parking lots an expensive proposition, and trade fell off dramatically during winter months, even in southern states. Drive-in lots had become hangouts for teenagers, and operators had to contend with large crowds of nonpaying youths and the drinking, fighting, and vandalism that often accompanied them. Cruising teens would make a loop from one drive-in to another, creating traffic jams that blocked not only the operators' lots but the adjoining streets as well. City residents began lodging complaints, and many municipalities enacted ordinances that held drive-in owners responsible for the activity on and around their premises and required landscaping, fences, and other facility changes.[4]

The drive-in had little chance of competing against the self-service outlets, where customers left their cars and stood in line for food. The limited hamburger-based menus were more cost-effective, customer turnover was twice as fast, and the number of employees required was much lower. In most cities, the number of drive-ins declined rapidly during the 1960s, and of those that remained, few served pit-cooked barbecue anymore. Once the king of the American roadside, barbecue had taken a backseat to the hamburger.

The Decline of American Barbecue

Operators who were committed to running a classic barbecue restaurant faced many challenges to keeping on doing business as they had. By the 1970s, hardwood was be-

Little Pigs of America, Pioneer of Barbecue Franchising

SOME ENTREPRENEURS, SEEING THE success of the hamburger chains, tried to follow suit with barbecue. In the early 1960s, the Memphis-based Little Pigs of America began selling franchises for barbecue restaurants nationwide. Asking for a total investment of $6,000, Little Pigs promised franchisees a net return of $18,000 per year, with no prior barbecue experience required. The company provided training for franchisees at their Memphis headquarters and also assisted with location selection and engineering a brick pit for the restaurant. A typical Little Pigs of America restaurant sold a pork basket for 59 cents, a pork plate for 69 cents, and a rib platter for $1.59.

The company boldly announced a goal of opening one thousand total restaurants, and by 1965 some two hundred franchised units had opened in the United States and Canada. (By comparison, in 1963 the eight-year-old McDonald's Hamburgers chain had opened unit number 500.) Despite its rapid initial growth, the company turned a profit in only one year, 1963, and filed for bankruptcy before the end of the decade, ending the brief run of what was America's largest barbecue chain. Many Little Pigs franchisees faded out after the parent company folded, but some stayed on in the business, and a few Little Pigs restaurants are still in operation, including well-known restaurants in Columbia, South Carolina, and Asheville, North Carolina.

Sources: "New Barbecue Establishment Opens," *Burlington (NC) Daily Times News,* April 24, 1965. "Profits for Mom & Pop," *Time,* May 24, 1963. *Securities and Exchange Commission News Digest,* Issue No. 66–64, April 4, 1966, 1.

coming scarce, driving up costs for log-burning pitmasters. Keith Stamey of Stamey's Barbecue in Greensboro, North Carolina, used to get his hickory from a woodman who delivered it in an old pickup truck. As business increased, he had to turn to sawmills and furniture factories for leftover scraps before finally securing a supplier who could regularly provide the volume they needed. "I won't tell you who they are," Stamey's son Chip told an interviewer recently. "Used to be that we wouldn't give out our recipes, but we're now more secretive about our wood than our recipes."[5] Some classic barbecue joints, like Melton's in Rocky Mount, North Carolina, turned away from wood altogether, installing gas cookers instead. Willie Bob Melton, the nephew of the original Bob Melton, explained that his restaurant switched to gas in the early 1970s because "wood was getting hard to get. You couldn't get anybody to cut your wood for you."[6]

The cost and availability of the wood wasn't the only issue. "More and more restaurateurs are turning to gas or electric heat as a way out of the labor predicament," Kathleen Zobel reported in 1977. "Besides being less trouble, it is a faster and cheaper method."[7] Even those pitmasters who were willing to put in the time and effort found it increasingly difficult to cook over wood, as health departments across the country began tightening their regulations on restaurants who used open pits. In many states—even those with a centuries-old tradition of barbecuing over wood—it became difficult to get a license to run a wood-burning barbecue operation. Alton Beck of Beck's Barbecue—a classic Lexington, North Carolina, joint—predicted in 1977 that good barbecue was on its way to extinction. "The state'll stop it," he told the *Charlotte Observer*. "You can't build a new pit now and use it in Lexington. The ones here now are operating under the grandfather clause."[8] In many states, when a barbecue restaurant was sold the new owner would convert to gas or electric cookers because it was simply too difficult to get a permit to operate the old wood pits.[9] When Allie Patricia Wall and Ron L. Layne surveyed South Carolina barbecue joints in 1979, they found that more than half used either electric or gas cookers.[10]

Entrepreneurs had started promoting electric barbecue cookers to restaurateurs as early as the 1930s. Most of the early models were essentially rotisserie ovens with electric heating elements, and they made little headway in the market. By the 1970s, however, the designs had evolved and began to gain wider adoption. These cookers were

Promotional postcard for the rotisserie oven from Dallas-based Barbe-Matic, Inc., which promised "Barbe-Matic's Lazy Susan Does it the Easy Way."

usually made of stainless steel with a lid that could be closed during cooking. On electric models, heating elements similar to an electric oven were positioned on the lid and near the bottom of the cooker, while on gas models gas jets provided the cooking heat. Most versions had a sloping bottom that drained grease to a pan underneath while the meat cooked. To give the meat smoke flavor, there was either a smoke box or a metal plate that would burn chips of hardwoods like hickory or oak to infuse the cooking chamber with smoke. With such equipment, an attendant could simply put the meat on a metal rack in the cooker, close the lid, and set the desired temperature on the thermostat, with no close watching or shoveling of coals required.[11]

Changes in the American economy and food system also affected barbecue in the latter part of the twentieth century. In the 1950s and 1960s, meat packing—once a local business—became increasingly industrialized and national in scope. In Texas, meat markets no longer slaughtered their own cattle and, therefore, didn't have low-demand cuts like chuck and shoulder leftover for barbecuing. Barbecue joints began ordering the cuts of their choice, which in most cases was untrimmed brisket.[12] Pork was changing, too. Although the vertical integration and health concerns over pork were still some years away (those changes occurred mostly in the 1990s), pork was beginning to fall out of favor with American consumers. U.S. per capita pork consumption fell from a peak of 81.1 pounds in 1944 to just 42.9 pounds in 1975, while both chicken and beef increased greatly, the latter reaching a peak of 88.2 pounds per person in 1975.[13]

Running a profitable barbecue operation in the era of fast-food chains was difficult, but traditional barbecue did not disappear completely from the American restaurant landscape. Instead, it became a more specialized product. A few diners and drive-ins today still include barbecue alongside their menu of hamburgers. The Beacon Drive-In in Spartanburg, South Carolina, and Doumar's in Norfolk, Virginia, are notable examples. Starting in the 1970s, however, most restaurants either dropped pit-cooked barbecue from their menus or decided to focus on barbecue exclusively. Barbecue restaurants tended to be modest establishments that didn't advertise widely and didn't get much attention from anyone except the local diners who had been eating at them for years.

By the 1970s, the definition of "barbecue" had changed dramatically for much of America. For many, it had less to do with the meat and the way it was cooked than it did with the sauce with which it was served. Over the course of the twentieth century barbecue sauces had grown progressively sweeter, particularly when large food producers began marketing bottled sauce in grocery stores. The prominence of sugar in these commercial recipes seems to have changed the way people ate barbecue and, before long, the way they defined what barbecue was. Sugary sauces were thicker than their vinegar-based forebears. Like ketchup, they could be poured directly onto meat in large quantities. Sugar caramelizes and burns when exposed to direct heat, so using such sauces to baste cooking meat would lead to a charred, blackened crust. As a result, backyard barbecue chefs started waiting until the end of cooking to pour on the sauce. The thick, sweet flavor of commercial sauces made the natural smoked flavor of the meat less noticeable, and cooks could devote less attention to the cooking process, since it wasn't as important to the final result. As the fuel used for backyard barbecuing evolved from hardwood to lump charcoal, then briquette charcoal, and finally electric cookers and gas grills, cooks could get a crispy grilled crust on the meat while relying on barbecue sauce for the flavor. The addition of smoke flavoring to barbecue sauces completed this process.

Originally, barbecue was defined by the cooking process: anything cooked slowly over an open fire could be said to be "barbecued." By the middle of the twentieth century, many Americans' definitions had shifted to focus on the sauce. The cookbooks of the 1950s and 1960s are filled with recipes for "barbecued chicken" that make no mention of a fire but rather involve a pan of chicken parts covered in barbecue sauce and baked in an oven. During the 1970s, "barbecue on bun" (oven-roasted pork shredded, covered with barbecue sauce, and served on a hamburger bun) became a staple of grade-school cafeterias. In 1981—three decades after Richard and Maurice McDonald removed the barbecue pits from their San Bernardino drive-in—barbecue returned to their McDonald's menu—sort of. The fast-food chain introduced the "McRib Sandwich," a pressed pork patty with rib-like marks seared into the meat, which was topped with sweet barbecue sauce, pickles, and onions and served on a long hoagie-style bun. Barbecue had strayed a long way from the pit.

The Rebirth of American Barbecue

Traditional American pit barbecue, of course, was never really gone. In most parts of America, the old classic joints continued right along selling barbecue as they always had, and—while their numbers were fewer than in prior decades—a new generation of restaurateurs continued to open businesses that followed the styles of their mentors. Barbecue had fallen back to a core set of specialized restaurants and had faded from the forefront of the public's awareness. But it was there all along, dormant, and ready to spring back into full flower once America was ready for it again.

In 1977, Max Brantley, then a reporter for the *Arkansas Gazette,* published an article about his favorite local barbecue spots. When he wrote the piece, he figured he was one of the few "barbecue zealots" left in Arkansas. Once the paper hit the streets, he discovered he was hardly alone and had, in fact, tapped into a simmering passion for the subject. "You think crime, pollution, bigotry, and official abuse of power are raging concerns of the day?" he wrote in a follow-up column. "Think again. Judging from the response to my articles, the next presidential candidate better have a barbecue plank in the platform." Brantley's barbecue piece generated more phone calls and letters than anything he'd previously written, many of them angrily taking issue with him for slighting or ignoring a favorite local spot.[14]

Other journalists joined Brantley in writing about old-school barbecue joints. In July 1977, Vic Gold published an article in the *Washington Post Potomac Magazine* that profiled the barbecue preferences of various members of Congress, noting, "the subject of barbecue evokes the worst in parochial elitism, even beyond that of specialized judges of continental haut cuisine or snobbish wine tasters." Gold, who hailed from Alabama by way of New Orleans, expressed his allegiance to "real barbecue," which he defined as the stuff being served by either Ollie's or the Golden Rule in Birmingham.[15]

North Carolina native Jerry Bledsoe responded to Gold (whom he called an "oyster sucker from Louisiana whose taste buds obviously are so Tabasco-seared he couldn't tell barbecue from baloney") with a five-part series for the *Charlotte Observer* profiling the legendary barbecue joints in the Tarheel state. In the final installment of the series, which covered barbecue in Lexington, North Carolina, Bledsoe noted that the town's barbecue places were not widely known, and he encouraged them to do something about it. "If Lexington had any ambition about it," he declared, "it would take immediate steps to protect, preserve, and promote this local treasure. It would proclaim itself the Barbecue Center of the World . . . and throw up the tents and have a big annual barbecue festival with music and dancing and other festivities to celebrate this regional delicacy that is becoming so rare."[16] Just a few years later, in 1984, the town did just that, staging the first annual Lexington Barbecue Festival, an event that today draws more than 150,000 visitors to sample the area's famous Piedmont North Carolina–style barbecue.

The "rediscovery" of barbecue was related to a more general cultural shift away from cosmopolitan aspirations and a renewed interest in local and regional traditions. For fifteen years, starting in 1967, Calvin Trillin wrote a series for the *New Yorker* called "U.S. Journal" for which he traveled around the country and wrote about topics that were intentionally unrelated to government or politics, including an occasional light article about eating in America. At first, he had difficulty tracking down local culinary specialties. People in the cities and towns he visited invariably pointed him to the same insipid "fancy" restaurants that tried to ape European cooking (Trillin took to calling these "La Maison de la Casa House, Continental Cuisine") rather than to a great local fried-chicken joint or crab shack. But that started to change. "At some point in the late seventies," Trillin later recalled, "a lot of Americans came to the realization that their local customs—playing bluegrass music, say, or growing corn or eating enchiladas—were not as shameful as they had once been led to believe."[17]

Trillin captured these local food customs in a wide-ranging series of reports that sampled everything from Cajun boudin to the Buffalo chicken wing, and he devoted particular attention to classic pit-cooked barbecue, for which he was an unapologetic champion. In a 1972 article for *Playboy* magazine, he asserted, "It has long been acknowledged that the single best restaurant in the world is Arthur Bryant's Barbecue at Eighteenth and Brooklyn in Kansas City."[18] In "Stalking the Barbecued Mutton," Trillin explored the unique barbecue style of western Kentucky, a style he feared was rapidly losing out to the competition of Kentucky Fried Chicken and similar fast-food chains. "With the franchisers and décor-mongers closing in," he wrote, "any authentic local specialty obviously needs celebrating.... 'Kentucky is the Barbecued-Mutton Capital of the World,' I would tell the first eater of influence I could find, 'Spread the word.'"[19]

A new breed of guidebooks writers did exactly that, bringing to market for the first time books meant to help curious eaters find and explore America's legendary barbecue restaurants. Dozens of barbecue books had been published during the 1950s and 1960s, but they were all aimed at the backyard chef, providing recipes and grilling tips with virtually no mention of traditional pit-barbecue restaurants. In 1979, Allie Patricia Wall and Ron L. Layne published *Hog Heaven: A Guide to South Carolina Barbecue,* which appears to be the first barbecue guidebook. Wall and Layne toured the Palmetto State, eating at over a hundred barbecue places and documenting not only their location and hours of operation but also the barbecue style, cooking technique, and description of the business.

Hog Heaven was restricted in scope to a single state. In 1988, Vince Staten and Greg Johnson published *Real Barbecue,* a guidebook to the top one hundred barbecue restaurants in the whole nation. "At that time," Staten remembers, "there were hundreds of handbooks for those seeking out the great French restaurants of America but no glovebox guide to great barbecue."[20] The book didn't sell particularly well—Staten estimates that the first edition sold fewer than eight thousand copies—but it helped establish a genre that flourished. Today, dozens of barbecue guidebooks—including a revised and expanded version of *Real Barbecue* that was published in 2007—help new generations of barbecue lovers explore the many regional variations of this inherently American food. In 1996, when Lolis Eric Elie set off with photographer Frank Stewart on the culinary tour that he chronicled in *Smokestack Lightning: Adventures in the Heart of Barbecue Country,* he hypothesized that "this art, so vital to our national identity, was dying or at least endangered." When he revisited the subject in his preface to the 2005 revised edition, Elie admitted that his assumption had not been completely accurate. Many of the old-time places had since closed up and many of the older generation of pitmasters had passed away, but he had not anticipated "the strongly nostalgic trend in the country these days, a longing for the old ways. A longing so strong it has brought real barbecue to relative prominence in places where it was previously little more than a novelty."[21]

Barbecue Competitions

The Memphis in May World Championship Barbecue Cooking Contest, the country's largest barbecue competition, was first held in 1978 on a vacant lot just north of the Orpheum Theatre. It was just the second year of the Memphis in May festival, a two-day Memorial Day weekend celebration, and Rodney Barber, the chairman of the events committee, and Jack Powell, a Tennessee chili cookoff champion, thought it would be ideal to have a barbecue contest to show off Memphis's most beloved food.[22]

Cover of Vince Staten's and Greg Johnson's *Real Barbecue* (1988), the first national barbecue guidebook.

Bessie Louise Cathey, who cooked ribs on a ramshackle backyard barrel cooker, beat out twenty-seven other contestants for the $500 grand champion prize. The next year, the contest moved to Tom Lee Park along the Mississippi River, where it is still held today, and within a few years more than two hundred teams were competing, and the competition had to move to an invitational format.[23]

Other contests emerged to rival Memphis in May. The Taylor International Barbeque Cookoff was started in 1978, and the first American Royal Barbecue was held in 1980 as part of the century-old American Royal Livestock Show. (The inaugural contest was won by Rich Davis, a Kansas City physician and child psychiatrist, who would later leave his medical practice and turn his "KC Masterpiece" barbecue sauce into a national brand.) By 1985 Calvin Trillin observed, "There are so many barbecue cooking contests in the summertime a competitive barbecuer can haul his rig from fairgrounds to fairgrounds, like a man with a string of quarterhorses."[24] But things were just getting started.

In the mid-1980s, the Memphis in May organizers started sanctioning contests throughout the region, and the Memphis Barbecue Network was born. Sanctioned events used the same rules as the Memphis in May contest, and winners were guaranteed a spot at the World Championship in May. A rival sanctioning body, the Kansas City Barbeque Society (KCBS), got its start in 1985, when twenty die-hard barbecuers came together to stage a "Spring training" cook-off. At the time, there were only three barbecue competitions in the Kansas City area—all of them in the summer and fall—so the KCBS created their own event to keep their hands in during the off-season. Before long, they were receiving calls from organizers of other barbecue competitions who wanted the KCBS to provide rules for their events, and the society became a sanctioning body, too.

According to Carolyn Wells, the KCBS's executive director, the competition circuit grew at a steady 10 to 20 percent through the 1980s and 1990s. In 1996, Robb Walsh counted more than one hundred competitions in the state of Texas alone.[25] But, things really took off following the September 11 terrorist attacks, as Americans looked inward and sought ways to spend more recreational time with family and friends.[26] The rise of the Food Network and its round-the-clock barbecue specials added more converts. Today the KCBS is the country's largest competition barbecue sanctioning body, with over eight thousand members and some three hundred sanctioned events on the calendar for 2009.

In the early days, barbecue contests were pretty bare-bones: contestants slept in pup tents and cooked on Weber kettles and homemade contraptions. Today, they travel the country in RVs and cook on professionally manufactured, high-tech barbecue rigs. Today's high-tech smokers have draft induction fans, electric thermostats, and augers that deliver a precisely calibrated stream of wood pellets to the firebox. Such innovations have caused a lot of controversy between the barbecue purists, who maintain that burning logs and tending the fire all night is essential to the art, and the pragmatists, who like getting a good night's sleep. But, as the KCBS's Wells says, "*Everything* in barbecue is controversial."[27]

The pits aren't the only things that have changed. In the early days, competitive barbecuing was a fairly transparent excuse for boozing it up all night with the boys. (Calvin Trillin wrote that barbecue contests "are a big attraction for the people I think of as the party-as-a-verb crowd."[28]) Today's competitors are a fun-loving lot, but—particularly on the KCBS circuit—they've toned it down a good bit and made the weekends more suitable for the entire family. For many participants, in fact, the family-friendly atmosphere is a large part of the appeal. It's common these days for entire families—including grandparents and small children—to travel together from one weekend competition to another, and they make strong friendships with members of other teams. The result is a close-knit community whose members share stories, swap tips on recipes and technique, and cheer on one anothers' victories in the competitions.

While contributing to the ever-growing popularity of barbecue, the competitions, some have argued, are blurring traditional regional differences and making barbecue more homogenous. They point to the standardized competition rules like those of the Kansas City Barbeque Society, which call for judging four categories of meat (chicken, pork ribs, pork, and beef brisket), and the fact that contestants from all over the country are competing side by side without much concern for the local barbecue style. Others have claimed that the expensive customized barbecue rigs and meticulous techniques like using syringes to inject the meat with flavorings have taken barbecue far from

The rig for the Blackjack Barbecue team at the 2008 Southern National Barbecue Championship and Bluegrass Festival, Mount Pleasant, South Carolina. As competition barbecue has increased in popularity, the contestants' gear has become more elaborate and high-tech.

its original roots. "It was once the province of lower-middle-class and working-class people," author John T. Edge has said, "and now it's the equivalent of the bass boat for the middle classes."[29]

Despite the concerns of the traditionalists, a few things about barbecue competitions are clear. First, they have helped introduce barbecue not only to a new population of eaters but also to a new population of cooks, creating a new generation of pitmasters dedicated to the practice of slow-smoking meats. And, the contests provide a contemporary example of barbecue's enduring power to bring people together. That is certainly the case for the members of circuit teams and the tight bonds they form with their fellow competitors. It is also the case for the communities where the contests are held. Barbecue competitions are usually paired with some other event, such as a music festival or a local community celebration, and the proceeds raised are generally donated for a charitable cause. The gleaming stainless steel custom pits and the Winnebagos and the corporate sponsorships may be new, but the phenomenon of thousands of people coming together to eat barbecue outdoors is as old as the country itself.

Barbecue Sauce

About the same time that barbecue competitions were becoming popular across the nation, a new category of "premium" barbecue sauces entered the market. The first of these was KC Masterpiece, a brand created by Rich Davis, the Kansas City physician and child psychiatrist who was the winner of the inaugural American Royal Barbecue in 1980. Davis got into the condiment business by marketing a product called Muschup, a combination of mustard and ketchup in a single bottle. Not surprisingly, Muschup was a commercial failure, but fortunately Davis had decided to sell his "KC Soul Style Barbecue Sauce" alongside his flagship product. The barbecue sauce sold three thousand cases in the first year. Davis changed the name to "KC Masterpiece," and in 1986 he sold the brand to the Kingsford Division of the Clorox Company (makers of Kingsford charcoal), which took it nationwide. KC Masterpiece remains the top-selling barbecue sauce in the premium category.

Other manufacturers soon launched their own premium brands. In 1987 Kraft brought out its Bulls-Eye line, creating two tiers of brands—the original Kraft Barbecue Sauce selling at around $1.50 per bottle and Bulls-Eye selling in the two- to three-dollar range. Kraft launched Bulls-Eye with a half-million-dollar promotional campaign that featured sponsorship of professional rodeo events along with extensive print, radio, and television ads. The efforts paid off, and by the early 1990s Bulls-Eye was competing head-on with KC Masterpiece at the top of the premium barbecue sauce category. It took Heinz a little longer to get into the game, but in 2001 it licensed the brand of bourbon-maker Jack Daniels to use on its own premium barbecue sauce. You can still buy the original orange-tinted Kraft and Open Pit barbecue sauces, but, as the market has matured, variety is the order of the day, and each major manufacturer now offers an array of flavors, such as honey and garlic, mesquite smoke, and hot and spicy. Over $350 million worth of bottled barbecue sauce is sold each year.

Clorox, Kraft, and Heinz are the major players in the market, but there's plenty of room left for the smaller guys. Many barbecue restaurateurs have supplemented their regular business by bottling and selling their signature sauces. Arthur Bryant's and Gates's (from Kansas City), Big Bob Gibson (from Alabama), Corky's (from Memphis), Scott's (from North Carolina), McClard's (from Arkansas), and Stubb's (from Texas) are just a few of the historic barbecue restaurants whose sauces can now be purchased at grocery stores across the country. Celebrities have jumped on the bandwagon, too. Comedian Jeff Foxworthy has his Redneck Barbecue Sauce, syndicated radio hosts John Isley and Billy James have their "John Boy and Billy's Grillin' Sauce," and TV chef Emeril Lagasse markets four flavors of "BAM B Q" sauce.

As the varieties have expanded, the lines have blurred between processed mass-market sauces and homemade originals. Most restaurants simply place bottles of Heinz ketchup and French's mustard on their tables and make no pretense of creating their own versions. Barbecue sauce is different. A recent industry study by *Restaurants & Institutions* magazine showed that it is the condiment that operators most frequently "customize." French's Cattlemen's Barbecue Sauce, the top-selling food service brand, is marketed directly to restaurants as being "extendable," with advertisements promising restaurateurs, "You can add on-hand ingredients to Cattlemen's Barbecue Sauces to increase servings or create signature sauces without sacrificing depth of flavor." "Private label" sauces, produced by large manufacturers and repackaged by restaurants and other retailers, are a big business, too. That tasty "secret-recipe" sauce down at your local barbecue joint may not be as local as you think.

Amid this explosion of variety, the famed regional distinctions in barbecue sauce are beginning to fade. On the shelves of a typical South Carolina grocery store one can find dozens of different brands of barbecue sauce, only a handful of which will be the region's traditional mustard-based style. Most of the big barbecue chains—and even some of the smaller independents—now put upwards of six different types of sauce on their tables, to better serve the individual tastes of their patrons. Few youngsters today are likely to grow up knowing only one type of sauce, so few will have a single type that becomes permanently emblazoned in their mind as the only "true" barbecue sauce.

Barbecue Chains and Franchises

In the 1960s and 1970s, several entrepreneurs had tried to establish chain barbecue restaurants but met with only limited success. Regionalism has frequently been pointed to as their main barrier. Because barbecue styles and preferences differ so greatly from one state to another, the theory goes, it is difficult to create a single barbecue product that appeals to customers in multiple regions. Other explanations include the inefficient, manually intensive nature of operating a barbecue restaurant—tending open wood pits is a skilled job and is not easily trainable for new workers—and the corresponding difficulty of maintaining a consistent, repeatable product.

But something changed around the same time that Americans were rediscovering the joys of their local barbecue joints, and barbecue restaurant chains began to find success not only in maintaining a large number of profitable units but also in spanning wide geographical areas. The most successful of these barbecue entrepreneurs, Floyd "Sonny" Tillman, opened his first barbecue restaurant in Gainesville, Florida, in 1968. He later changed the name from "Fat Boys" to "Sonny's Real Pit BBQ," and the restaurant became a popular spot for University of Florida students, particularly the football players. After opening three locations in Gainesville, Sonny began franchising in 1977. By 1988, when Tillman sold the company to outside investors and retired, the restaurant had seventy-seven locations in six states.[30] Today, with more than one hundred thirty restaurants in operation, Sonny's is the nation's largest barbecue chain.

All of the Sonny's restaurants are in the South, but its territory cuts across nine states with very divergent barbecue styles, including the Carolinas, Georgia, Kentucky, and Tennessee. And it's not alone in being able to span regional boundaries. "I think that the chain approach to barbecue is going to undress that regional preference theory a little bit," says Marc Chastain, vice president of franchising for Rib Crib Barbecue.[31] By 2008, the Oklahoma-based chain had forty-one restaurants in a region stretching from Mason City, Iowa, down to Lubbock, Texas, and had opened its first East coast franchise in Lakeland, Florida. Orlando-based Smokey Bones BBQ grew to over seventy restaurants by 2007, while Minnesota-based Famous Dave's, with one hundred eighteen outlets in twenty-nine states, has perhaps the widest geographic reach, stretching from Manchester, New Hampshire, to Tacoma, Washington.

Many of these chains blur regional distinctions with their menus. Famous Dave's restaurants are designed to look like Minnesota fishing camps, with a lot of rough-hewn wood and camping gear and fishing posters on the walls. The menu, however, features styles that range from "Georgia Chopped Pork" to "Texas Brisket." Bandana's Bar-B-Que, a twenty-seven-store chain based in St. Louis, Missouri, advertises a "Southern style" barbecue that the founder David Seitz learned as a boy in Jacksonville, Florida, but the Bandana's name as well as the restaurant's heavy cowboy-theme drips Texas. Charleston, South Carolina–based Sticky Fingers features Memphis-style dry-rubbed ribs and promotes "a flavor so good you'll think you're walking down Beale Street with B.B. King!" The walls of the restaurants are covered with photographs of bluesmen, and Delta-style electric blues is always playing over the sound system. But the chain's fifteen restaurants are found mostly in the Carolinas; the only two outlets in Tennessee are in Chattanooga, some three hundred miles east of Memphis.

The recent success of barbecue chains is due to more than just a blurring of regional tastes. It is also the result of changes within the restaurant industry itself. One important factor is equipment. The Little Pigs of America chain, which folded in the mid-1960s after a few brief years of rapid growth, helped its franchisees build their own wood-burning brick pits. At his first barbecue restaurant in Gainesville, Sonny Tillman cooked over an open pit with blackjack oak. As he started to expand operations, though, he switched to the gas-fired smoker manufactured by Southern Pride, whose equipment is now used by most of the country's top-grossing barbecue chains. The new high-tech, self-contained smokers include electric rotisserie racks, gas-fired wood boxes (which burn hickory and other woods to impart smoky flavor), and automatic time and temperature controls. Using these smokers, restaurateurs can cook hundreds of pounds of meat overnight with the precision and control to ensure a consistent, repeatable product. Some chains have even adopted pressure smokers, which seal the smoke into a cooking chamber and cook the meat under pressure. Such equipment can cook forty-five pounds of ribs in just an hour and a half, a boon for restaurateurs with high-volume operations.[32]

Curtis' All-American Barbecue in Putney, Vermont, shows that traditional barbecue still appeals to diners in every corner of the nation. (Courtesy of Mike Murphy.)

But the growth in barbecue restaurants is not only due to new chains and franchises. "In Louisville," Vince Staten writes, "there has been a barbecue restaurant explosion in the last fifteen years. There was only one good place in town when we wrote [the restaurant guidebook] *Real Barbecue.* Now there are a half-dozen, all of them owned and operated by guys who do it for the love of 'cue."[33] The competition barbecue phenomenon has produced more than its fair share of restaurateurs, with hobbyists who mastered the art on the competition circuit deciding to set up shop and sell barbecue in a restaurant setting full time. Increasingly, classically trained chefs with years of experience in fine dining restaurants are trading their white jackets and toques for overalls and opening their own barbecue restaurants complete with wood-fired pits. Though traditional pit-cooked barbecue is becoming harder to find and the boundaries of regional styles are become less and less distinct, there is no shortage today of restaurants where diners can enjoy smoked pork, brisket, and ribs.

The Legacy of American Barbecue

In the mid-1970s, it seemed that barbecue as an American foodway was slowly sliding toward extinction. But that trend was successfully reversed, and barbecue is now available in more parts of the country and in a wider variety than ever before. From the competition barbecue circuit to national barbecue chains to a never-ending array of bottled sauces, barbecue is as popular today as it ever has been.

Traditionalists grumble over the fading of regional variations and the gradual replacement of hardwood by electric and gas cookers, and they have a point. In its twenty-first-century incarnation, barbecue has moved a long way away from the days when pitmasters at roadside stands cooked whole hogs over hardwood coals and served the meat with a homemade sauce from a distinctive local recipe. Though still not lost, the classic styles of the Golden Age of American barbecue become harder to find with each passing year.

But, looked at over the full sweep of barbecue's history, these recent changes are hardly surprising, for barbecue has always been a dynamic tradition. Since the very beginning it has grown and changed along with American society, reflecting the evolving variety of the culture and the people. The widely celebrated regional barbecue styles—styles that barbecue fans will drive for hours down country roads to seek out—are less than a century old, and they represent just one of the many phases in the long history of barbecue. At the time those barbecue stands were introduced, after all, traditionalists grumbled about how new-fangled and heretical they were.

Barbecue is one of the most American of foods, and it's the one most intimately linked to the contours of the nation's history. It excites the passions of contemporary eaters, and it remains strong in Americans' memories, evoking nostalgia for "old-fashioned barbecue" eaten in years past. Barbecue's power to bring people together and establish community bonds has made it highly enduring. The tradition will continue to evolve over time, but barbecue seems destined to remain an essential part of American foodways for many years to come.

Notes

Chapter 1

1. Edward Ward, *The Barbacue Feast: or, the three pigs of Peckham, broiled under an apple-tree* (London: 1707), 7–9.

2. Robert Beverley, *History of Virginia In Four Parts* (1705; repr., Richmond, VA: J. W. Randolph, 1855), 138. Available online at the University of Virginia Electronic Text Center, http://jefferson.village.virginia.edu/vcdh/jamestown (accessed November 8, 2002).

3. John Brickell, *The Natural History of North-Carolina* (Dublin, 1737), 340, 362. Available online at The Colonial Records Project, North Carolina Office of Archives and History, http://www.ah.dcr.state.nc.us/sections/hp/colonial/bookshelf/natural/Indians1.htm (accessed April 26, 2003).

4. Beverley, *History of Virginia*, 137.

5. *Diaries of Benjamin Lynde and of Benjamin Lynde, Jr.* (Cambridge, MA: Riverside Press, 1880), 138.

6. Wilson Waters, *History of Chelmsford, Middlesex County, Massachusetts* (Lowell, MA: Courier-Citizen Company, 1917), 784. *The Holyoke Diaries,* ed. George Francis Dow (Salem, MA: Essex Institute, 1911), 50, 56.

7. William D. Williamson, *The History of the State of Maine* (Hallowell, ME: Glazier, Masters, 1832), 340.

8. *Boston Post Boy,* August 17, 1767, 3.

9. *Boston News-Letter and New-England Chronicle*, May 25, 1769, 2.

10. The cultural historian David Hackett Fisher has identified these differences in feasting habits as part of the four distinct "folkways" in Colonial America, a term that encompasses a wide range of cultural characteristics such as dialect, architecture, and social customs. These folkways are associated with geographic regions—New England, the Tidewater South, the Dela-

ware Valley, and the Southern Highlands—and their characteristics derive from the regions in Britain from which each group came—East Anglia, southern England, the North Midlands, and the Borderlands, respectively. See David Hackett Fisher, *Albion's Seed: Four British Folkways in America* (New York: Oxford University Press, 1989), 353.

11. Daniel W. Gade, "Hogs," in Kenneth F. Kiple and Kriemhild Coneè Ornelas, eds., *Cambridge World History of Food* (New York: Cambridge University Press, 2000), 536–41.

12. Virginia DeJohn Anderson, *Creatures of Empire* (New York: Oxford University Press, 2004), 98.

13. "Hogs," *Cambridge World History of Food,* 536–41.

14. Anderson, *Creatures of Empire,* 115, 121.

15. In Virginia, the social historian Rhys Isaac has noted, "most of the dominant values of the culture were fused together in the display of hospitality, which was one of the supreme obligations that society laid upon heads of households." Rhys Isaac, *The Transformation of Virginia, 1740–1790* (New York: Norton, 1982), 71.

16. John Kirkpatrick to George Washington, 21 July 1758 in *Letters to Washington and Accompanying Papers,* ed. Stanislaus Murray Hamilton (New York: Houghton, Mifflin, 1899), 3:379.

17. Donald Jackson and Dorothy Twohig, eds., *The Diaries of George Washington, Vol. III 1771–75* (Charlottesville: University Press of Virginia, 1976), 204.

18. For descriptions of early Virginia elections, see Charles S. Sydnor, *American Revolutionaries in the Making: Political Practices in Washington's Virginia* (1952; repr., New York: Free Press, 1965), 26–29, and Rhys Isaac, *The Transformation of Virginia, 1740–1790* (New York: Norton, 1982), 111.

19. Sydnor notes, "Many of the candidates may have been perfectly circumspect in their preelection behavior, but all of them, with hardly an exception, relied on the persuasive powers of food and drink dispensed to the voters with open-handed liberality." Sydnor, *American Revolutionaries in the Making,* 51.

20. Richard R. Beeman, "Deference, Republicanism, and the Emergence of Popular Politics in Eighteenth-Century America," *William and Mary Quarterly, 3rd Series* 49 (July 1992): 148.

21. Isaac, *Transformation of Virginia,* 112. Beeman, "Deference, Republicanism and the Emergence of Popular Politics," 415.

22. Washington to Wood, July 28, 1758, quoted in Beeman, "Deference, Republicanism and the Emergence of Popular Politics," 418.

23. Richard Beeman and others have recently argued that although the hierarchical nature of the elections were predicated on the concept of voters' "deference" to their social superiors, practices such as treating marked the beginning of a trend of voters' using the ballot to advance their own interests. The Virginia gentry professed the classical Republican ideal of a disinterested elite governing for the public good with the deferential consent of the common citizens, but barbecues and other forms of treating were early signs that voters were exerting a certain amount of power and that their will would have to be respected. This changing tide was noticeable in Tidewater Virginia, where the social structure was relatively stable and well defined, but it would be even more evident on the frontier, where the social order was less certain and ordinary citizens were much more likely to demand that their representatives cater to their personal interests. In these environments, public gatherings such as barbecues would take on increased importance as venues where ambitious men could establish themselves in politics.

24. William John Grayson, "Autobiography of William John Grayson," ed. Samuel Gaillard Stoney, *South Carolina Historical and Genealogical Magazine* 49 (1948): 25.

25. Grayson, "Autobiography," 26. Grayson recalled one violator, a young man newly arrived from Scotland, who refused to drink to excess and was sentenced to a one-mile footrace. Given a five-yard head start, he had to outrun the entire "barbacue posse." If caught, he had to submit to the drinking; if he won, he could "do as he pleased." Perhaps because of his relative sobriety, the Scotsman "outran his pursuers without trouble."

26. "On the Fall of the Barbacue-House at Beaufort, S.C. During the Late Tremendous Storm." *Charleston Courier*, November 1, 1804, 2.

27. John Hammond Moore, *The Confederate Housewife* (Columbia, SC: Summerhouse Press, 1997), 15. Moore's two-page discussion of barbecue in antebellum South Carolina is one of the few scholarly treatments of the subject, and I am indebted to it for helping me find the trail of early newspaper accounts of barbecues.

28. Findlay, "On the Fall of the Barbacue-House At Beaufort."

29. Grayson, "Autobiography," 37.

30. William Henry Foote, *Sketches of North Carolina, Historical and Biographical, Illustrative of the Principles of a Portion of Her Early Settlers* (New York: 1846), 49.

31. Charles Woodmason, *The Carolina Backcountry on the Eve of the Revolution,* ed. Richard S. Hooker (Chapel Hill: University of North Carolina Press, 1953), 55.

32. Spartanburg Unit of the Writer's Program of the WPA, *A History of Spartanburg County* (Spartanburg, SC: Band & White, 1940), 21.

Chapter 2

1. "Occoney Station, July 4th," *Miller's Weekly Messenger,* July 9, 1808, 3.

2. John James Audubon, *Delineations of American Scenery and Character* (New York: G. A. Baker, 1926), 241. The exact date of the barbecue attended by Audubon is uncertain. The description, which was one of a set of essays originally published interspersed among the bird articles and illustrations in *Ornithological Biography,* was composed sometime during the 1830s, and in it Audubon comments that "although more than twenty years have elapsed since I joined a Kentucky Barbecue, my spirit is refreshed every 4th of July by the recollection of that day's merriment." This suggests the event occurred sometime during the 1810s.

3. This advertisement was quoted in full in the *Salem (MA) Gazette* on June 30. The northern editor took great delight in mocking the prospect of such an event: "Now, reader, suffer your fancy for one moment to revel on this picture of felicity—a hot July day—mercury at 94°— the earth parched and thirsty—every breeze like the breath of a furnace, wafting dust into your throat, nose, and eyes—around the festal board a thick clutter of ladies who had been liberally 'furnished with foreign liquors' & gentlemen who had 'free access to the use of domestic liquors'—before you on the groaning table, mountain high, an entire Swine broiled and roasted, its skin crisp and brown—making you perspire at the very thought of the flames by which it had been scorched—why, it is enough to make the 'solid flesh to melt' and dissolve into a thin dew!" *Salem Gazette,* June 30, 1815, 3.

4. *Camden (SC) Journal,* July 2, 1831, 3.

5. *Jackson (TN) Gazette,* July 10, 1824, 3.

6. *Greenville (SC) Mountaineer,* July 13, 1834, 1.

7. Manuscript from the Folklore Project of the WPA's Federal Writers' Project. Available online in American Life Histories: Manuscripts from the Federal Writers' Project, 1936–1940, http://memory.loc.gov/american/wpaintro/wpahome.htm (accessed October 10, 2008).

8. *Greenville Mountaineer,* July 12, 1834.

9. *North-Carolina Gazette,* July 10, 1778, quoted in Alan D. Watson, ed., *Society in Early North Carolina: A Documentary History* (Raleigh, NC: Division of Archives and History, 2000), 314.

10. The *Camden Journal,* for example, noted in its account of the local 1826 Independence Day celebration, that the barbecue dinners "closed the day in the enjoyment of republican plenty, with republican care and hospitality." *Camden Journal,* July 8, 1826, 3.

11. *Jackson Gazette,* June 5, 1824.

12. *Camden Journal,* July 2, 1831, 3. Committees of Arrangements were common practice

not only for July Fourth celebrations but for a variety of civic and social events such as banquets and dances.

13. Robert B. McAfee, *The Life and Times of Robert B. McAfee and His Family and Connections. Written by Himself* (1845). Transcribed by Jenny Tenlen. Available at http://www.drizzle .com/~jtenlen/mcafee/rbmcafee.html (accessed April 26, 2003).

14. David Crockett, *A Narrative of the Life of David Crockett of the State of Tennessee* (Philadelphia: Carey and Hart, 1834), 137.

15. In his study of early politics in Madison County, Alabama, Daniel S. Dupre found that "Each year newspaper notices of several barbecues a week enticed people away from their labors with the promise of food, drink, excitement, and sociability." Daniel S. Dupre, *Transforming the Cotton Frontier: Madison County, Alabama 1800–1840* (Baton Rouge: Louisiana State University Press, 1997), 179.

16. Quoted in Dupre, *Transforming*, 172.

17. Quoted in Dupre, *Transforming*, 179–80.

18. Library of Congress Printed Ephemera Collection, Portfolio 29, Folder 13. Available online at the *American Memory* Web site, http://hdl.loc.gov/loc.rbc/rbpe.02901300 (accessed March 8, 2008).

19. "Improved Mode of Electioneering," *Norwich (CT) Courier*, October 12, 1825, 2.

20. "Barbecuensis," letter to the editor, *Southern Advocate*, July 13, 1827, quoted in Dupre, *Transforming*, 182. Gander-pulling was a particularly cruel form of frontier entertainment in which a large gander was tied to a fence post or similar platform so that participants could charge past on horseback, competing to be the first to grab the bird's neck and wrench it from its body.

21. Ibid., 172, 185.

22. *Southern Advocate*, April 28, 1828, quoted in Dupre, *Transforming*, 184.

23. *Huntsville Democrat*, March 14, 1828, quoted in Dupre, *Transforming*, 184.

24. "Barbecuensis" reflected this fear when he argued that the purpose of barbecues was "to humble the proud—to exalt the based—to enrich the poor, and impoverish the rich, and finally to bring every member of the human family, of every rank and degree, upon one broad level of universal equality." "Barbecuensis," letter to the editor, *Southern Advocate*, July 20, 1827, quoted in Dupre, *Transforming*, 183.

25. Dupre, *Transforming*, 188.

26. Dupre, *Transforming*, 187.

27. *National Party Conventions, 1831–1988* (Washington, DC: Congressional Quarterly, 1991), 5.

28. *Pendleton (SC) Messenger,* September 7, 1838, 3.

29. Philip Hone, *The Diary of Philip Hone,* ed. Alan Nevins (New York: Dodd, Mead, 1927), 264.

30. Floyd C. Shoemaker, *Missouri—Day by Day* (State Historical Society of Missouri, 1942), 399.

31. During the Jackson administration, Calhoun had defended the Bank of the United States against the assaults by the president, who was determined to dissolve the institution and place its deposits in selected state banks. In 1838, however, Calhoun changed his position and supported Martin Van Buren's plan to keep in place federal currency not in a national bank but in government-owned vaults, or "subtreasuries." Calhoun did not consider this shift to be inconsistent, since he viewed the deposit of federal funds in any bank—whether a national one or multiple state banks—to be a source of political corruption. But his sudden switch to the administration's subtreasury system created confusion and turmoil among South Carolina's political leaders, who had previously been stalwart defenders of the Bank. Some—most notably U.S. senator William Preston and Representative Waddy Thompson Jr.—began negotiations with national Whig leaders such as Henry Clay over the possibility of creating a Whig party in South Carolina. The prospect of such party developments appalled Calhoun, who feared it would undermine the state's unity on issues of states' rights.

32. Clyde N. Wilson, ed., *The Papers of John C. Calhoun: Volume X, 1837–1839* (Columbia: University of South Carolina Press, 1981), 406.

33. Wilson, *Papers,* 10:410.

34. Wilson, *Papers,* 10:411.

35. Samuel Eliot Morison, *The Oxford History of the American People* (New York: Oxford University Press, 1965), 456.

36. Elizabeth R. Varon, "Tippecanoe and the Ladies, Too: White Women and Party Politics in Antebellum Virginia," *Journal of American History* 82 (September 1995): 498.

37. When a Democratic journalist sneered that, given a barrel of hard cider and a $2,000 pension, Harrison would prefer his log cabin to the White House, the Whigs turned the insult around and declared they were running a "Log Cabin, Hard Cider" campaign, portraying Harrison as a plain farmer/soldier against Van Buren as a decadent politician addicted to luxury.

Soon, there were "log-cabin badges and log-cabin songs, a *Log Cabin* newspaper and log cabin clubs, big log cabins where the thirsty were regaled with hard cider that jealous Democrats alleged to be stiffened with whisky; little log cabins borne as floats in processions, with latchstring out, cider barrel by the door, coonskin nailed up beside, and real smoke coming out the chimney." Morison, *Oxford History,* 458.

38. Franklin Gorin, *The Times of Long Ago* (Louisville, KY: John P. Morton, 1929), 102.

39. Edmund L. Starling, *History of Henderson County, Kentucky* (Henderson, KY: 1887), 172.

40. David F. Wilcox, ed., *Quincy and Adams County: History and Representative Men* (Chicago: Lewis, 1919), 613.

41. James Edmonds Saunders, *Early Settlers of Alabama* (New Orleans: L. Graham & Son, 1899), 311.

Chapter 3

1. Quoted in Varon, "Tippecanoe and the Ladies, Too," 509.

2. "Hon. Preston S. Brooks at Home," *Charleston Daily Courier,* October 7, 1856, 1.

3. Lewis W. McKee and Lydia K. Bond, *A History of Anderson County, KY* (Baltimore: Regional Publishing Company, 1975), 141.

4. *Cheraw (SC) Gazette,* July 12, 1837, 43.

5. Frederic Richard Lees, *An Argument for the Legislative Prohibition of the Liquor Traffic* (London: William Tweedie, 1857), 287.

6. *The American Annual Register for the Year 1832–33* (New York: William Jackson, 1835), 310.

7. Ian R. Tyrell, "Drink and Temperance in the Antebellum South: An Overview and Interpretation," *Journal of Southern History* 48 (November 1982): 489.

8. Several versions of the anecdote, likely apocryphal, can be found in temperance books and journals. See, for example, John W. Berry, *Uniac, His Life, Struggle, and Fall* (A. Mudge & Sons, 1871), 88–89, and Peter Turner Winskill, *The Temperance Movement and Its Workers: A Record of Social, Moral, Religious, and Political Progress* (London: Blackie & Sons, 1892), 52–53.

9. *South Carolina Temperance Advocate,* July 23, 1846.

10. Lee L. Willis III, "The Road to Prohibition: Religion and Political Culture in Middle Florida, 1821–1920" (PhD Diss., Florida State University, 2006).

11. "Temperance Barbecue of July Fourth in Norwich Township," *Weekly Ohio State Journal,* July 19, 1843, 2.

12. Mary E. Moragne, *The Neglected Thread: A Journal from the Calhoun Community 1836–1842,* ed. Delle Mullen Craven (Columbia: University of South Carolina Press, 1951), 42.

13. *Greenville (SC) Mountaineer,* July 14, 1843, 1.

14. *Greenville (SC) Mountaineer,* July 12, 1844, 1.

15. For a representative version of this narrative, see the Web site of the Brunswick County/ Lake Gaston Tourism Association, http://www.tourbrunswick.org/brunswick_stew.htm (accessed September 14, 2008).

16. Quoted in Brunswick County, Virginia: Information for the Homeseeker and Investor (Richmond, VA: Williams Printing Company, 1907), 22.

17. "'Brunswick Stew': The Origin of One of Our Most Delicious Stews," *Petersburg (VA) Index-Appeal.* Rpt. *Macon (GA) Telegraph,* August 19, 1886.

18. "Tar Heel" claims Matthews started making the stew in 1816; M. E. Brodnax says Matthews earned his reputation "about 1828."

19. Marion Harland, *Marion Harland's Autobiography: The Story of a Long Life* (New York: Harper & Brothers, 1910), 124–125.

20. Willie Lee Nichols Rose, *A Documentary History of Slavery in North America* (Athens: University of Georgia Press, 1999), 107–110.

21. The details of the Nat Turner barbecue can be found in Thomas Wentworth Higginson, "Nat Turner's Insurrection," *Atlantic Monthly* (August 1861): 173.

22. Louis Hughes, *Thirty Years a Slave: From Bondage to Freedom* (Milwaukee: South Side Printing Co., 1897), 50.

23. Works Project Administration. Slave Narratives (online database). Provo, UT: The Generations Network, Inc., 2000.

24. Virginia Tunstall Clay-Clopton, *A Belle of the Fifties: Memoirs of Mrs. Clay of Alabama, covering Social and Political Life in Washington and the South, 1853–66,* ed. Ada Sterling (New York: Doubleday, Page & Company, 1904), 217.

25. Mahala Jewel Slave Narrative, WPA Slave Narrative Project, Georgia Narratives, Volume 4, Part 2. Written by Grace McCune, Athens.

26. Hughes, *Thirty Years,* 46–47. Hughes's account of the Fourth of July barbecue at Pontotoc may sound nostalgic, but his memoir as a whole is sober and unforgiving. The section im-

mediately preceding the barbecue provides a detailed description of the barbarous punishments used on the plantation, including stocks and rawhide whippings.

27. Walter L. Fleming, *Civil War and Reconstruction in Alabama* (New York: Columbia University Press, 1905), 243.

28. Frederick Douglass, *Narrative of the Life of Frederick Douglass* (1845; repr., New York: Penguin, 1982), 116.

29. Interview with Estrella Jones, Augusta Georgia, Works Project Administration, Slave Narratives (online database). Provo, UT: The Generations Network, Inc., 2000.

30. See John F. Stover, *American Railroads,* 2nd ed. (Chicago: University of Chicago Press, 1997), 28–31.

31. *Charleston Courier,* July 16, 1847, 2.

32. Stover, *American Railroads,* 35.

33. Robert T. Hubard to Edward W. Hubard, June 30, 1860, Hubard Family Papers, University of North Carolina Southern History Collection, Series 1.9–1.10, Reel 18.

34. *Charleston News & Courier,* June 21, 1842, and June 29, 1842.

35. Karl Jack Bauer, *The Mexican War, 1846–1848* (Lincoln: University of Nebraska Press, 1992), 69–70.

36. J. H. Wallace, *History of Kosciusko and Attala County,* 1917. Available online at http://attala.msgenweb.org/history-kosciusko.html (accessed September 28, 2008).

37. Oran Perry, ed., *Indiana in the Mexican War* (Indianapolis: State of Indiana, 1909).

38. "Public Dinner to Col. Moore," *Austin City Gazette,* November 11, 1840, 3.

39. Quoted in Ernestine Sewell Linck and Joyce Gibson Roach, *Eats: A Folk History of Texas Foods* (Fort Worth: Texas Christian University Press, 1989), 146.

40. Advertisement, *Clarksville (TX) Northern Standard,* August 5, 1848, 3.

41. "Barbecue on the Fourth of July," *Victoria (TX) Advocate,* June 7, 1850, 2.

42. "Fourth of July on the California Trail," *Philadelphia North American and United States Gazette,* October 3, 1849, 1.

43. "News from California," *Pittsfield (MA) Sun,* August 29, 1850, 2.

44. "Celebration of the Fourth in Suisun Valley," *San Francisco (CA) Daily Placer Times and Transcript,* July 11, 1853, 1.

45. "The Political Barbecue at San Jose," *San Francisco Alta California,* 6 October 1856, 7.

46. *Lowell (MA) Daily Citizen and News,* November 25, 1856, 2.

47. Fanny G. Hazlet and Gertrude Hazlet Randall, "Historical Sketch and Reminiscences of Dayton, Nevada," *Nevada Historical Society Papers, 1921–1922* (Reno: Nevada Historical Society, 1922), 16.

Chapter 4

1. Charles Sumner, "The Crime Against Kansas." Available online at Wikisource, http://en.wikisource.org/wiki/The_Crime_against_Kansas (accessed February 15, 2009).

2. "Hon. Preston S. Brooks at Home," *Charleston Daily Courier*, October 7, 1856, 1.

3. "Mr. Breckenridge Accepts an Invitation to Speak," *Washington, D.C., Constitution*, August 28, 1860.

4. "The Breckinridge Barbecue," *New York Herald*, September 4, 1860, 1.

5. "The Great Kentucky Meeting," *Washington, D.C., Constitution*, September 7, 1860, 2.

6. "The Douglas Barbecue," *New York Herald*, September 13, 1860, 3.

7. Background information on Bryan Lawrence is taken from genealogists' notes posted on the RootsWeb message board, http://news.rootsweb.com/th/read/IRL-KILKENNY/2003–03/1046703947 (accessed September 21, 2008).

8. "From Our Own Correspondent," *Washington, D.C., Constitution*, September 14, 1860, 2.

9. "From Our Own Correspondent," 2.

10. H. M. Hamill, *The Old South: A Monograph* (Dallas: Smith & Lamar, 1904), 58–59.

11. Hamill, *The Old South*, 59–60. This account is corroborated by Mollie Hollifield, *Auburn: Loveliest Village of the Plain* (Auburn: n.p, 1955), 10–14.

12. "From Port Sullivan," *Austin State Gazette*, March 9, 1861, 1.

13. "Hurrah for San Augustine," *Austin State Gazette*, March 16, 1861, 1.

14. Robert E. Corlew, *Tennessee: A Short History* (Knoxville: University of Tennessee Press, 1981), 291.

15. Corlew, *Tennessee*, 294.

16. B. G. Brazelton, *A History of Hardin County* (Nashville: Cumberland Presbyterian, 1885), 60–61.

17. *New York Herald*, June 17, 1861.

18. "Crittenden Festival," *Philadelphia Inquirer*, July 4, 1861.

19. Frank H. Heck, "John C. Breckenridge in the Crisis of 1860–1861," *Journal of Southern History* 21 (1955): 339–344. W. M. Railey, *History of Woodford County* (Frankfort: Roberts, 1928), 91.

20. "Presentation to the Pennsylvania Twenty-Third," *Philadelphia Inquirer,* December 16, 1861.

21. "Mr. Cushing," *Houston Telegraph,* May 22, 1863, 4.

22. "Barbecue and Fair," *Houston Telegraph,* August 10, 1863, 2.

23. "The Richmond Dinner," *Washington (AR) Telegraph,* August 19, 1863.

24. Thomas Wentworth Higginson, *Army Life in a Black Regiment* (1870; repr., New York: Penguin, 1997), 28.

25. Susie King Tayor, *A Black Woman's Civil War Memories,* ed. Patricia W. Romero and Willie Lee Rose (1902; repr., New York: L. Marcus Wiener, 1998), 49.

26. Eliza Frances Andrews, *The War-Time Journal of a Georgia Girl, 1864–1865* (New York: Appleton, 1908), 324.

27. Andrews, *The War-Time Journal of a Georgia Girl,* 324–29.

28. Andrews, *The War-Time Journal of a Georgia Girl,* 330.

Chapter 5

1. Quoted in William H. Wiggins Jr., *O Freedom! Afro American Emancipation Celebrations* (Knoxville: University of Tennessee Press, 1987), xvii.

2. Wiggins, *O Freedom,* xix.

3. Quoted in Robb Walsh, *Legends of Texas Barbecue Cookbook* (San Francisco: Chronicle Books, 2002), 114–15.

4. See the Emancipation Park page at the City of Houston Web site, http://www.houstontx.gov/parks/emancipation.html (accessed November 9, 2008).

5. "The Day Elsewhere," *Dallas Morning News,* June 20, 1893, 8.

6. "Emancipation Day," *Dallas Morning News,* June 19, 1898, 4.

7. The first appearance of the word "Juneteenth" in newspaper accounts of Emancipation Day celebrations is likely that in the *Fort Worth Star Telegram,* June 16, 1903, which notes "Prominent Negroes declare that the 'Juneteenth' celebration, which will be held here next Friday, will be the biggest thing that the colored people of Washington county have ever attempted."

8. "Mrs. Ella Boney," American Life Histories: Manuscripts from the Federal Writers' Project, 1936–1940, American Memory, http://memory.loc.gov/ammem/index.html (accessed October 18, 2008).

9. "Letter from Putnam," *Macon Telegraph,* July 19, 1866.

10. Ibid.

11. "Mississippi. The Democratic Canvass," *Memphis Daily Avalanche*, June 17, 1868, 1.

12. *Harper's Weekly*, September 26, 1868, 616.

13. The forty-three figure is cited in "Grand Radical Barbecue," *Arkansas Gazette*, July 28, 1868, 1.

14. Keith S. Bohannon, "'These Few Grey-Haired, Battle-Scarred Veterans': Confederate Army Reunions in Georgia, 1885–1895," *The Myth of the Lost Cause and Civil War History*, ed. Gary W. Gallagher and Alan T. Nolan (Bloomington: Indiana University Press, 2000), 99.

15. Matthew J. Graham, *The Ninth Regiment New York Volunteers* (Hawkins' Zouaves) (New York: 1900), 466, 473.

16. Mattie Thomas Thompson, *History of Barbour County, Alabama* (Eufaula, AL: 1939): 415.

17. *Perry (IA) Chief*, August 12, 1887, 12.

18. *Mexia (TX) Evening News*, June 4, 1900, 1.

19. "What a Real Barbecue Is," *Springfield (MA) Republican*, August 9, 1896, 8.

20. "Death of Celebrated Cook," *Columbia (SC) State*, June 23, 1908, 4.

21. "The Colonel in the City," *Columbus (GA) Daily Enquirer*, August 23, 1887, 8.

22. "In the Barbecue County," *Atlanta Constitution*, August 26, 1889.

23. *Atlanta Constitution*, August 28, 1890, 2.

24. Maude Andrews, "The Georgia Barbecue," *Harper's Weekly*, November 9, 1895, 1072.

25. *Atlanta Constitution*, October 8, 1901, 9.

26. Robert Willingham, "An Overview of Local History," Washington-Wilkes Web site, http://www.washingtonwilkes.org/page6184.html (accessed January 8, 2008).

27. "Death Comes to Mr. F. T. Meacham," *Statesville (NC) Landmark*, May 19, 1930, 1. See also the following issues of the *Statesville (NC) Landmark*: April 25, 1921; April 28, 1921; November 28, 1921; March 16, 1922; May 1, 1922; July 6, 1922, 1.

28. "Boss of Burgoo and Barbecue," *New York Sun*, June 3, 1906, 7.

29. See, for example, *The WPA Guide to Kentucky*, ed. F. Kevin Simon (1939; repr., Lexington: University Press of Kentucky, 1996), 354.

30. According to Confederate regiment rolls and enlistment records, there were at least two Jauberts who served in the Confederate army. On July 1, 1862, a Gustavus Jaubert enlisted at Chattanooga, Tennessee, in Company B of John Hunt Morgan's Second Cavalry Regiment, Kentucky. A Gus Jaubert enlisted in the First Kentucky Infantry in Louisville, Kentucky, entering as a private on April 23, 1861, and being promoted to 4th Corporal on April 30, 1862. In

a 1906 profile of Jaubert, the *New York Sun* reported that Jaubert served four years in the First Kentucky Infantry. Since Gus Jaubert himself was interviewed for this profile, it seems likely that the burgoo king did not serve under Morgan.

31. R. Gerald Alvey, *Kentucky Bluegrass Country* (Oxford: University Press of Mississippi, 2000), 270.

32. "Boss of Burgoo and Barbecue," 7.

33. *Lexington (KY) Central Record,* November 4, 1904, 1.

34. "Louisville Encampment," *Decatur (IL) Evening Bulletin,* 13 September 1895, 9. "Boss of Burgoo and Barbecue," 7.

35. *Frankfort (KY) Roundabout,* July 2, 1904, 7.

36. "Burgoo & Boom," *Time,* November 26, 1934.

37. Ibid.

38. Horace Ward, "Kentucky in Stew Over Real Burgoo," *Kingsport (TN) News,* April 20, 1948, 10.

39. Edward Ward, T*he Barbacue Feast: or, the three pigs of Peckham, broiled under an apple-tree* (London: 1707), 7–9.

40. Lettice Bryan, *The Kentucky Housewife* (Cincinnati: Shepard & Stearns, 1839), 95–96.

41. Mrs. A. P. Hill, *Mrs. Hill's New Cook Book* (1872). Reprinted as *Mrs. Hill's Southern Practical Cookery and Receipt Book* (Columbia: University of South Carolina Press, 1995), 171.

42. *My Ride to the Barbecue: or, Revolutionary Reminiscences of the Old Dominion* (New York: S. A. Rollo, 1860), 58–59.

43. "At a Barbecue," *Harper's Weekly,* October 24, 1896, 1051.

44. Alex E. Sweet and J. Armoy Knox, *On a Mexican Mustang, Through Texas, From the Gulf to the Rio Grande* (Hartford, CT: S. S. Scranton, 1883), 437.

45. Andrews, "The Georgia Barbecue," 1072.

46. "At a Barbecue," 1051.

47. John R. Watkins, "Barbecues," *Strand Magazine* 16 (1809): 463.

48. Andrews, "The Georgia Barbecue," 1072.

Chapter 6

1. U.S. Census Bureau, *1990 Census of Population and Housing,* http://www.census.gov/population/censusdata/table-4.pdf (accessed March 22, 2009).

2. Perhaps the earliest use of the term *restaurant* in conjunction with *barbecue* appears in

1901. Sheriff John W. Callaway became such a fixture at public events in Georgia that a member of the Georgia State Fair management said, "It would hardly seem like an exhibition or a fair in Atlanta if Sheriff Callaway was not present with his barbecue restaurant." *Atlanta Constitution,* October 8, 1901, 9. *Restaurant* in this sense is referring to a temporary set-up, not a permanent restaurant. The term *barbecue stand* would be commonly used until the 1920s to describe businesses that sold smoked meats.

3. Fire Reports in *Dallas Morning News,* May 24, 1897, October 24, 1897, November 4, 1898.

4. Reed and Reed, *Holy Smoke,* 60.

5. "Barbecue Stand," *Charlotte Observer,* March 30, 1899.

6. "People's Column," *Charlotte Observer,* April 12, 1899.

7. *Faucett v. State*, 134 P. 839 10 Okla. Cr. 111 No. A-1207. (Criminal Court of Appeals of Oklahoma, 1913.)

8. *Kintz v. State*, 12 Okla. Cr. 95 152 P. 139 (1915).

9. *Winterman v. State*, 179 S.W. 704 No. 3648 (Court of Criminal Appeals of Texas, 1915).

10. *Spartanburg (SC) Carolina Spartan,* August 13, 1868. Quoted in Works Progress Administration, *A History of Spartanburg County* (Spartanburg: Band & White, 1940), 159.

11. In some areas, such as the Midlands of South Carolina, many barbecue restaurants are still only open Thursday through Saturday nights.

12. Martha McCulloch-Williams, *Dishes and Beverages of the Old South* (New York: McBride, Nast, 1915), 275.

13. Quoted in Reed and Reed, *Holy Smoke* 254.

14. See Garner, *North Carolina Barbecue,* 7–8, 88; and Jerry Bledsoe, "Even Yankees Know of Melton's Barbecue," *Charlotte Observer,* August 21, 1977, E1.

15. Reed and Reed, *Holy Smoke,* 34–36.

16. Garner, *North Carolina Barbecue,* 8–13; Greg Johnson and Vince Staten, *Real Barbecue* (New York: Harper & Row, 1988), 75.

17. *Columbia (SC) State,* July 4, 1923.

18. *Columbia (SC) State,* September 1, 1930, 8.

19. Classified advertisement, *Atlanta Constitution,* November 20, 1924, 19.

20. Joe York, *BBGBBQ* (documentary film). Available online at the Southern Foodways Alliance Web site, http://www.southernfoodways.com/documentary/film/bbgbbq.html (accessed March 22, 2009).

21. Amy Evans, Interview with Pat Davis Sr., *The Mississippi Hot Tamale Trail,* http://www.tamaletrail.com/OH_abes.shtml (accessed May 28, 2007).

22. Brian Fisher, "Interview with James Willis," BBQ Oral History Project and the Southern Foodways Alliance Web site, http://www.southernfoodways.com/oral_history/tnbbq/M09_leonards.shtml (accessed March 22, 2009).

23. Marcie Cohen Ferris, "We Didn't Know from Fatback," *Cornbread Nation 2,* ed. Lolis Eric Elie (Chapel Hill: University of North Carolina Press, 2004), 97–103.

24. Rick Montgomery and Shirl Kasper, *Kansas City: An American Story* (Kansas City: Kansas City Star Books, 1999), 102–13, 121.

25. Ibid., 169.

26. Ibid., 184. Perry first appears in the City Directory at the 1514 E. Nineteenth Street address in 1916.

27. "Henry Perry Has Cooked Good Barbecue for 50 Years," *Kansas City Call,* February 26, 1932, 1.

28. Doug Worgul and other chroniclers of Kansas City barbecue have recorded that Charlie Bryant became a business owner when he bought Perry's stand after the Barbecue King died in 1940. But Bryant's obituary in the *Kansas City Call* as well as city directories from the period make clear that Bryant was operating his own restaurant a few blocks away from Perry's throughout the 1930s. Obituary of Charlie Byant, *Kansas City Call*, November 10, 1952, 1.

29. Quoted in Doug Worgul, *The Grand Barbecue: A Celebration of the History, Places, Personalities, and Techniques of Kansas City Barbecue* (Kansas City: Kansas City Star Books, 2001), 25.

30. Worgul, *The Grand Barbecue,* 21.

31. Worgul, *The Grand Barbecue,* 37–38.

32. Robb Walsh, *Legends of Texas Barbecue Cookbook* (San Francisco: Chronicle Books, 2002), 16.

33. *Houston, Texas, City Directory 1917* (Houston: R. L. Polk, 1917).

34. Robb Walsh, "The Art of Smoke," *Houston Press* (2002). Available online at http://www.robbwalsh.com/03writings/artsmoke.shtml (accessed March 22, 2009).

35. Robb Walsh, "Barbecue in Black and White: Carving the Racism out of Texas Barbecue Mythology," *Houston Press,* May 5, 2003.

36. Walsh, *Legends,* 154.

37. Ibid.

38. Walsh, *Legends,* 157.

39. "Central Texas BBQ Dynasties," *Austin Chronicle,* November 9, 2001, food section.

40. A detailed description of the preparation of traditional Texas barbacoa can be found in Mario Montaño, "The History of Mexican Folk Foodways of South Texas: Street Vendors, Offal Foods, and Barbacoa de Cabeza" (PhD diss., University of Pennsylvania, 1992).

41. Quoted in Worgul, *Grand Barbecue,* 31.

42. Sadie B. Hornsby, "The Barbecue Stand," Federal Writers' Project Papers #3709, Southern Historical Collection, Manuscripts Dept., Wilson Library, University of North Carolina at Chapel Hill.

43. Hornsby, "The Barbecue Stand," 12.

44. John A. Jakle and Keith A. Sculle, *Fast Food: Roadside Restaurants in the Automobile Age* (Baltimore: Johns Hopkins University Press, 1999), 40.

45. Rose and Bob Brown, "A Good Roasting," *Collier's,* September 4, 1937, 28.

46. Quoted in Jakle and Sculle, *Fast Food,* 43.

47. "The Great American Roadside," *Fortune,* September 1934, 62.

48. *Burlington (NC) Daily Times,* April 12, 1930, 3, 6; July 30, 1930, 1; August 1, 1930, 5; November 21, 1930, 2; February 11, 1932, 6.

49. Michael Karl Witzel, *The American Drive-In* (Osceola, WI: Motorbooks International, 1994), 25–27. Dwayne Jones, "What's New with the Pig Stands—Not the Pig Sandwich!" *National Park Service Cultural Resource Management* #9 (1996). Available online at http://crm.cr.nps.gov/archive/19–9/19–9–5.pdf.

50. Edgerton, *Southern Food,* 150.

Chapter 7

1. Nell B. Nichols, "A Back-yard Barbecue," *Woman's Home Companion,* August 1924, 51.

2. Doris Hudson Moss, "Real Barbecues," *American Home,* August 1936, 29, 51.

3. George A. Sanderson and Virginia Rich, *Sunset's Barbecue Book* (San Francisco: Sunset Magazine, 1939), 5.

4. Sanderson and Rich, *Sunset's Barbecue Book,* 5.

5. Kevin Starr, *The Dream Endures: California Enters the 1940s* (New York: Oxford University Press, 2002), 7.

6. D. S. Graham Jr., "Outdoor Grills for the California Home," *Touring Topics,* November 1933, 28.

7. Genevieve Callahan, "Here's the News in Barbecues," *Better Homes and Gardens,* May 1941, 50.

8. "Backyard Barbecue Solves War's Entertainment Problem," *Deming (NM) Headlight,* June 19, 1942, 4.

9. "Outdoor Grills," Rpt. *Fitchburg (MA) Sentinel,* August 11, 1942, 6.

10. Sylvia Lovegren, *Fashionable Food: Seven Decades of Food Fads* (New York: Macmillan, 1995), 121.

11. Harold Coggins, "My Barbecue Pit," *Atlantic Monthly* (June 1947), 114.

12. In a nod to barbecue's heritage, the book does include directions for old-fashioned "pit barbecue" that describes the typical large portions of meat cooked on iron spits over a hand-dug pit in the ground.

13. Sanderson and Rich, *Sunset's Barbecue Book,* 55–58.

14. Rufus Jarman, "Dixie's Most Disputed Dish," *Saturday Evening Post,* July 3, 1954.

15. From Weber Company History, available online at http://weber.mediaroom.com/index.php?s=pageA (accessed June 30, 2007). The history includes the claim that "George's post-World War II invention was the beginning of the 'American Backyard Barbecue' as we know it today," but the backyard barbecue had been in full swing for more than a decade by the time Stephen invented his first kettle grill.

16. Robert L. Wolke, *What Einstein Told His Cook 2* (New York: W. W. Norton, 2004), 318–319.

17. "Immense Revenue from By-Products for Ford's Plants," *Appleton (WI) Post-Crescent,* February 20, 1925, 26.

18. *Sheboygan Press,* July 1, 1930, 13, and June 2, 1931, 2.

19. In recent years there has been a return to lump charcoal by barbecue enthusiasts, who find it provides better flavor and are skeptical of the various fillers and additives in briquettes. But, lump charcoal's share of the market remains tiny.

20. "Gas Grills Find Favor With Chefs," *Dallas Morning News,* April 23, 1964, 6:2.

21. "Arkla Air Conditioning Co. Moves Into Air Cooled Equipment Field," *Dallas Morning News,* June 12, 1966, K13.

22. Alina Tugend, "Grilling Burgers on a Ferrari in the Backyard," *New York Times,* July 21, 2007, C5.

23. *Atlanta Constitution,* January 31, 1909, 11.

24. S. R. Dull, *Southern Cooking* (Atlanta: Ruralist, 1928).

25. Dorothy Malone, *Cookbook for Brides* (New York: A. A. Wyn, 1947), 47.

Chapter 8

1. Brian Fisher, "Interview with Nick Vergos," October 16, 2002, BBQ Oral History Project and the Southern Foodways Alliance Web site, http://www.southernfoodways.com/oral _history/tnbbq/M14_rendezvous.shtml (accessed March 22, 2009).

2. Fisher, "Interview with Nick Vergos"; Steven Raichlen, *BBQ USA: 425 Recipes from All Across America* (New York: Workman, 2003), 36.

3. Greeks in Birmingham, Southern Foodways Alliance Web site, http://www .southernfoodways.com/documentary/oh/greek/index.shtml (accessed March 22, 2009). Reed and Reed, *Holy Smoke,* 70.

4. North Carolina Barbecue Society, NCBS Historic Barbecue Trail, http://www .ncbbqsociety.com/trail.html (accessed March 8, 2009).

5. Rufus Jarman, "Dixie's Most Disputed Dish," *Saturday Evening Post,* July 3, 1954, 89.

6. David Cecelski, "E. R. Mitchell: Backyard barbecue," *Raleigh News & Observer,* October 8, 2000. Available online at *Southern Oral History Program,* http://www.sohp.org/research/lfac/ N&O/6.5b29-ER_Mitchell.html (accessed December 6, 2008).

7. Roy G. Taylor, *Sharecropper: The Way We Really Were* (Wilson, NC: J-Mark, 1984), 118–19.

8. August Kohn, *The Cotton Mills of South Carolina, 1907* (Columbia: South Carolina Department of Agriculture, 1907), 164.

9. Reed and Reed, *Holy Smoke,* 52.

10. "Thousand Textile Union Members at Barbecue," *Charlotte Observer,* June 7, 1919, 3.

11. Samuel Mitrani, "Labor Day," in Eric Arnesen, ed., *Encyclopedia of U.S. Labor and Working-class History* (New York: Taylor & Francis, 2007), 760–61.

12. "Sam Rayburn to Address Labor Day Rally," *Dallas Morning News,* August 12, 1955, 13.

13. "Gala Labor Day Celebrators to Close Busy Summer Season," *Dallas Morning News*, August 1956, 2:1.

14. Reed and Reed, *Holy Smoke,* 53.

15. "History" from the Mallard Creek Barbecue Web site, http://mallardcreekbbq.com (accessed November 9, 2008).

16. Kathleen Purvis, "Pressing the flesh, dishing the pork," *Charlotte Observer,* October 27, 2004, 1, 8.

17. Jarman, "Dixie's Most Disputed Dish," 90.

18. Quoted in Garner, *North Carolina Barbecue,* xiv.

19. "His Inaugural to be Old-Fashioned," *Danville (VA) Bee,* December 30, 1922, 8. "Governor Asks Provisions for 200,000 Guests," *Duluth News-Tribune,* December 24, 1922.

20. "50,000 Already Present for Walton Ceremonies," *Dallas Morning News,* January 9, 1923, 4.

21. Amy Dee Stephens, "It Started with a Deer," *Outdoor Oklahoma* 61 (January–February 2005): 12.

22. "22,000 Gallons of Soup, Made from Barbecue Leftovers," *San Antonio Express,* January 11, 1923.

23. "50,000 Already Present for Walton Ceremonies," *Dallas Morning News,* January 9, 1923, 4.

24. Huey Long was assassinated in 1935, but his machine remained in power in the state through the election of Richard W. Leche—the first Louisiana governor to be sentenced to prison. They then appointed Earl Long, Huey's brother, to fill Leche's seat.

25. "Mammoth Barbecue to Mark Louisiana's Inauguration," *St. Petersburg Times,* May 13, 1940, 5.

26. "Barbecue in Austin," *Time,* February 3, 1941.

27. William Anderson, *The Wild Man from Sugar Creek* (Baton Rouge: Louisiana State University Press, 1975), 64.

28. Quoted in Anderson, *Wild Man,* 69.

29. Jarman, "Dixie's Most Disputed Dish," 37.

30. Hal K. Rothman, *LBJ's Texas White House: "Our Heart's Home"* (College Station: Texas A&M University Press, 2001), 166–167.

31. Rothman, *LBJ's Texas White House,* 169.

32. Robb Walsh, *Legends of Texas Barbecue Cook Book* (San Francisco: Chronicle, 2002), 33.

33. "Fort Worth Rites Set for 'Barbecue King,'" *Dallas Morning News,* January 30, 1968, 5.

34. "Washington Texans Whoop It Up At Maryland Barbecue," *Dallas Morning News,* October 7, 1951, 2. "Annual Barbecue Set on June 14 by Texans in Capital," *Dallas Morning News,* May 31, 1952, 3.

35. Walter Jetton with Arthur Whitman, *Walter Jetton's LBJ Barbecue Cook Book* (New York: Pocket, 1965), 9.

36. Brendan Gill, "Barbecue," *New Yorker,* August 29, 1964, 22

37. "Fort Worth Rites Set for 'Barbecue King,'" 5.

38. "Civil Rights Act of 1964," Transcript available online at http://www.ourdocuments.gov (accessed December 26, 2008).

39. Richard C. Courtner, *Civil Rights and Public Accommodations: The Heart of Atlanta and McClung Cases* (Lawrence: University Press of Kansas, 2001), 64–65.

40. *Katzenbach v. McClung,* available online at http://laws.findlaw.com/us/379/294.html (accessed December 26, 2008).

41. "Beyond a Doubt," *Time,* December 25, 1964.

42. "Bessinger Case Heard in Aiken," *Florence (S.C.) Morning News,* April 6, 1966, 3.

Chapter 9

1. R. David Thomas, *Dave's Way: A New Approach to Old-Fashioned Success* (New York: Putnam, 1991), 70.

2. Ibid., 72.

3. Witzel, *American Drive-In,* 106–16.

4. Philip Langon, *Orange Roofs, Golden Arches: The Architecture of American Chain Restaurants* (New York: Knopf, 1986), 74–75.

5. Reed and Reed, *Holy Smoke,* 245.

6. Quoted in Jerry Bledsoe, "Even Yankees Know of Melton's Barbecue," *Charlotte Observer,* 1977.

7. Kathleen Zobel, "Hog Heaven: Barbecue in the South," *Southern Exposure* 5 (Summer and Fall 1977): 61.

8. Quoted in Jerry Bledsoe, "Lexington: The Last Bastion of Real Barbecue," *Charlotte Observer,* August 23, 1977, 8A.

9. Rick Bragg, "Love this Barbecue or Leave It, Stranger," *New York Times,* February 15, 1995.

10. Allie Patricia Wall and Ron L. Layne, *Hog Heaven: A Guide to South Carolina Barbecue* (Lexington, SC: Sandlapper Store, 1979). Statistics compiled by the author from Wall's and Layne's restaurant surveys.

11. For a detailed description of the various types of pits used by barbecue restaurants in the 1970s, see Wall and Layne, *Hog Heaven,* 5–10.

12. Walsh, *Legends of Texas Cookbook,* 210.

13. U.S. Department of Agriculture, Economic Research Service, 2004.

14. Max Brantley, "The Ribs Hit the Fan," *Arkansas Gazette,* July 21, 1977. Rpt. *Cornbread Nation 2,* ed. Lolis Eric Elie (Chapel Hill: University of North Carolina Press, 2004), 108–10.

15. Vic Gold, "Beyond Grits," *Washington Post Potomac Magazine,* July 17, 1977.

16. Bledsoe, "Lexington: The Last Bastion," *Charlotte Observer,* 8A.

17. Calvin Trillin, Preface to *The Tummy Trilogy* (New York: Farrar, Straus and Grioux, 1994), xi.

18. Trillin, *Tummy Trilogy,* 17.

19. Calvin Trillin, "Stalking the Barbecued Mutton," *New Yorker,* February 7, 1977, 76.

20. Vince Staten, "Real Barbecue Revisited," *Cornbread Nation 2,* 138.

21. Lolis Eric Elie, *Smokestack Lightning: Adventures in the Heart of Barbecue Country* (1996; repr., New York: Ten Speed Press, 2005), viii–ix.

22. "History of World Championship Barbecue Cooking Contest," Memphis Commerical Appeal Bar*B*Q Blog, http://blog.commercialappeal.com/bbq/archives/2005/05/history_of_worl.html (accessed January 4, 2009).

23. Calvin Trillin, "Thoughts of an Eater with Smoke in His Eyes," *New Yorker,* August 12, 1985, 56.

24. Ibid., 58–59.

25. Robb Walsh, "Summer and Smoke," *Natural History,* August 1996, 68.

26. Carolyn Wells, Interview with the author, September 2, 2008.

27. Wells interview.

28. Calvin Trillin, "Barbecue and Home" in *Feeding a Yen: Local Specialties, from Kansas City to Cuzco* (New York: Random House, 2004), 181.

29. Quoted in Matt Guarente, "Griller Warfare," *The Independent,* June 15, 2003.

30. Anthony Clark, "Founder Reflects as Sonny's Turns 40," *Gainesville Sun,* September 7, 2008.

31. Allison Perlik, "Hot Spots: Taking Their 'Cue," *Restaurants & Institutions,* May 1, 2004.

32. Janice Matsumoto, "Pit Boss: Proper Equipment Can Turn Smoke into Sales," *Restaurants & Institutions,* May 15, 2002.

33. Staten, "Real Barbecue Revisited," 139.

References

Books on Barbecue

Caldwell, Wilber W. *Searching for the Dixie Barbecue: Journeys into the Southern Psyche.* Sarasota, FL: Pineapple Press, 2005.

Elie, Lolis Eric, editor. *Cornbread Nation 2: The United States of Barbecue.* Chapel Hill: University of North Carolina Press, 2004.

Elie, Lolis Eric, editor. *Smokestack Lightning: Adventures in the Heart of Barbecue Country.* New York: Farrar, Strauss, and Giroux, 1996.

Garner, Bob. *North Carolina Barbecue: Flavored by Time.* Winston-Salem, NC: John F. Blair, 1996.

Griffith, Dotty. *Celebrating Barbecue: The Ultimate Guide to America's Four Regional Styles of 'Cue.* New York: Simon & Schuster, 2002.

Johnson, Greg, and Vince Staten. *Real Barbecue.* New York: HarperCollins, 1988.

Reed, John Shelton, and Dale Volberg Reed with William McKinney. *Holy Smoke: The Big Book of North Carolina Barbecue.* Chapel Hill: University of North Carolina Press, 2008.

Wall, Allie Patricia, and Ron L. Hayne. *Hog Heaven: A Guide to South Carolina Barbecue.* Lexington, SC: Sandlapper Store, 1979.

Walsh, Robb. *Legends of Texas Barbecue Cookbook.* San Francisco: Chronicle Books, 2002.

Ward, Edward. *The Barbacue Feast: or, the three pigs of Peckham, broiled under an apple-tree.* London: 1707.

Worgul, Doug. *The Grand Barbecue: A Celebration of the History, Places, Personalities, and Techniques of Kansas City Barbecue.* Kansas City, MO: Kansas City Star Books, 2001.

Articles on Barbecue

Andrews, Maude. "The Georgia Barbecue." *Harper's Weekly.* November 9, 1895, 1072.

Bass, S. Jonathan. "'How 'bout a Hand for the Hog': The Enduring Nature of the Swine as a Cultural Symbol of the South." *Southern Cultures* 21, no. 3 (Spring 1995): 301–20.

Hitt, Jack. "A Confederacy of Sauces." *New York Times Magazine.* August 26, 2001, 28–31.

Jarman, Rufus. "Dixie's Most Disputed Dish." *Saturday Evening Post.* March 7, 1954, 36–91.

Lovegren, Sylvia. "Barbecue." *American Heritage* 54, no. 3 (June 2003): 36–44.

Walsh, Robb. "Barbecue in Black and White: Carving the Racism out of Texas Barbecue Mythology." *Houston Press,* May 5, 2003.

Walsh, Robb. "Summer and Smoke." *Natural History* 105, no. 8 (August 1996): 68–72.

Zobel, Kathleen. "Hog Heaven: Barbecue in the South." *Southern Exposure* 5 (Summer and Fall 1977): 61.

Online Resources

Southern Foodways Alliance, Oral History Project, http://www.southernfoodways.com/documentary/oh/index.html.

Historical Context

Brickell, John. *The Natural History of North-Carolina.* Dublin, 1737.

Courtner, Richard C. *Civil Rights and Public Accommodations: The Heart of Atlanta and McClung Cases.* Lawrence: University Press of Kansas, 2001.

Dupre, Daniel S. *Transforming the Cotton Frontier: Madison County, Alabama, 1800–1840.* Baton Rouge: Louisiana State University Press, 1997.

Egerton, John. *Southern Food: At Home, On the Road, In History.* New York: Alfred A. Knopf, 1987.

Fisher, David Hackett. *Albion's Seed: Four British Folkways in America.* New York: Oxford University Press, 1989.

Foote, William Henry. *Sketches of North Carolina, Historical and Biographical, Illustrative of the Principles of a Portion of Her Early Settlers.* New York: 1846.

Hilliard, Sam Bowers. *Hog Meat and Hoecake: Food Supply in the Old South, 1840–1860.* Carbondale: Southern Illinois University Press, 1972.

Isaac, Rhys. *The Transformation of Virginia, 1740–1790.* New York: Norton, 1982.

Jakle, John A., and Keith A. Scully. *Fast Food: Roadside Restaurants in the Automobile Age.* Baltimore: Johns Hopkins University Press, 1999.

Lovegren, Sylvia. *Fashionable Food: Seven Decades of Food Fads.* New York: Macmillan, 1995.

Moore, John Hammond. *The Confederate Housewife.* Columbia: Summerhouse Press, 1997.

Root, Waverly, and Richard de Rochemont. *Eating in America: A History.* New York: Morrow, 1976.

Sydnor, Charles S. *American Revolutionaries in the Making: Political Practices in Washington's Virginia.* 1952; Reprint, New York: Free Press, 1965.

Witzel, Michael Karl. *The American Drive-In.* Osceola, WI: Motorbooks International, 1994.

Woodmason, Charles. *The Carolina Backcountry on the Eve of the Revolution.* Edited by Richard S. Hooker. Chapel Hill: University of North Carolina Press, 1953.

Index